Impact of parametric design on young Architects

Ayda Aglmand Azarian, Niloofar Amel, Pourya Ahmadzadeh, Elmira Amiri,

Foad Bonakdar, Mehdi Bahari, Mitra Dolatshahi, Mahsa Fakhr Jahani, Afsane Fardyar,

Negin Hosein Alizadeh, Sahand Latifi, Leila Manzouri, Samira Mahooutchian,

Negar Mikhi, Amir Ali Navadeh Shahla, Sajjad Sabour, Saede Sadegpour, Nasim Tabrizi,

Mohamad Reza Talebi, Mohammad Reza Torabi

Improved & Collected by Ali Khiabanian
Translated by R.Kafouri

© All Rights Reserved

All rights reserved. No part of this book may be reproduced or transmitted in any form or by any means, electronic or mechanical, including photocopying and recording, or by any information storage and retrieval system, without permission in writing from the author.

Title: The Role of Brain Hemispheres in Architectural Design

Authors: Ayda Aglmand Azarian, Niloofar Amel, Pourya Ahmadzadeh, Elmira Amiri, Foad Bonakdar, Mehdi Bahari, Mitra Dolatshahi, Mahsa Fakhr Jahani, Afsane Fardyar, Negin Hosein Alizadeh, Sahand Latifi, Leila Manzouri, Samira Mahooutchian, Negar Mikhi, Amir Ali Navadeh Shahla, Sajjad Sabour, Saede Sadegpour, Nasim Tabrizi, Mohamad Reza Talebi, Mohammad Reza Torabi

Improved & Collected by: Ali Khiabanian,

Translator (from Persian): R. Kafouri

Cover design: Sjjad Sabour

ISBN: 9781942912095

LCCN: 2015917898

Publisher: Supreme Art, Los Angeles, CA

Prepare for Publishing: Asan Nashr,

www.ASANASHR.com

Table of Contents

Introduction 6

Chapter 1 13
_Introduction to museum design 13
_Objectives of museum 14
_Types of museum 14
_Points about museum architecture 15
_Introduction Field 18
_Administrative field 19
_Research field 20
_Training field 20
_Architectural Projects 21
_Museum of Modern Art 22
_Archaeological Museum 40
_Tabriz Music Museum 48
_Tabriz Digital Museum 63
_Tabriz Children's Garden Museum 71
_Sensory perception of children from space 72
_Children and architecture 72
_The space designed for children should include: 73
_Children & colors 74
_Children and colors psychology 75
_Effect of environmental conditions 76
_Tabriz Theater 87
_Women Cultural Center of Tabriz 95
_Parametric Art Museum 105
_Parasite Brighton pier- Parasite Millennium Bridge London 108

Chapter 2 "Conceptual visualization based on parametric design" 119
_Exhibition spaces design based on Iranians architecture tradition-theories 120
_Parametric Space 127
_Samples of parametric designs inspired by shell 131
_Exhibiting spaces design, inspired by snail and the forms created during previous projects ... 135

_Humanity's history museum design, inspired by human chest 138
_Pelagic animals' museum design inspired by frog skeleton 142
_Fire temple 147
_Parametric presence inside the cube 156
_Parametric forms 160
_From patterns to parametric design 162
_Parametric Tower 168
_Alternatives Forms for Water museum concept 170
_Design of semi-open exhibition space 173
_Aqua museum 175
_Pelagic animals' museum 176

Chapter 3 "Pattern Design" 178
_Pezeshkan Tower facade design 179
_Façade design 190
_Symbols designed as vault ornaments based on Persian patterns 194
_Facad Design (Store) 200
_Table Design 203
_Refrences 216

Introduction

This is my ninth book published on architecture. I begin with an indescribable enthusiasm and unasked questions are posed or, it is better to say, closed windows are opened to me after publication. What may be found inside the building makes me excited. The excitation and curiosity direct me to create novel works. It comes back to 2002-03 when I was working on my M.A. thesis. It was really difficult to access high speed internet (32kb/s) and foreign books especially about museum design. I spent several hours to search for materials about modern art and museums. My thesis was about "Modern Art Museum". I intended to connect architectural design and painting-which gradually became more serious- and take benefit of thought and attitude of modern artists toward the space in choosing main concept of my plan. Considering limited resources, it deemed really difficult. However, it was very exciting for me. Spending several months to study west art history, I began my work with etudes of different art styles. I wanted to assay myself and embody my perceptions. The way- which was later named "conceptual sketch"- was very helpful in recognizing of my mental space and my perception from modern art. A complex, curious, and sometimes, disturbed mind became clear gradually. To begin architectural design of the project, I re-experienced conceptual sketches on the project site. I tried to coordinate restrictions and objectives of the project with avant-garde and complex space of my mind. I designed freely and edited the sketches carefully to enclose myself in the frame of the physical plan. The process was continued until I began to model the designed forms. I began a new challenge in learning and experiencing curved and broken volumes using Auto CAD and 3Ds MAX software, a beginning not lasted by now!. At that time, 3D software was often used for drawing in Iran rather than for design. In simple words, no one thought parametrically, i.e. playing with parameters to create new form and space or develop the form animatedly. The materials will be seen in coming pages and animation of the project design process, Museum of Modern Art, may be found in YouTube.

My M.A. thesis reminded me two important points:

- It should have a specific, extensible, and scientific design process and be able to offer creative responses.

- Role and importance of computer and software in design process

After two years of continuous work on my thesis, I found so many things that I do not know. Although I passed my thesis with excellent grade, the two above-mentioned points involved my mind and resulted in many sketches, models, computer forms, and books two of which were translated to and published in English by Supreme Century Press:

- Conceptual sketches in architectural design (2014)
- The role of brain hemispheres in architectural design (2015)

The problem did not stop. My interest in color and form attracted my attention to Iranian art and architecture. Here, a question affected my achievements:

What was the relation between the designed buildings and Iranian local culture and architecture?

The process was continued until 2010 when I seriously began to practice architectural design using 3Ds MAX software in Islamic Azad University of Tabriz. The practices were completed and held as workshops in Inter-discipline Design Universe (my office). The outcomes encouraged us to name our design method and the created form and space as "parametric design".

Since there were few Persian resources about parametric design, I involved in translation and research about the subject in addition to scientific experiences. I tried to express Iranian drawings, patterns, and architectural space in a modern language. The studies resulted in compiling of a book: "The role of creativity in architectural design process with parametric approach"

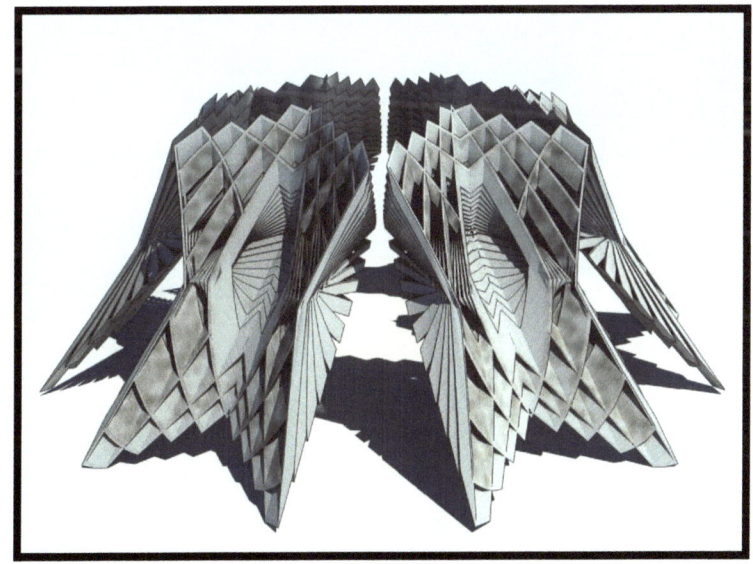

In the ceremony of Iran Architecture Luminaries Association (2013), this book was introduced as winner of the book reward of Dr. Mozayeni. Some designs of the book are presented here and it is hoped that it is translated into English as a complete collection.

After publication of the book, I put the obtained experiences into effect in M.A. theses with more power and organized plan, the projects such as museum, city theater, and cultural center designed in chapter one of the book and I was their advisor or supervisor and helped students in parametric design or computer modeling. As it will be seen, sketch is one of the important tools and stages in design process of the projects. The spaces designed without Marquette and sketches are demonstrated in other chapters. I convinced the students to design with software and become familiar with thought and design method of computers.

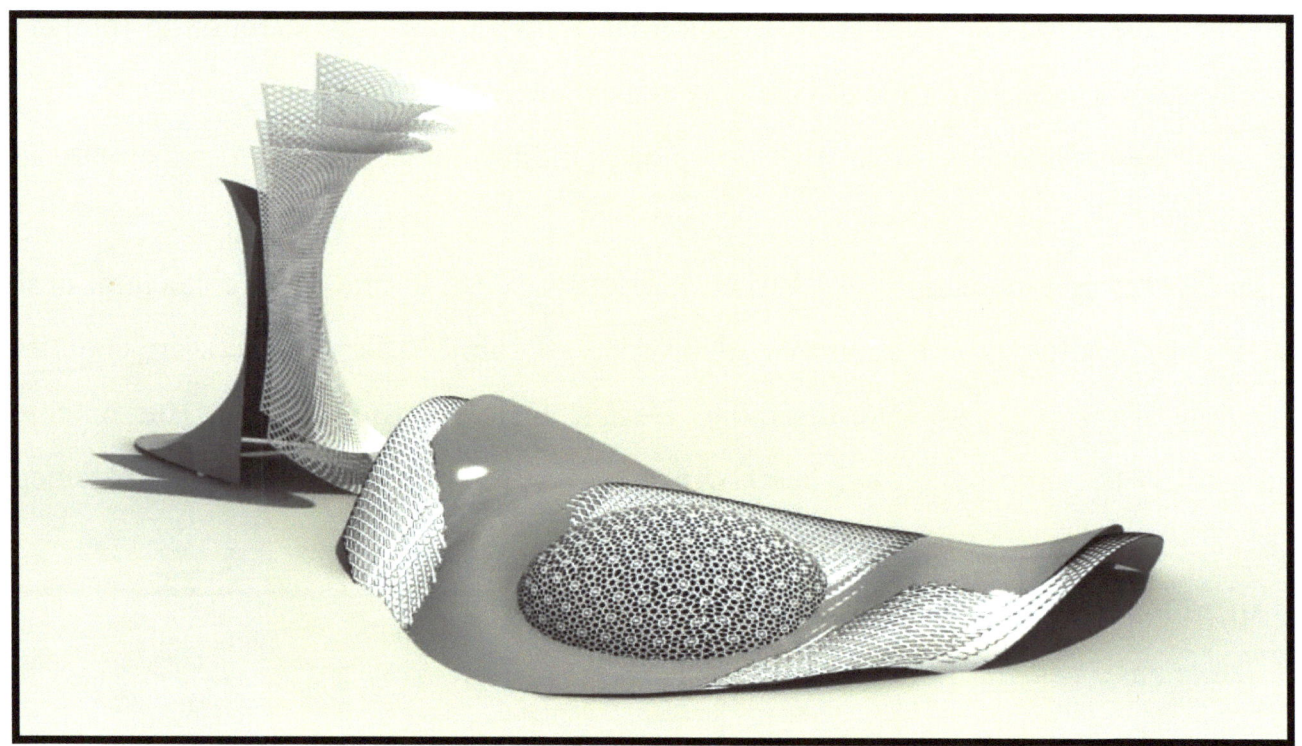

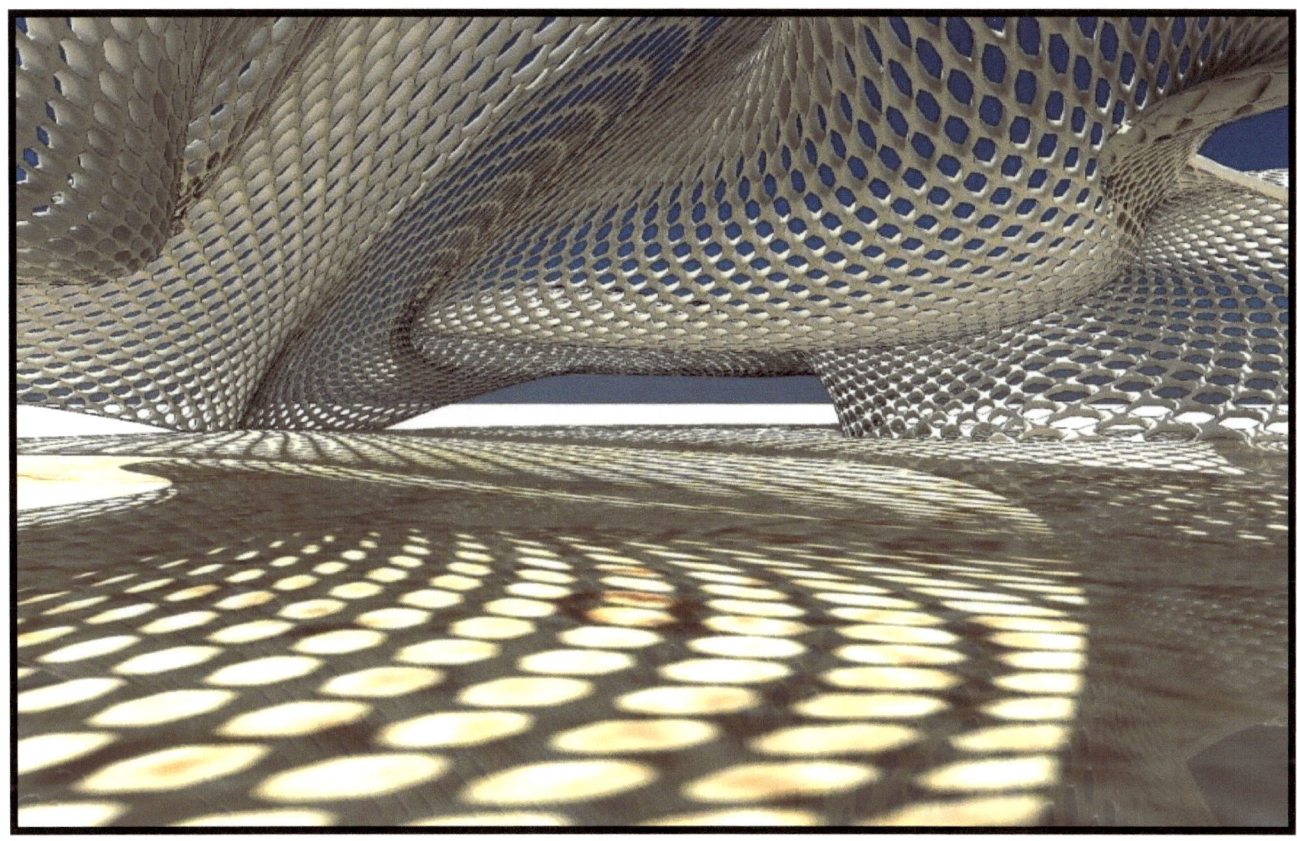

Chapter two contains design of conceptual spaces and forms with subjects of projects of the previous chapter. It includes practices helping in more understanding of design using computer and creation of new spaces in addition to better recognition of exhibition and museums space.

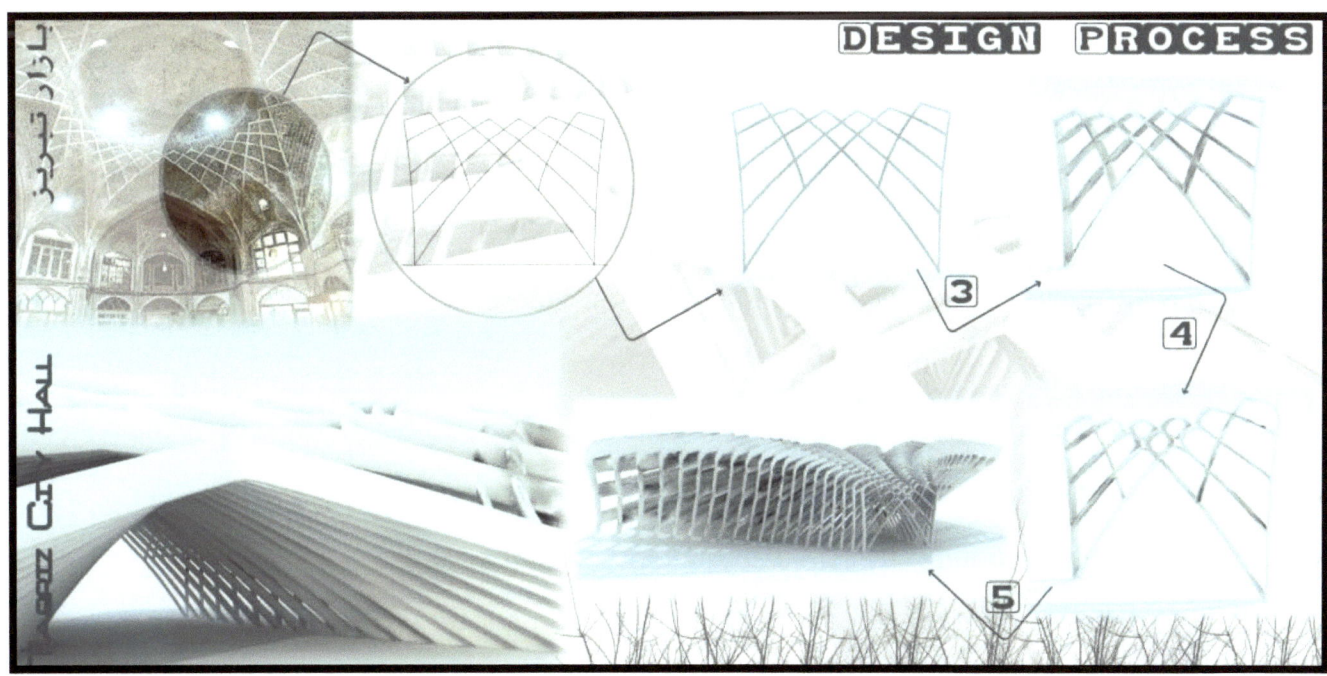

Contents of chapter three were not specified from beginning. During compiling the book and considering that pattern design is an important stage in parametric design and we are faced with a diversity of patterns in most projects of the book, I decided to add the practices I did with my students at the beginning of the way.

While writing this preface, it seems that the book should be studied from the end.

The book contains general descriptions about features of museum design as well as a summary of project design process which was selected and rewrote from M.A. thesis of the students. There are several books about museums and cultural spaces design and very important works have been made during years. However, what was important for me was attitude of architecture students of Tabriz (as one of the metropolises of Iran) toward museum and cultural spaces design. Although Tabriz is enriched culturally and artistically and has introduced globally famous artists in poem, music and visual arts, it has very few museums. Importantly, how students may have creative and accurate attitude, experience parametric design using architectural software, transfer their attitude and approach, if possible, to Iranian genuine architecture, deal with perception and recreation of Iranian architecture relying on a parametric tool and language, and localize it while using west technology in a world full of diversity of architectural styles. For this reason, a trace of Iranian genuine architecture especially in details of façade and color of glasses is found in the projects and exercises which was created by attitude and space provided by computers.

It is rarely seen in Iran universities. There are two dominant thoughts in Iranian architecture training, i.e. biased and inflexible attitude toward Iranian past architecture and a modern approach fondly looking at west architecture events. There is not any specific syllabus for design aimed at interacting between local architecture and global events. For this reason, most projects are designed and completed as thesis in my private office without any assistance of the university. It is a very difficult and challenging subject in design for which there has not been found any specific solution except to some important and creative works designed and made by Houshang Seihoun, Hossein Amanat, Darab Diba, and other outstanding architects since 1970s which were not repeated within the last 30 years.

Arched entrance decorated with paintings, Sheikh Lotfollah Mosque, Isfahan

However, computers and design software within the last two decades in Iran has opened new horizon for the architects to recognize Iranian architecture and approach European and American designers' thoughts and processes. Parametric architecture empowered the subject during recent years especially in design and probability of enforcing quick and easy variations of the patterns forms and dimensions. Obviously, patterns play a significant role in Iran art and architecture. There are various abstract forms in Iranian carpet, tiling, and decorations using mirrors in mosques and houses. The forms are repeated using symmetry technique and their form and dimensions change considering space structure and form of wall or dome.

This book does not claim to express a new language in an interactive design between Iranian architecture and special philosophical approach and west architecture, rather, it is a software-aided design practice trying to reach a better perception and recognition of Iranian architecture and modern achievements of western architects.

In fact, the book demonstrates the process of transition from manual to digital design in a country which was far from most software and technological progresses as well as essential trainings. An endeavor to keep pace with global design pulse and its training!

Ali Khiabanian

www.IDUarchitects.com

Email: Ali_Khiabanian@yahoo.com

Facebook Page: Parametric Architecture +

Chapter 1
Introduction to museum design

Objectives of museum

Objectives of museum may be summarized as follows:
1. To safeguard works of the ancients and exhibit and transfer them to future generations
2. To evaluate and compare the past and present historical, practical, technical, industrial, and artistic manifestations
3. To create and strengthen understanding among nations and peoples
4. To know and demonstrate contribution of nations and peoples in global civilization and culture
5. To promote and improve knowledge of students, researchers, and other groups
6. To prevent from destruction of local culture and create an obstacle against wandering and exotic cultures

Origin of the museums is hidden whether in royal or church treasures of the middle ages or in small rooms with rare objects and samples being prevalent during 16th and 18th centuries.

Types of museum

The first classification still used in most countries and reflected in ICOM specialized committees names refers to a distinction between fine arts, applied arts, archeology, history, anthropology, natural sciences, knowledge and technology, local regional, and specialized museums. However, museums evolution since World War II has gradually eliminated the borders found between disciplines and complexes. No, it seems reasonable to classify museums as follows:

1. Art museum: It contains fine works and objects of painting, architecture, sculpture and so and are classified as museums of painting, architecture and sculpture, decorative arts and handicrafts, utensils, calligraphy, book and bookbindery, ceramic and tile, carpet, carving, woodwork and wood industries, jewels, and textiles.
2. History museum: Ancient works and objects which are evidence of anthropological, archeological and historical background are placed in the history museums.

3. Specialized museum: They exhibit historical, artistic, and technical works at different occasions. They are also known as outdoor and local museums.
4. Science museum: It prepares and protects plants, animals, rocks, soils, fossils and anything are created without human involvement. It is classified to museum of natural history, land animals, plants, fish and marine creatures.

   Science museums are the most protected and active museums.

   Natural sciences museums should play a significant role in informing and convincing of people. At scientific level, these museums provide the researchers with documents and evidences (over than million samples) resulting in knowledge enhancement from perspective of different disciplines.
5. Technology and industry museum: It shows technical and industrial manipulations of human being about inventions, discoveries, vehicles, machineries and so and is known as museum of inventions, discoveries, machineries, and vehicles.

Points about museum architecture

1. What is done by the addresses in museum requires a space for a contradictory activity to remove their fatigue feeling.
2. Appropriate hierarchy of short-time resting places enhances the museum yield and encourages the visitors to stay and visit more.
3. People watch closely what is in museums. To be refreshed, it is better to create a distance between the visitors and what is visited in the museums. Also, paying attention to the surrounding perspectives, leaving free the line of sight of the surrounding perspectives and visual relation of these perspectives with display halls are of special importance.
4. Features of museum architecture should correspond with coordinated relations of space, light, and works.
5. Human activity place requires an open space with direct sunlight while objects should be displayed in rooms with artificial and controllable light. Architecture of the display space should be a response to association of these activities and contrary requirements.

6. In museums design, its social mission- direct communication with addresses- and security issues should be considered.
7. The designer's skill in museum design is manifested through appropriate association of contrary activities.
8. It should be considered that museum and its building is a mean to exhibit objects rather than the objects a mean to display museum building.
9. Museum architecture should be adjustable with and emphasize on issues such as allocating special pavilions or classes for the objects.
10. The relation between the objects and addresses forms the primary binder of every museum.
11. In museum architecture, walking path of the visitors should be separate from that of the employees
12. The entrance should be an independent architectural element in close relation with the museum.
13. The entrance is a bridge connecting people with what is found in museum.
14. Allocating independent entrance for some service places such as restaurants exposes the museum at accidental visit (those who have not come to visit museum) and is helpful in attracting the addresses and keeping the complex active.
15. Every visitor visits the museum to establish a personal communication with the objects.
16. At display scene, there is not any absolutely communicative space. The smallest area of museum should be served to provide information and display the works for the addresses.
17. In spatial organization of museum, the designer should try to establish a discipline that visitor can easily walk at different spaces of museum and perceive its hierarchy well.
18. The designer should try to prevent from any visual interruption at display scene and accompany vertical and horizontal movement of the addresses. Here, appropriate selection of the body elements is of special importance.

19. In designing the museum, the designer should define and create the space (to present the materials) in a way that the addresses can deeply understand the issues while the expected results and behaviors are realized.

Introduction Field

The field includes parts of museum allocated to introduction and exhibition of works. In fact, it is the most important and essential field with a direct relation with visitors. Galleries, amphitheaters, and libraries are of spaces constituting this field.

1. Galleries

    Galleries are the most important and evident part of the introduction field. Based on type of the exhibited works, i.e. temporary and permanent, galleries are classified as 1) permanent galleries exhibiting the works permanently (they do not change generally) and 2) temporary galleries where the works are displayed temporarily and only when the temporary and seasonal exhibitions are held. In carpet museum, permanent galleries are a place for displaying of about 200 ancient-artistic carpets and even tools used for carpet weaving and maintaining while temporary galleries are used for seasonal and subjective exhibitions held to display works and especially personal artistic carpets at different occasions and with different subjects. Works of temporary exhibitions are also offered for sale. The design process should consider the issue that the displayed carpets are in different sizes and dimensions varying from carpet tableau to very big carpets.

    To make the visitors familiar with specialized skills of carpet such as restoration, it is better to establish restoration workshops during galleries path as part of the exhibition. A place (restoration workshop) is allocated to restore the worn-out carpets by the master craftsmen. In the restoration workshop, a small laboratory will be required for physical and chemical researches equipped to, at least, the usual and ordinary tools.

    Galleries used to exhibit artistic works as well as scientific and cultural objects should have following conditions:
    - They should be safe places considering being protected against destruction, stealing, fire, moisture, extra dryness, intense sunlight, and dust.

- At ordinary conditions, human viewing angle (54° or 24° over the eye level) for an image located at a 10m distance and its surface is completely light is provided when height of the hanged image is 4900mm over the eye level and continues 700mm toward the lower part of the surface. Only in big images, human eye has to move from lower part of the image to the upper part of the viewing angle. The best place to mount small images (point: horizon level in image) is a place at the same level with the visitor's view.
- The objects should be placed in such an order that can be visited by people easily.

2. Amphitheaters

    Amphitheater should be separate from ordinary path of visitors, near to the main entrance hall or with direct access to it. It should be equipped to safety equipment (extra doors, independent electricity system, separate heating and cooling systems).

Administrative field

The field includes presidency department and different administrative sectors such as deputyships. It deals with administrative, financial, planning, and general policy making affairs of the complex.

Administrative field has two different departments:

1. Presidency department: It is responsible for supervising over execution of plans of different sectors, coordinating among deputyships and managements, final approval of plans and projects, preparing and codifying of general policies as objectives of the complex, supervising over performance of other fields. The field is consisted of three departments of presidency, plan, budget and organization, and security.

2. Administrative and financial deputyship department: It is responsible for preparing and codifying of policies of the subordinated units as objectives of the complex, notifying the approvals and governing regulations to the related units, supervising over good performance of the administrative, financial and service affairs of the complex while observing the related rules and regulations, supervising over preparing and supplying needs of the complex, installation, repair, and environmental health affairs, and

supervising over good performance of the contracts. This department is consisted of four main sectors including financial management, personnel management, technical, repair, and maintenance management, and general management.

Research field

This field is a space where the interested researchers may study about carpets theoretically or practically and take advantage of the facilities provided there. Research plays a significant and undeniable role in technological and scientific advancements. Iranian carpet industry is very poor considering scientific and artistic researches. Thus, it is better to provide carpet research sector beside the museum. The research field is consisted of two main fields:

1. Scientific research field: Here, the researchers study the issues related to spinning, dyeing and carpet weaving skills in workshops and laboratories.
2. Theoretical research field: Here, the researchers theoretically study the issues related to history of carpet and its design, and carpet from economical viewpoint, in general, and, spinning and weaving, specifically, as well as chemistry and dyeing.

To realize research objectives in museum, the research field should have some spaces such as research department, laboratories, and specialized workshops.

Training field

Scientific training of carpet is of important elements of this museum which may be helpful in recognition of this art, propagate it, and made it available for public. This is realized by training sectors of the museum which are responsible for holding of training classes and workshops about carpet history, design, weaving, dyeing, and restoration. Considering its objectives and duties, this sector is consisted of classes, workshops, and laboratories.

Architectural Projects

Museum of Modern Art

Design by Ali Khiabanian

River
River
River

ورودی اصلی مجموعه
مسیر فرعی
فضای سبز
پارکینگ
ورودی موزه
رستوران مجموعه
خروجی به طرف سایت
مسیر فرعی
آمفی تئاتر روباز
فضای آموزشی مجموعه
باغ مجسمه
رودخانه
شهرک مسکونی

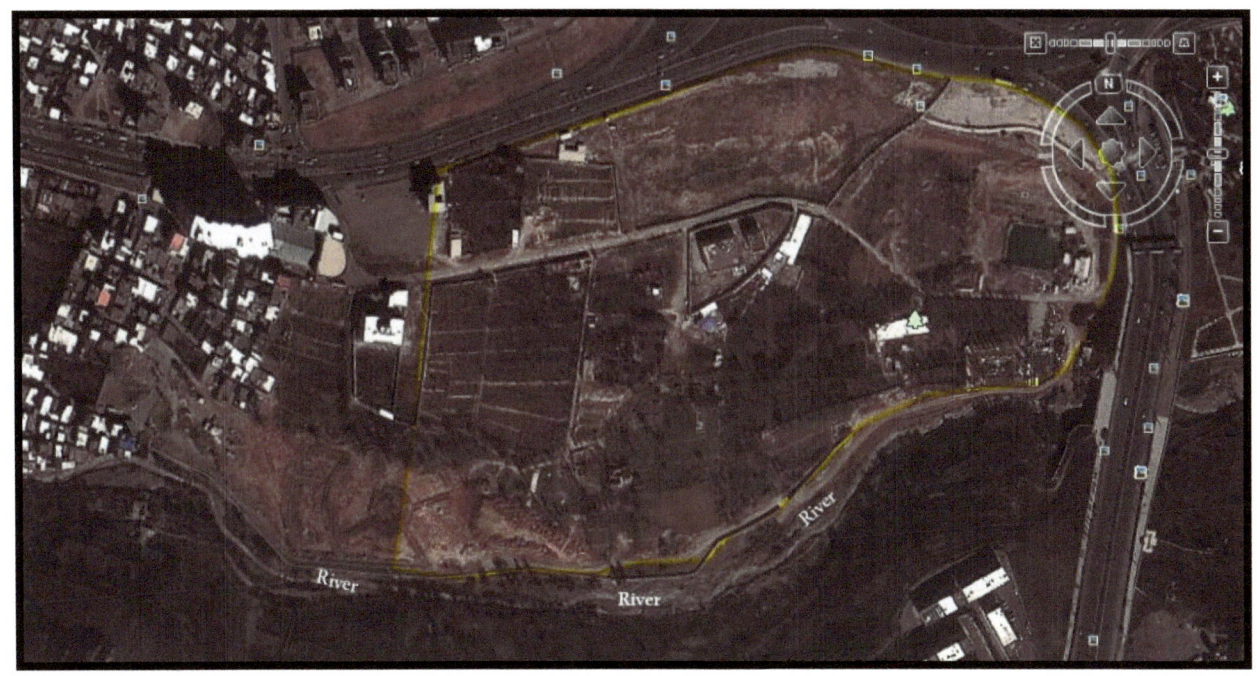

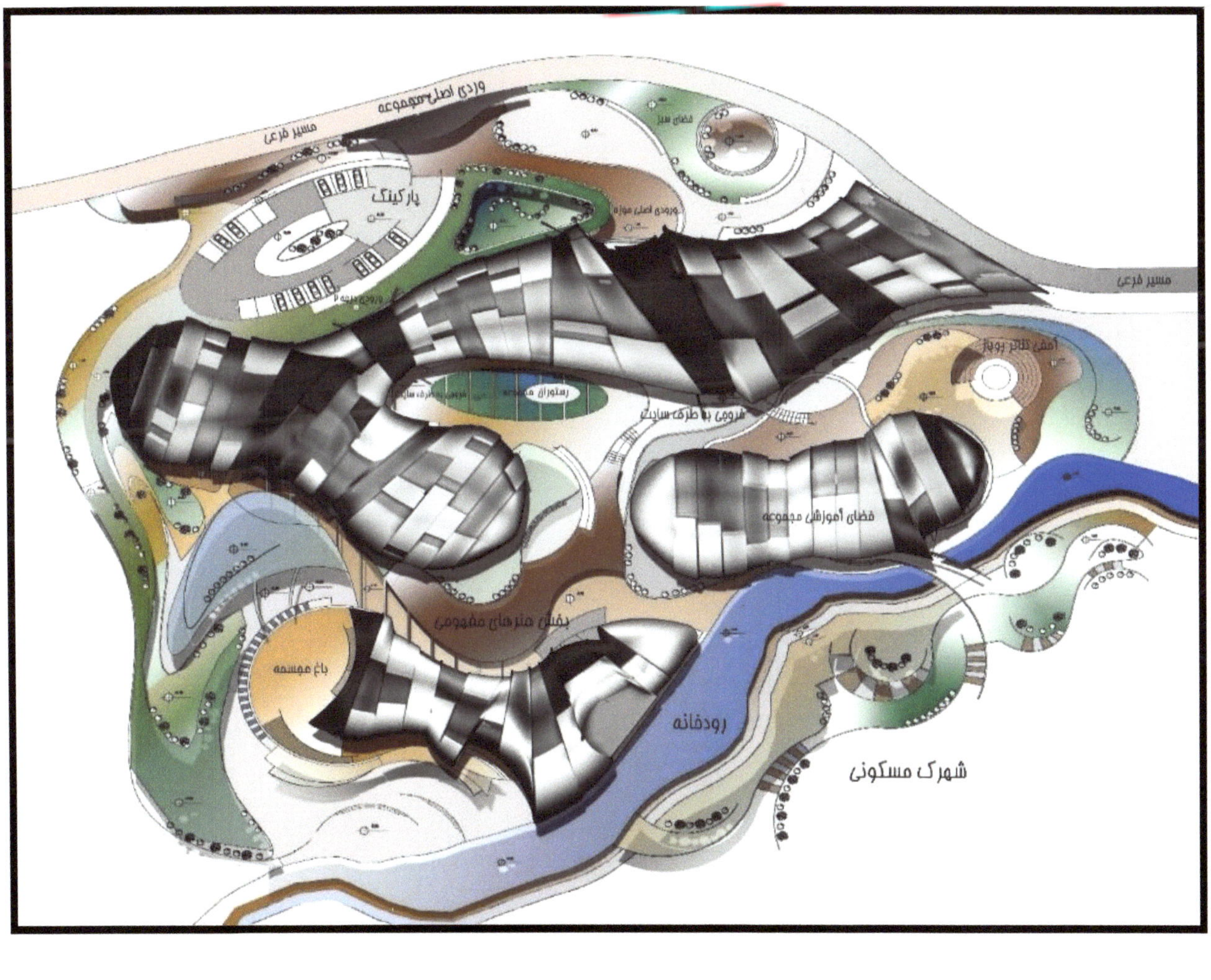

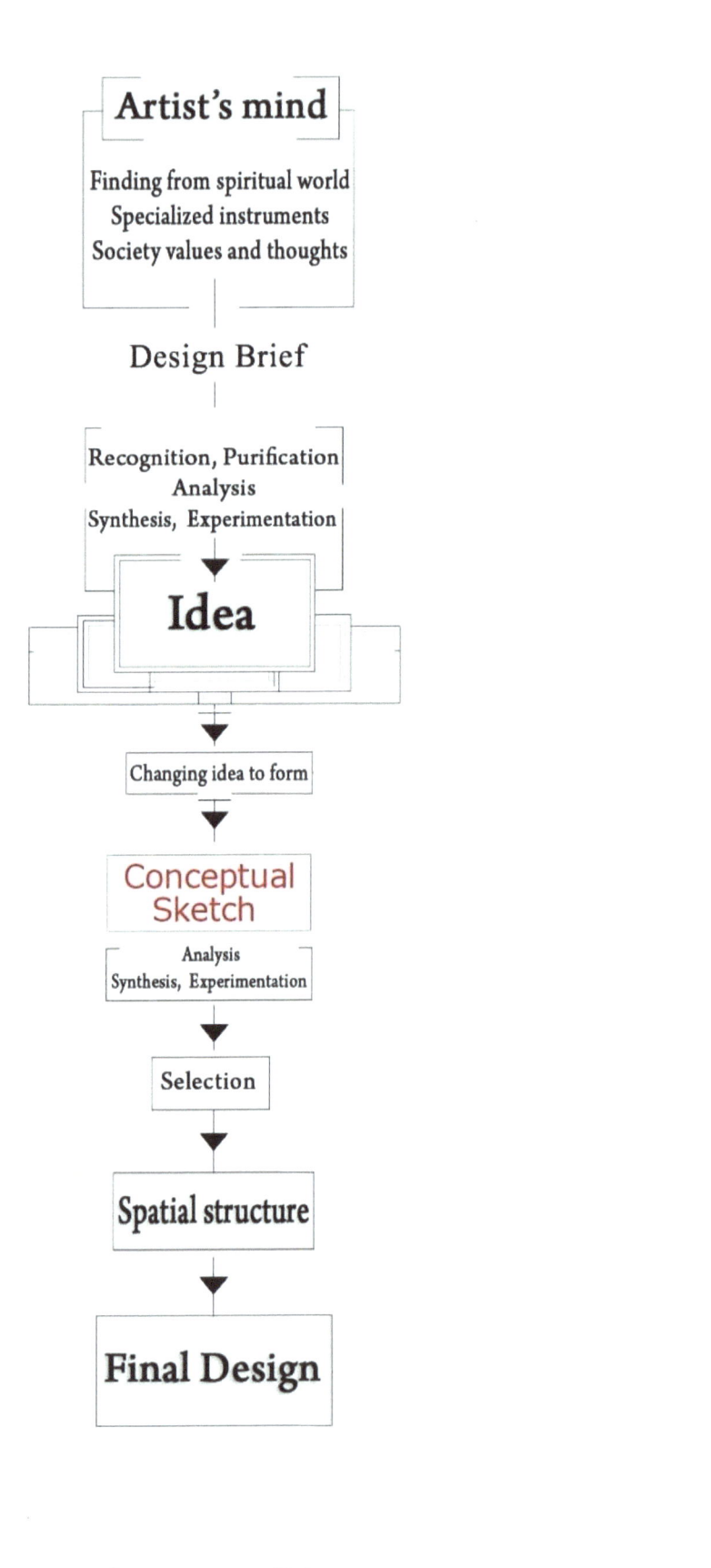

Design Process Diaram

Diagram of the previous page was described in detail in "The role of brain hemispheres in architectural design". Taking benefit of design process and being bounded to it, similar to other books, is really important for me in this book, too. As it is seen in the projects, conceptual sketches play important role in this process. "Conceptual sketch" stage (within the red rectangular) is related to embodiment of ideas and thoughts formed in architectural imaginations. However, they are not sufficiently clear and the sketches help them to express themselves better.

Conceptual sketches of these projects are not merely limited to manual design; rather they are presented as 3D models in computer or volumetric works using 3D pens or prints. At this stage, there is a traverse between manual sketches and modeling.

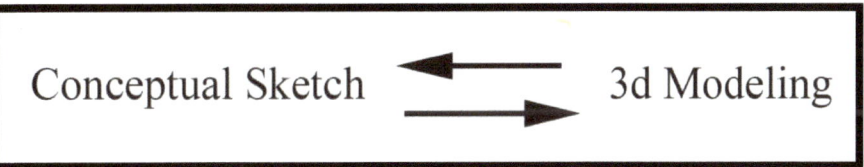

The sketches are modeled with a new perspective or designed based on 3D models to enrich their volume or space. This traverse which is regarded as a transversal movement during the design process is of special importance. I call it "interaction between design and computer".

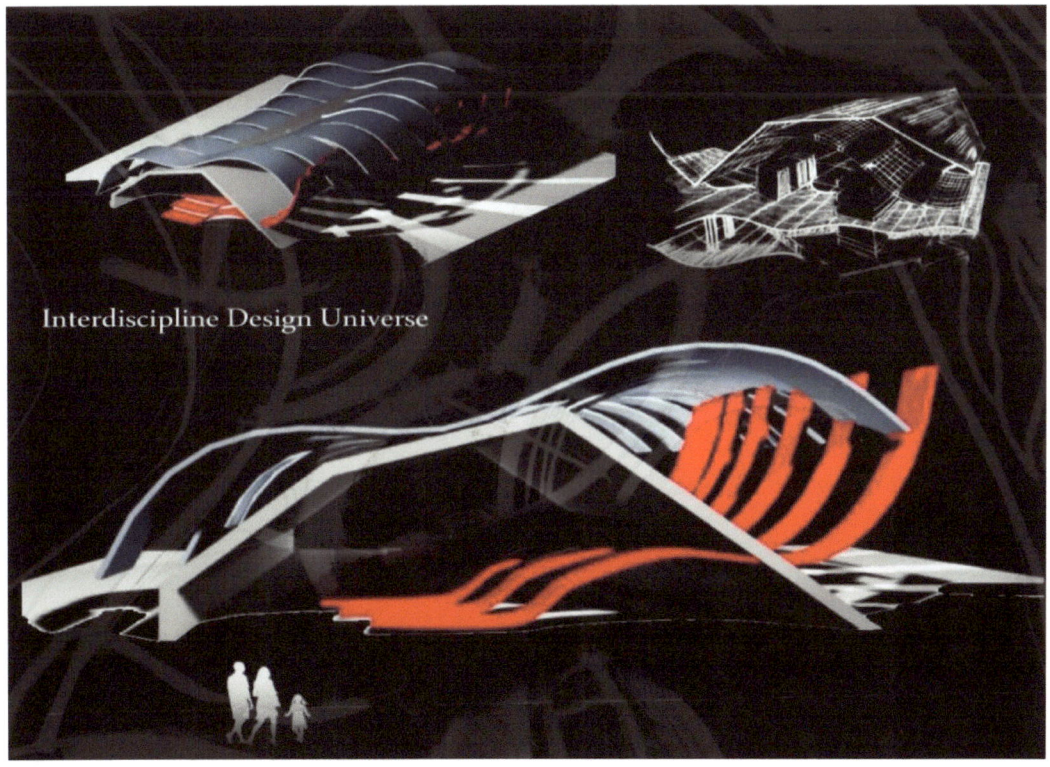

I think "interactive design" accurately defines digital design where two or more minds try to create a novel phenomenon. It helps interaction and coordination of design and computer as well as better understanding of software. The method which is now used in projects design at Inter-discipline Design Universe, directed us toward another direction or, in better words, a mutation in design, to design merely on computer without any sketch or Marquette. The next chapters exactly support results of interactive design between computer and designer mind where design process is began on computer based on a predetermined concept.

Animation link of museum design process:

https://www.youtube.com/watch?v=P1G73uvuEtI

Design Process

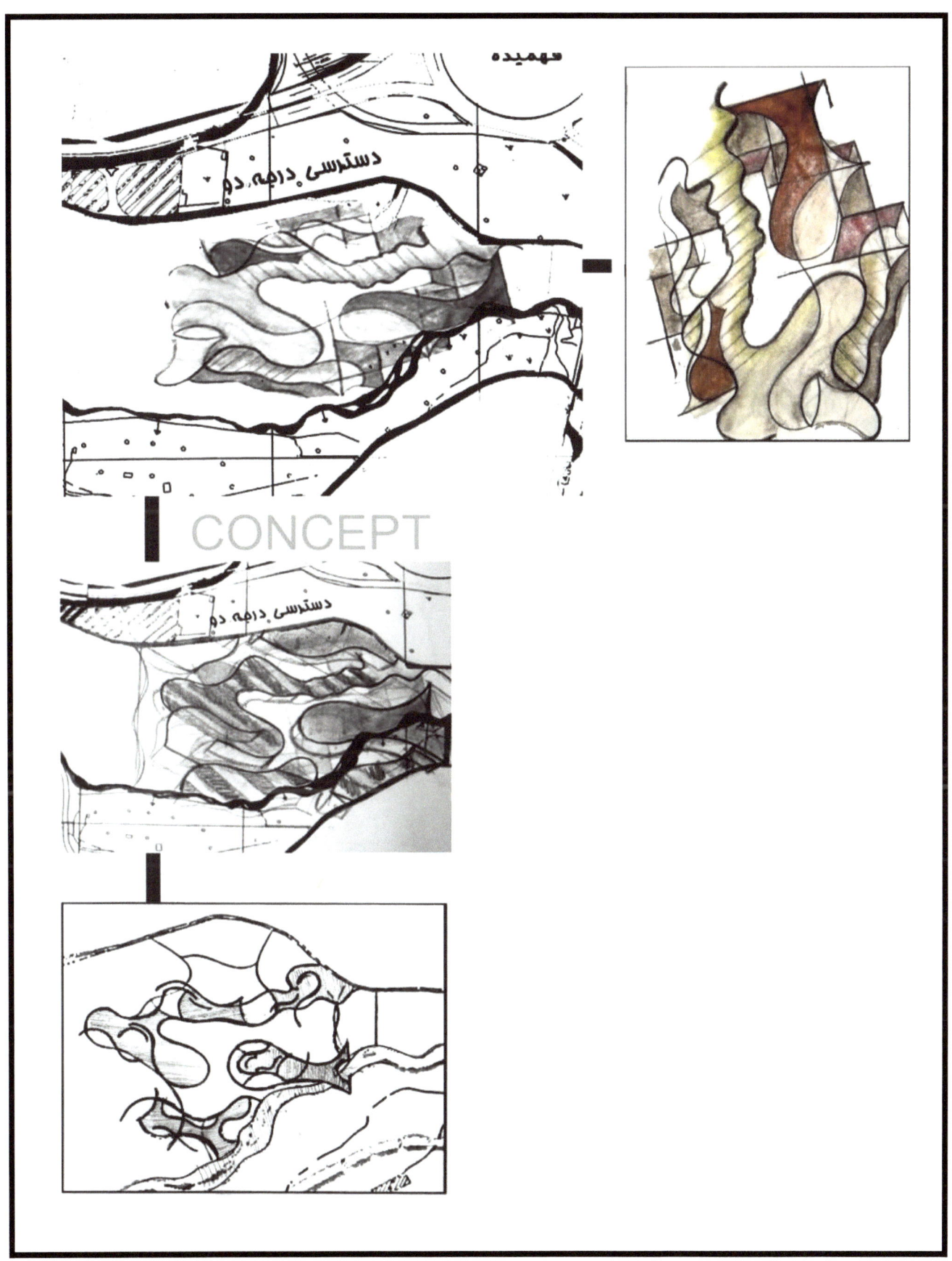

CONCEPT

**Effort to use site's original lines :
Attention to interference and continuation of lines from inside of form to site plan and vice versa (in order to make communication)**

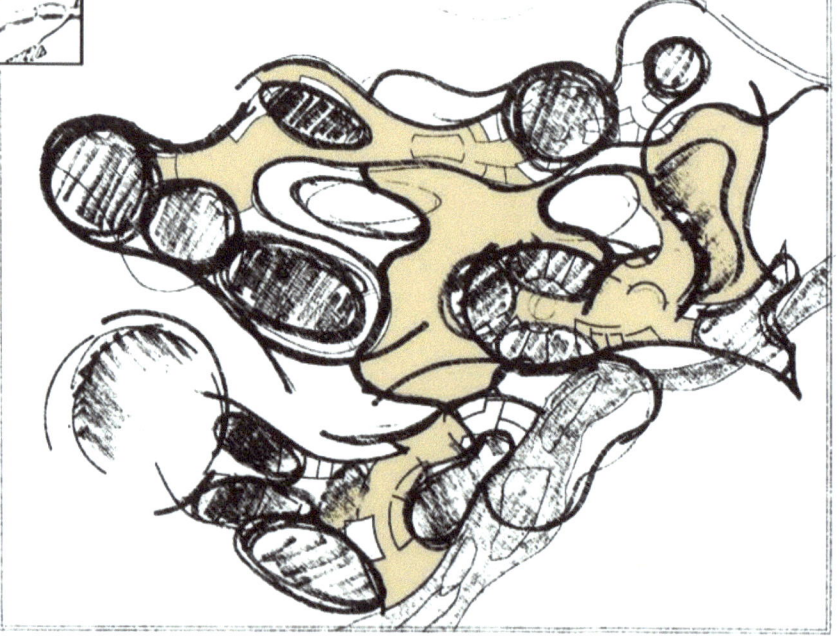

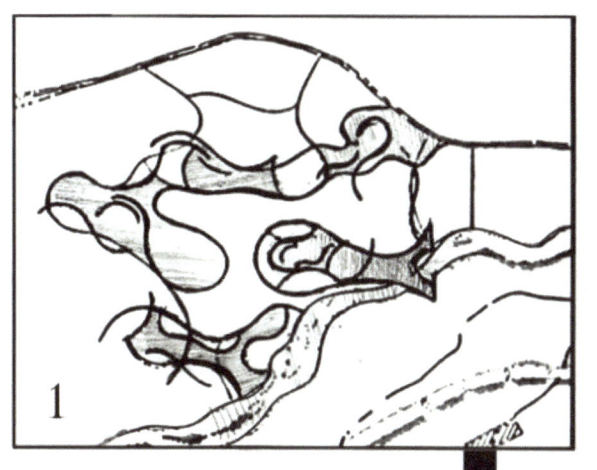

Siteplan geeneral lines (After studying the alternatives and sketches)

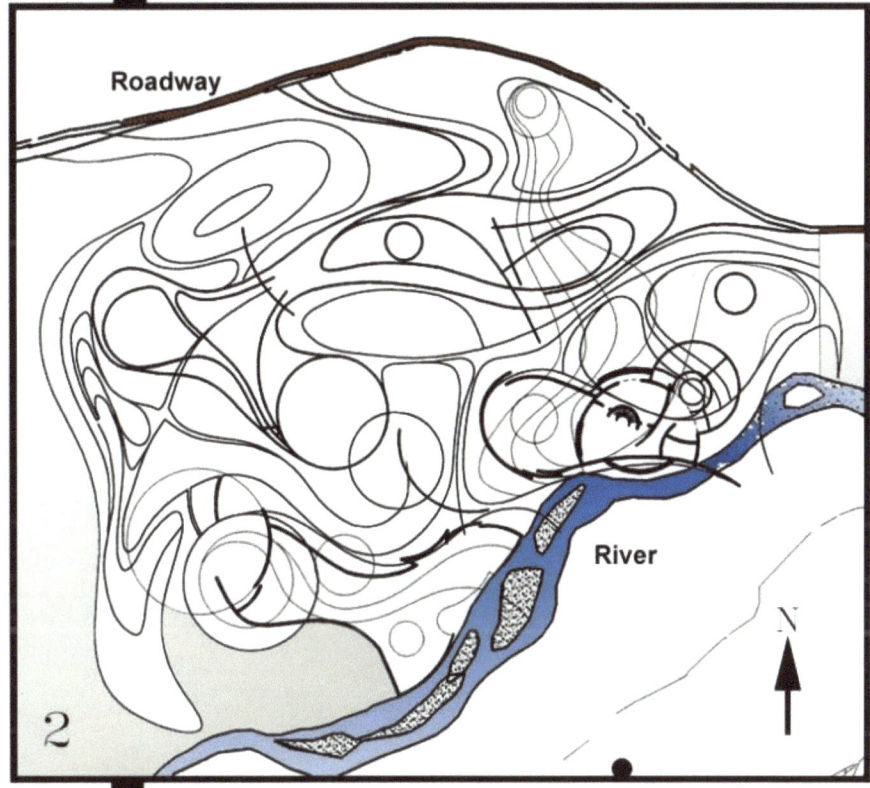

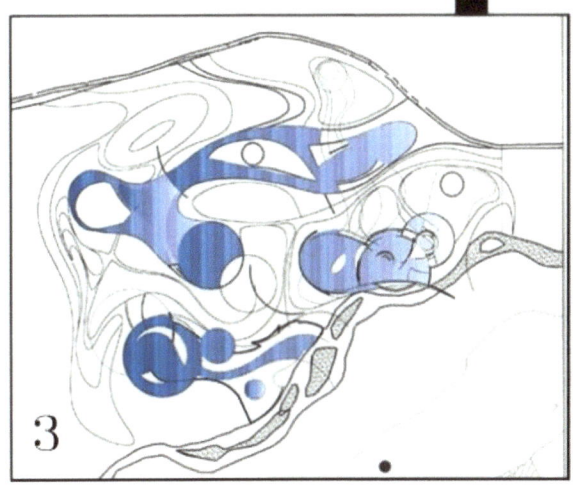

Overlaying forms on the siteplan (According to proposed design area)

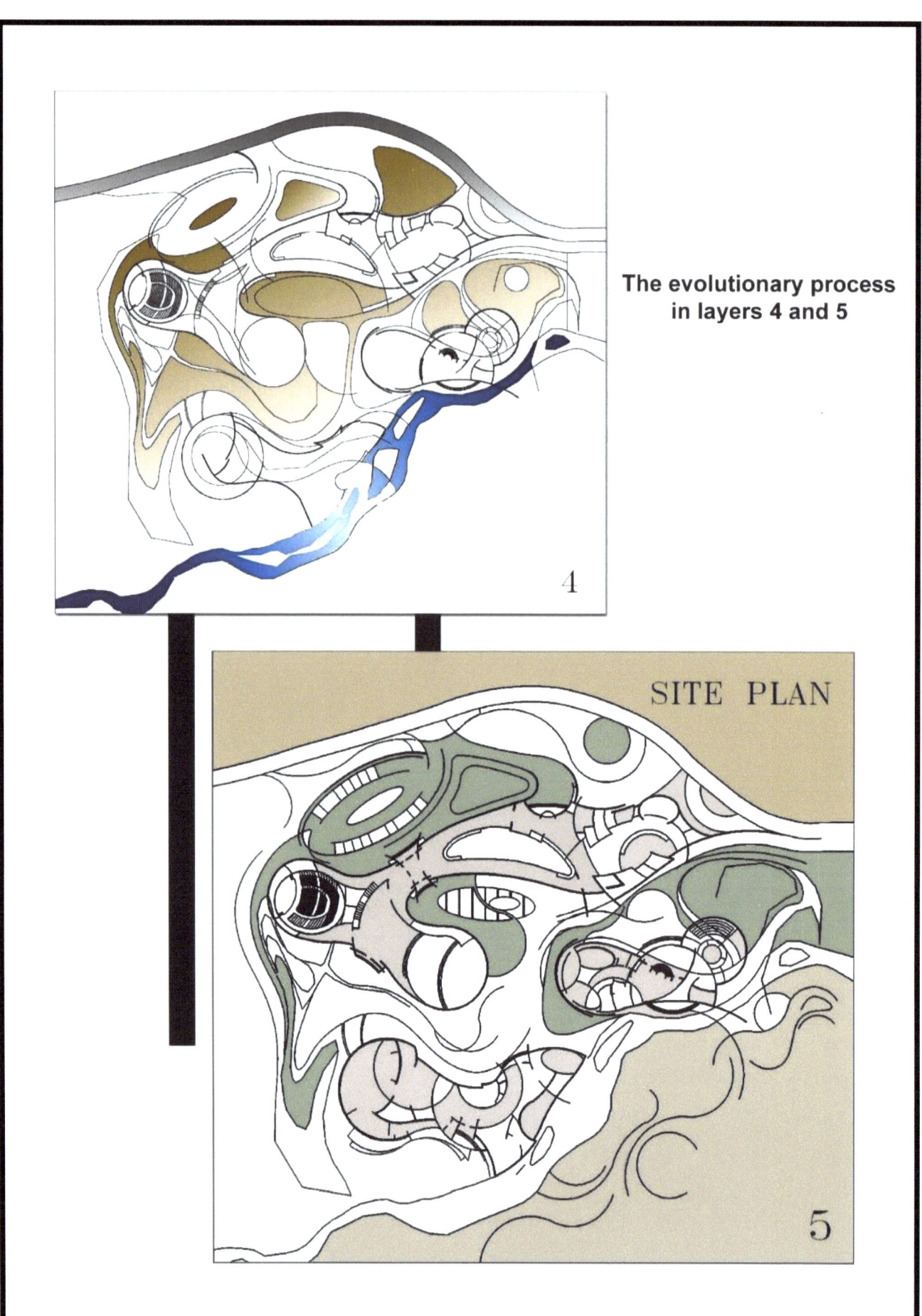

The evolutionary process in layers 4 and 5

Design Process

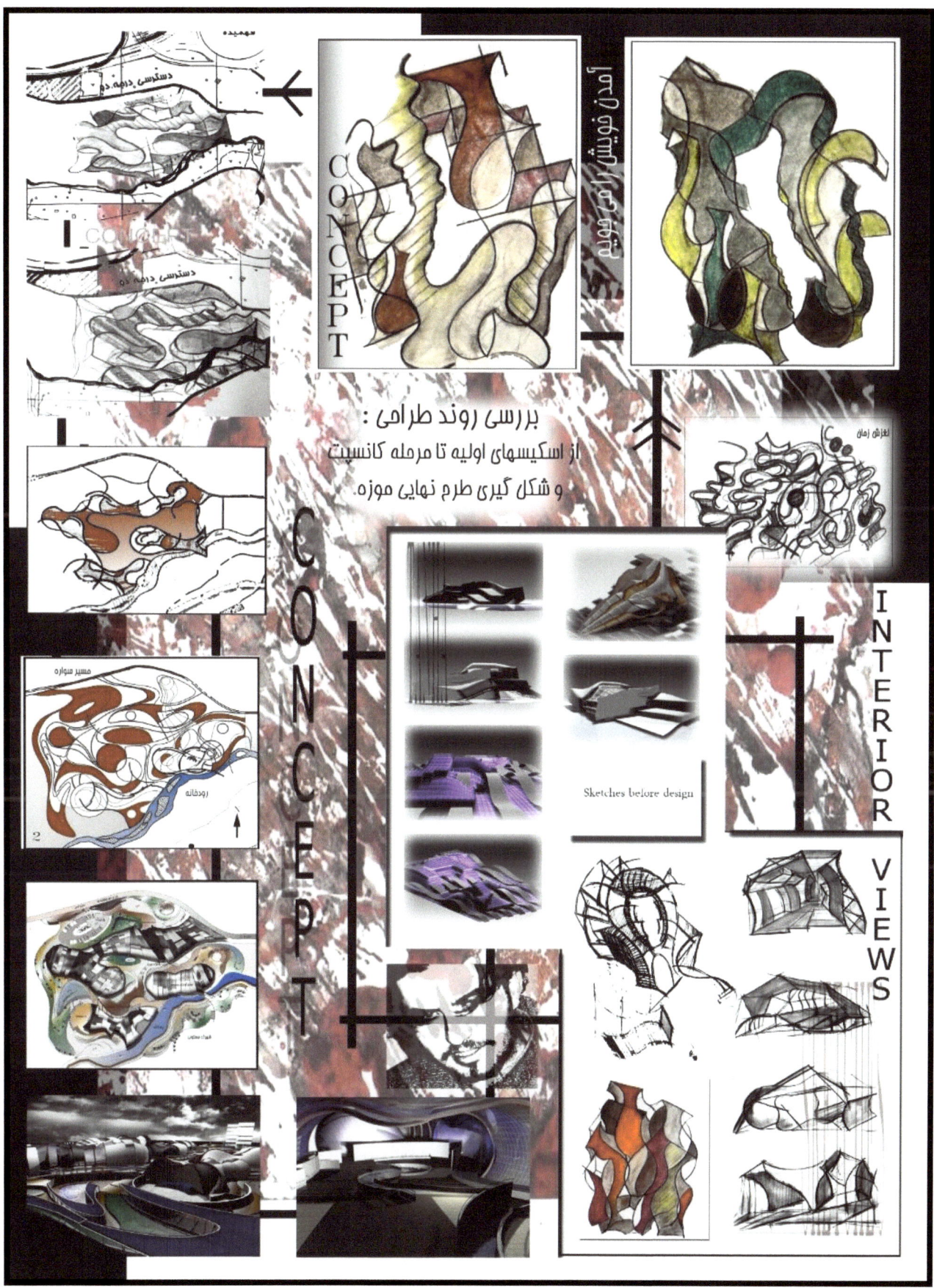

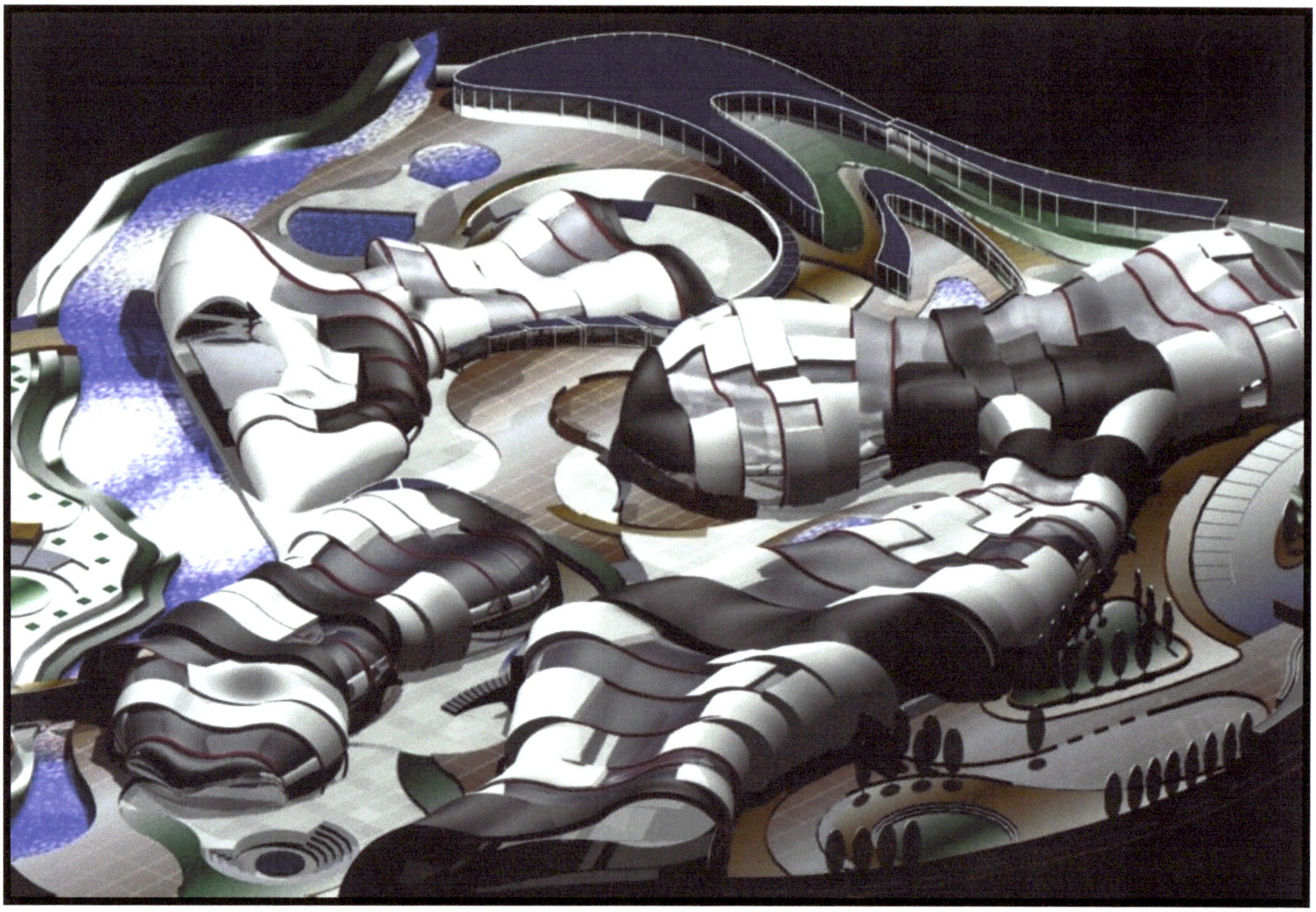

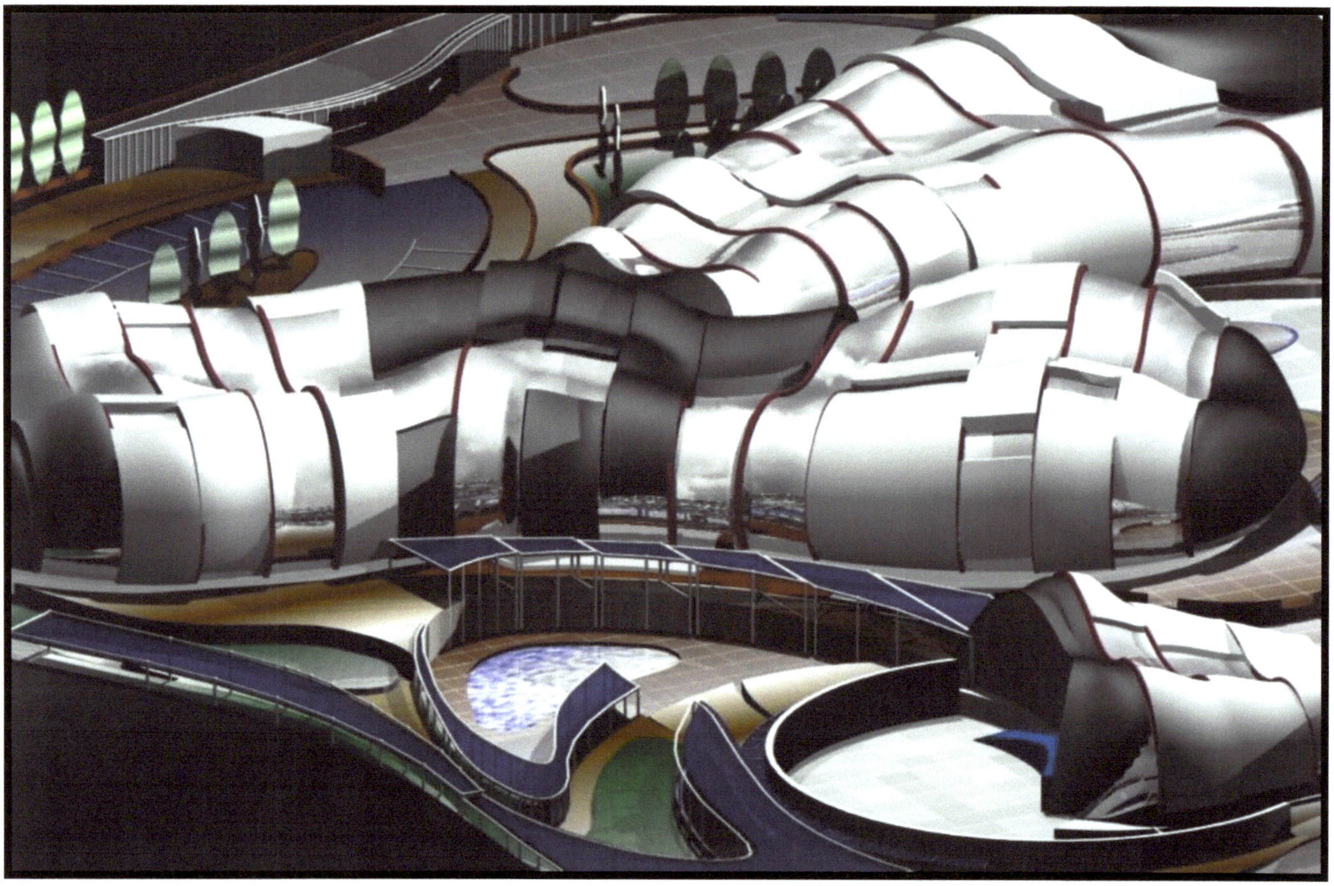

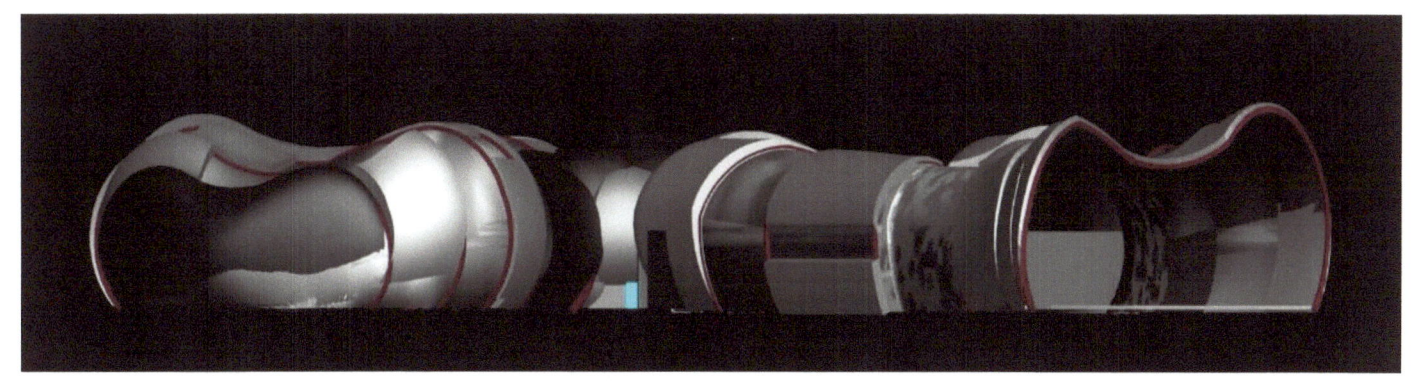
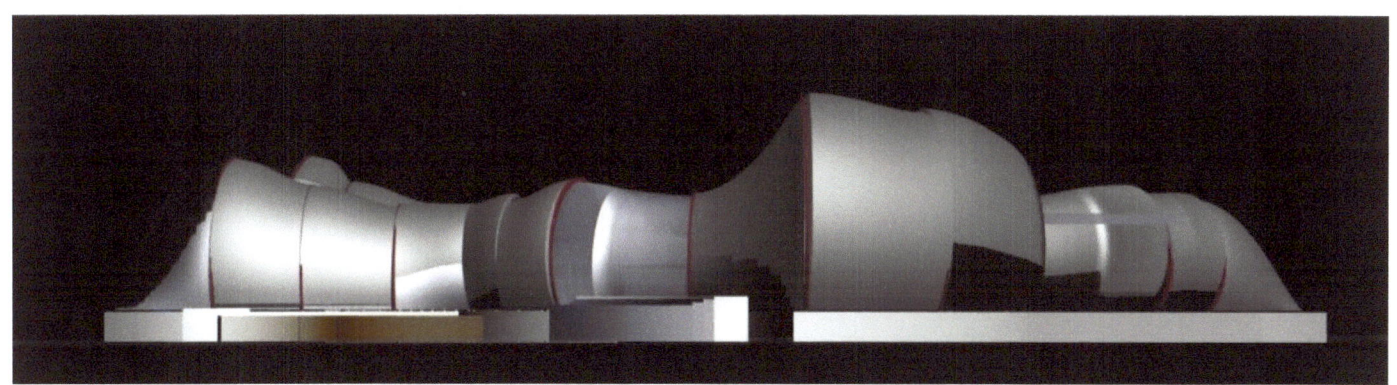
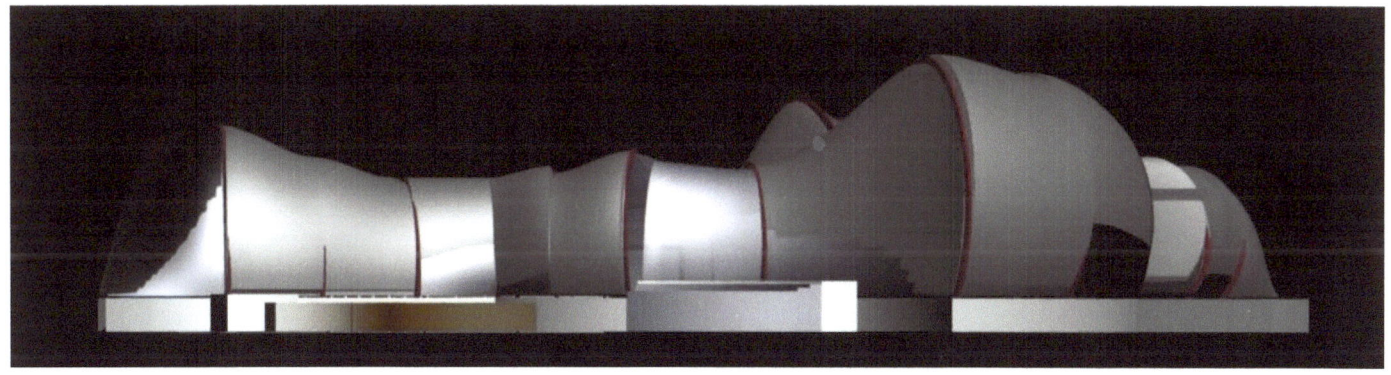
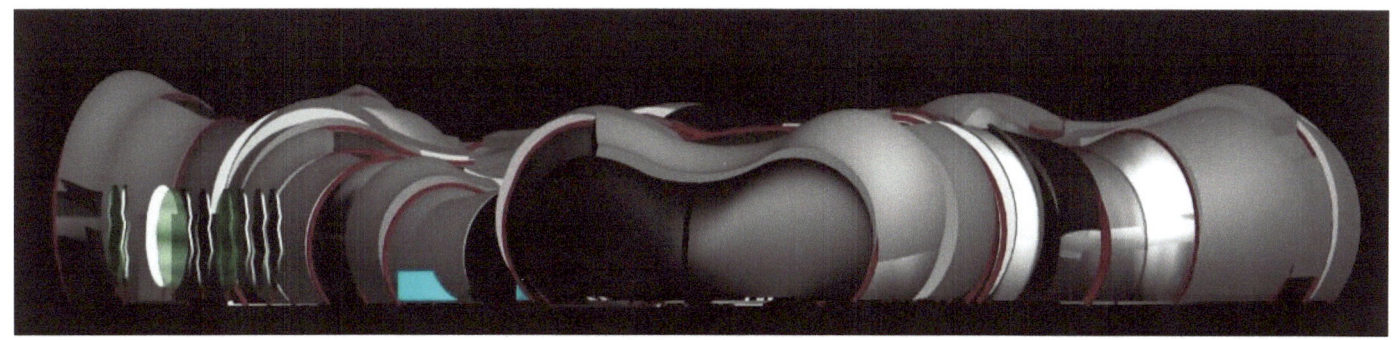

Elevations

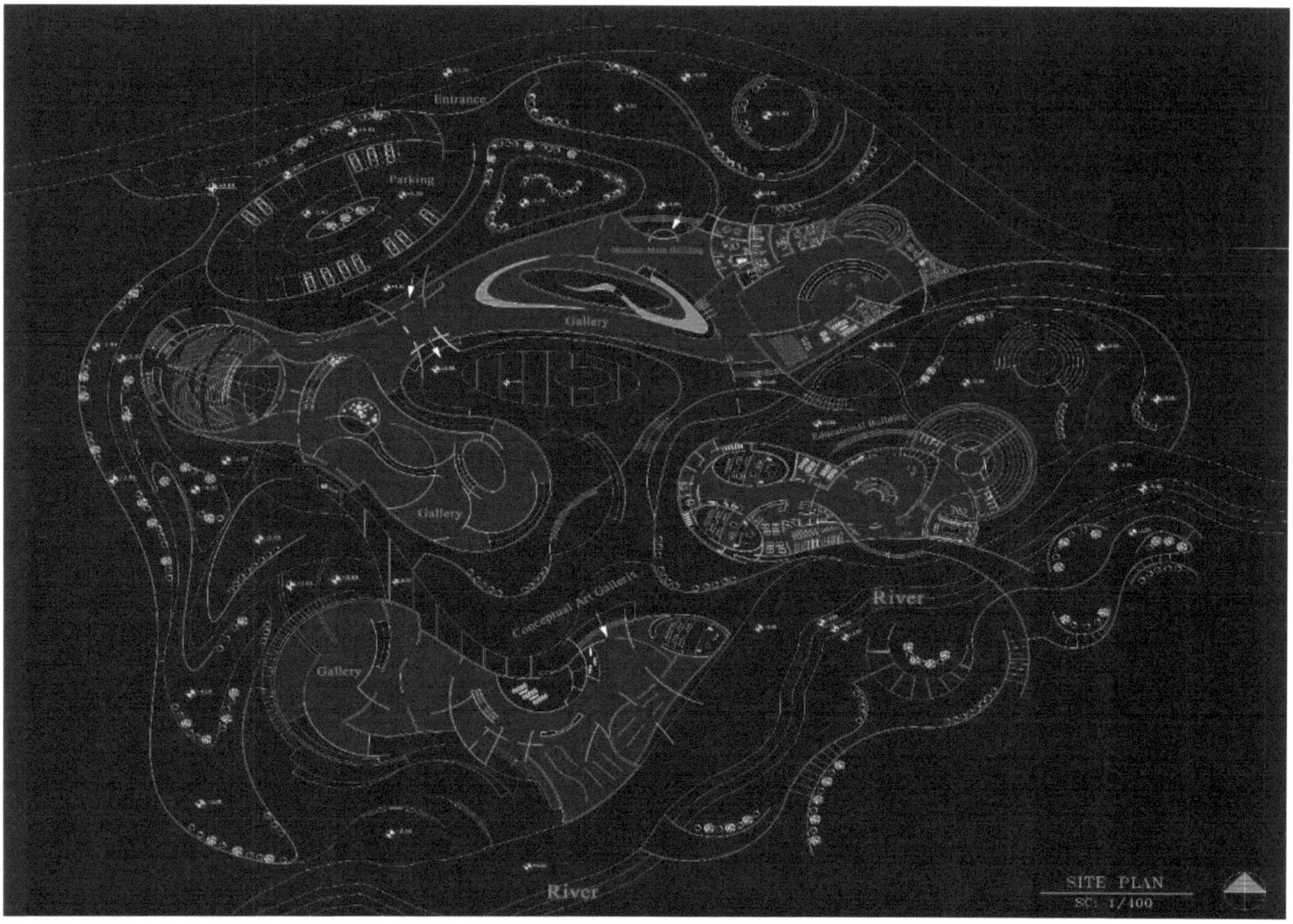
Entrance
Parking
Gallery
Gallery
Conceptual Art Gallery
Gallery
River
River
SITE PLAN
SC: 1/400

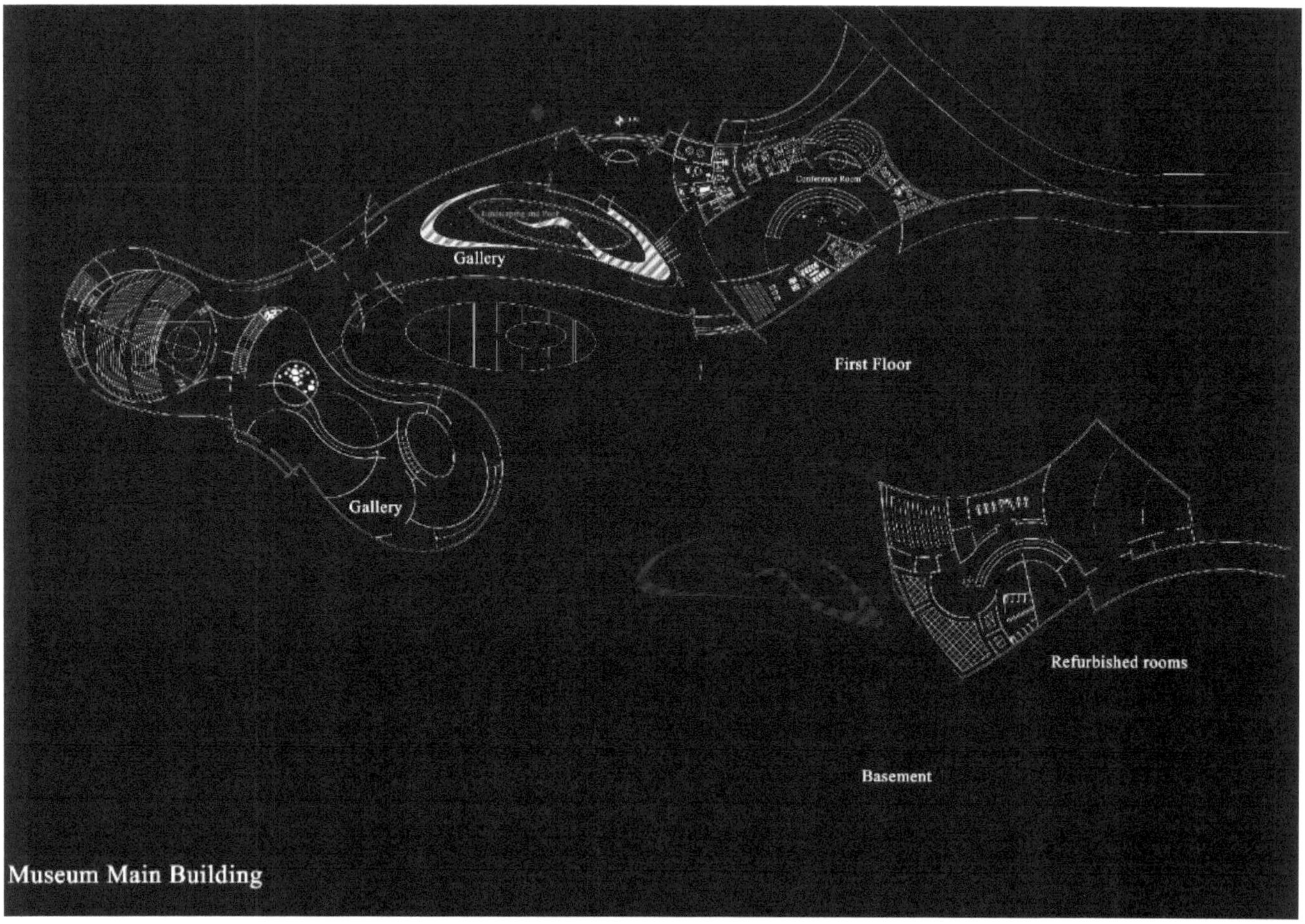
Gallery
First Floor
Gallery
Refurbished rooms
Basement
Museum Main Building

Museum Second Building
(Temporary Galleris)

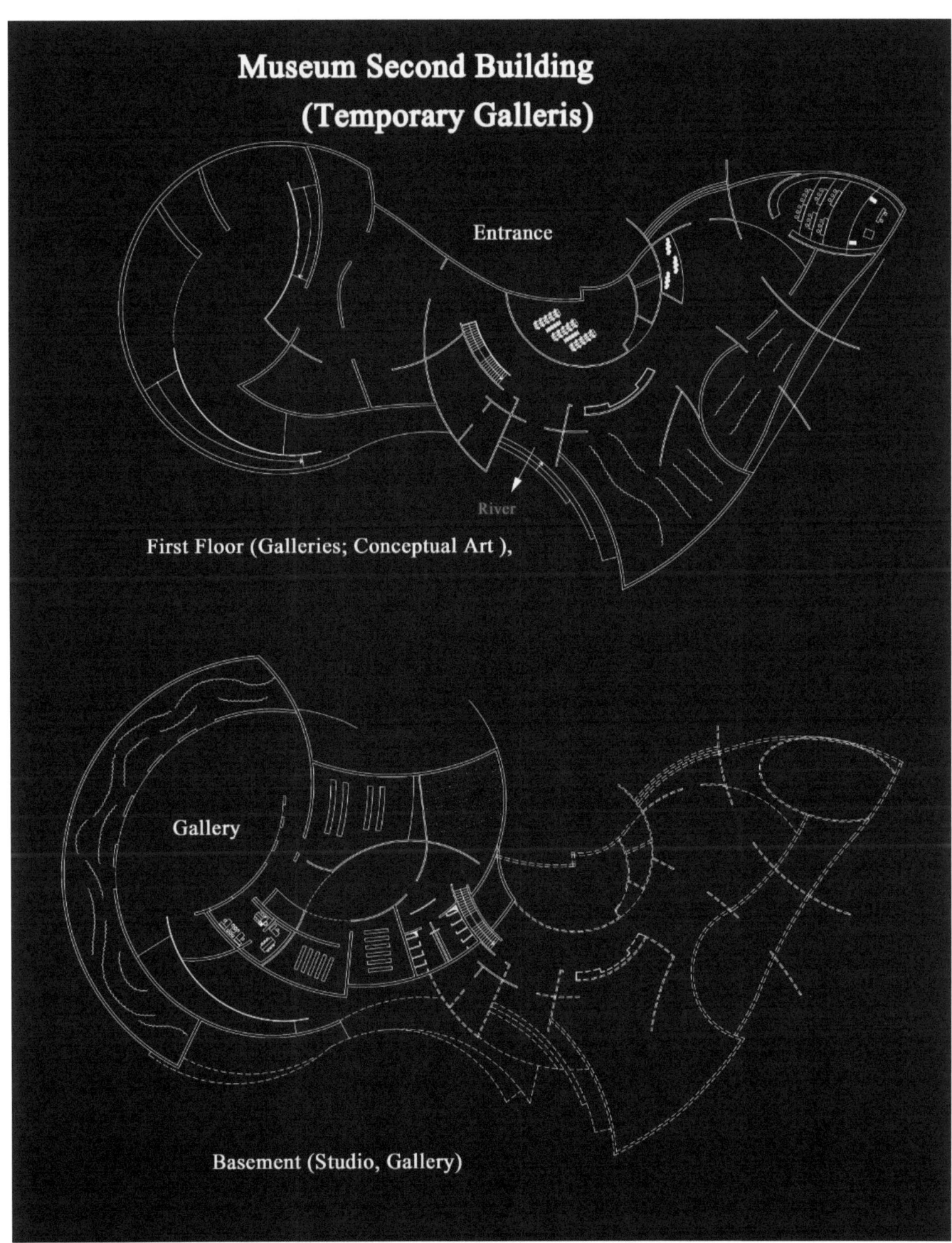

Educational Building

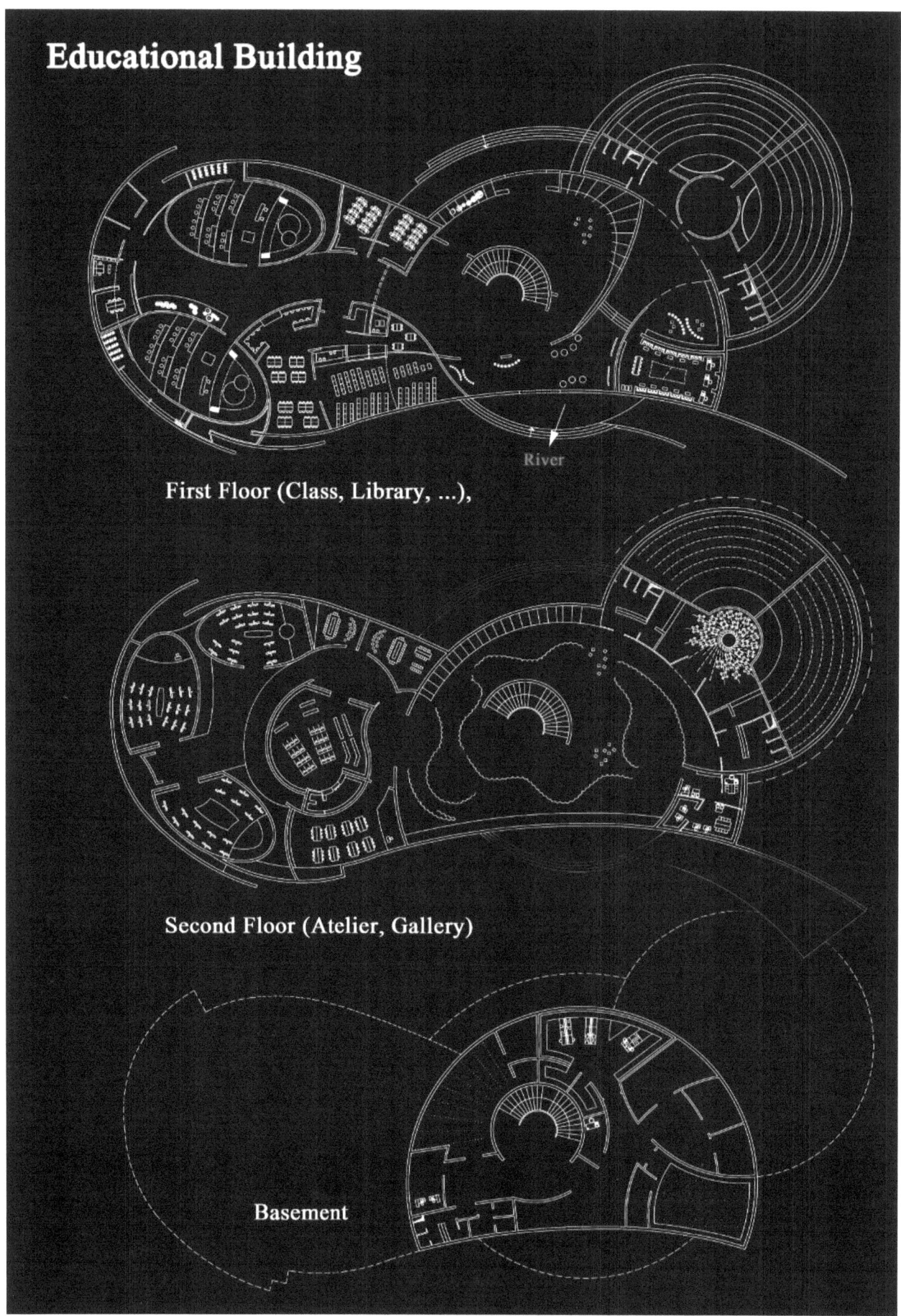

First Floor (Class, Library, ...),

Second Floor (Atelier, Gallery)

Basement

Museum of Modern Art

Sections

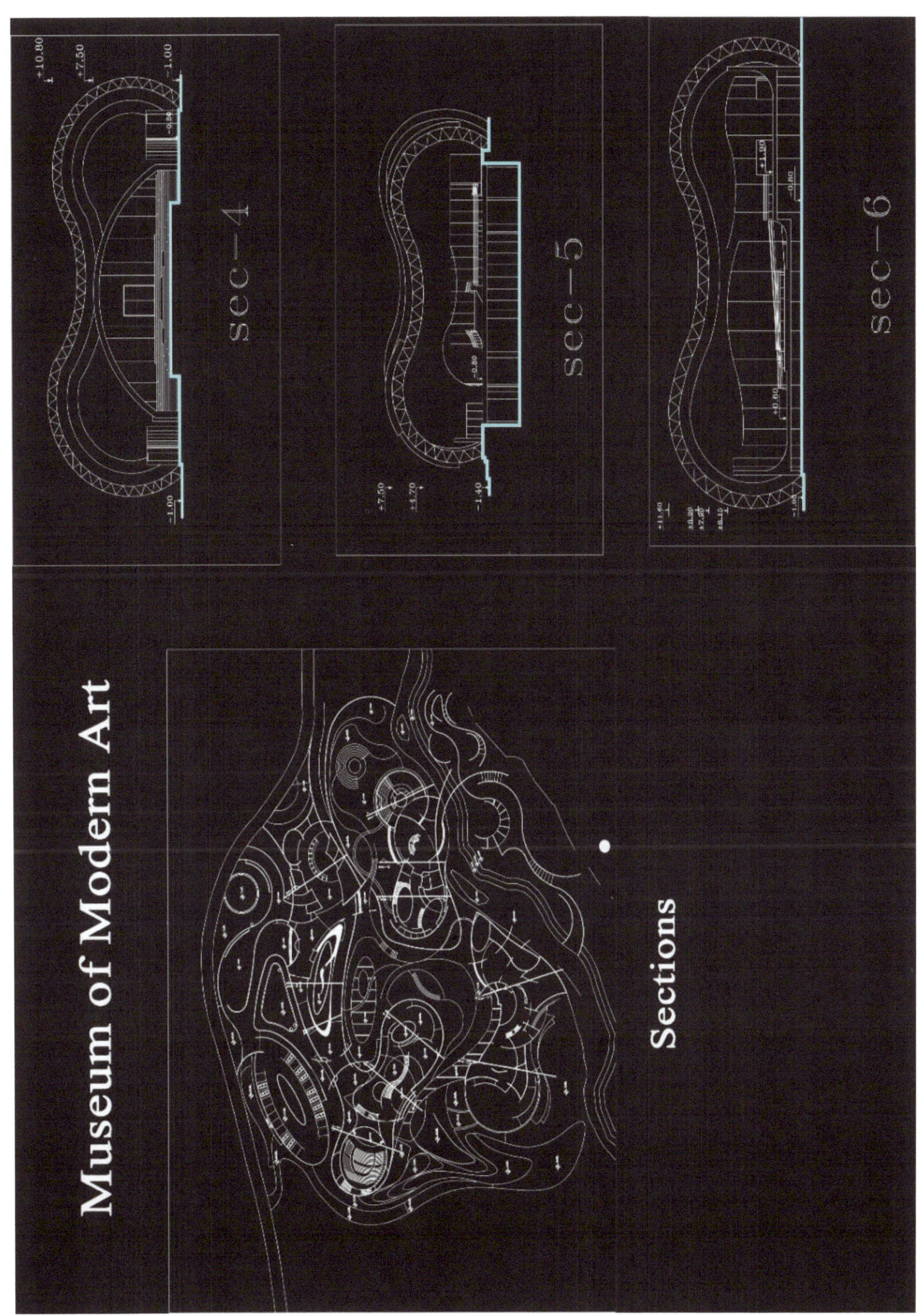

Archaeological Museum

Mohammad Reza Torabi

Master of architecture

An architectural work belongs to its past, on one hand, and its future, on the other hand. Architecture is formed at present. In a figurative meaning, it is an in-between space or a changing compound passing from past to future. Here, the in-between space serves as an intermediary between adjacencies and is not a separator element. Rather it is a potential to reach the flexibility and an interwoven which operate by the forces radiating from the bed and its adjacencies as continuity and urban space interaction not as a contrast. The complex design mainly aims at creating flexibility, connecting the adjacent elements, interweaving urban space context, releasing the work from the inflexible space, and promoting the clients 'knowledge about the work.

Here, in-between space plays a role in organizing and combining two different contexts and making every urban space and building dynamic. It is a container for different functions. Pleasures of such spaces find a bilateral nature due to its constructive objectives and become both a process and a product of process. Concurrent with formation process, in-between space is helpful in rating and orienting of distinct concepts and is finally manifested as a whole.

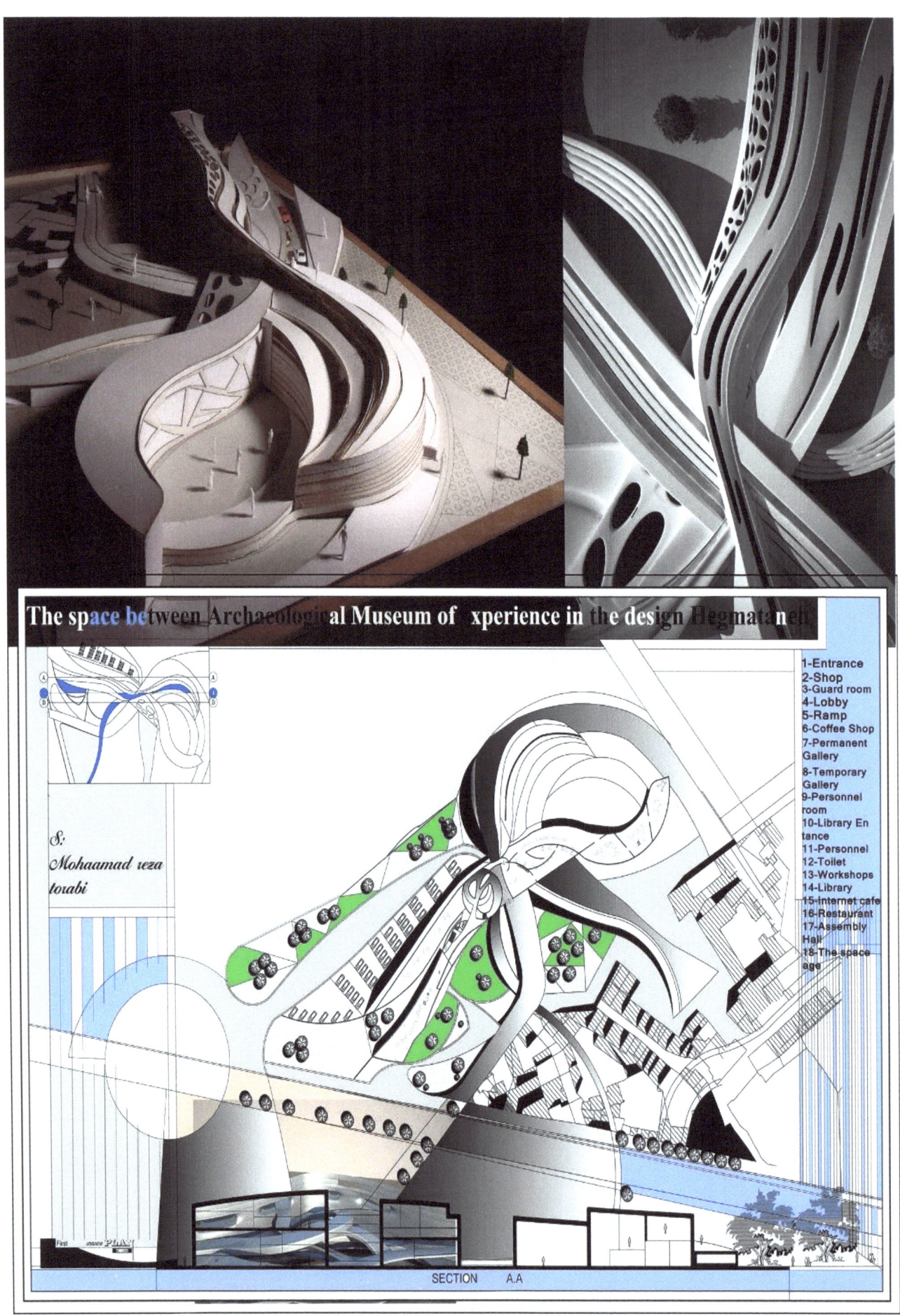

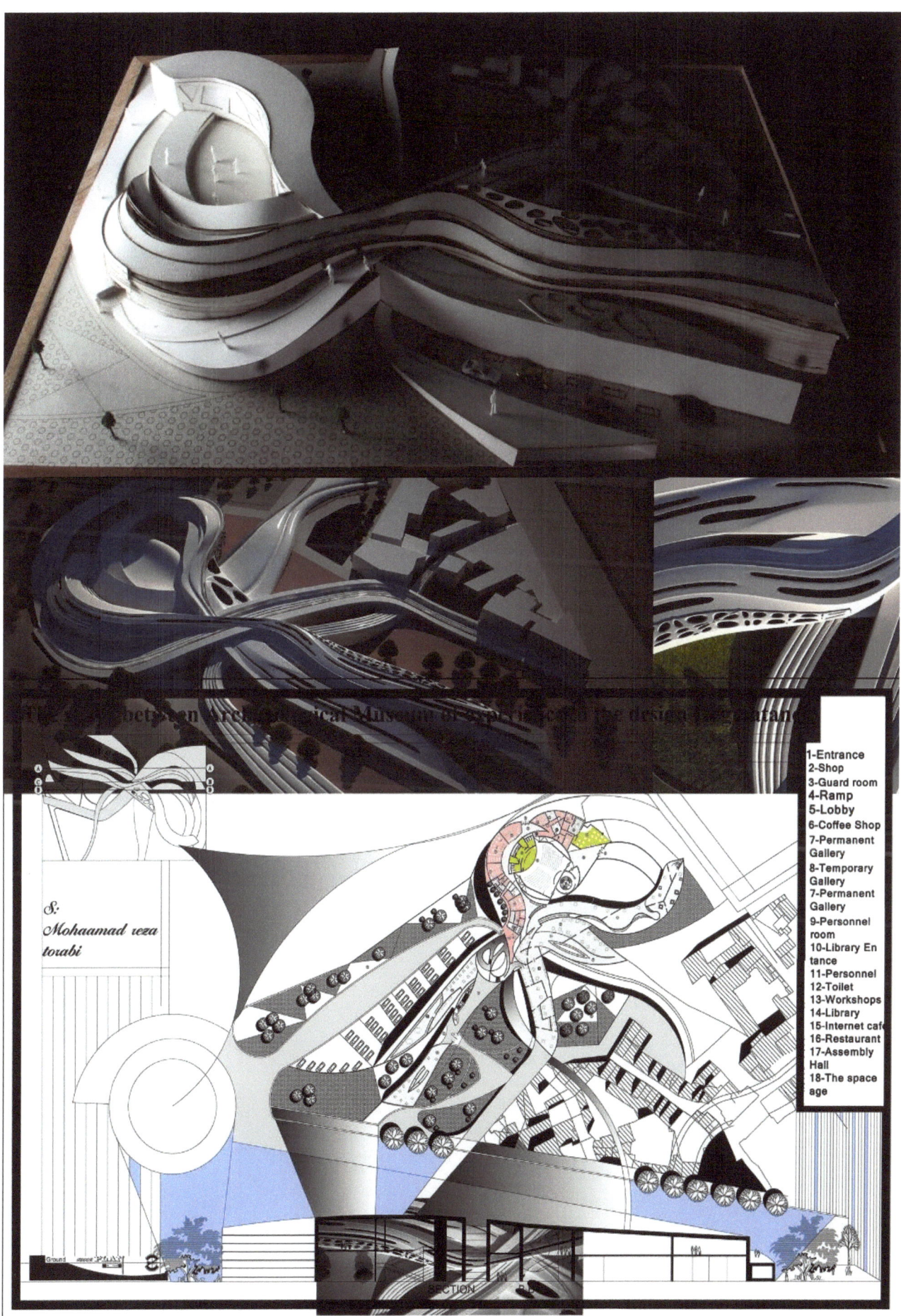

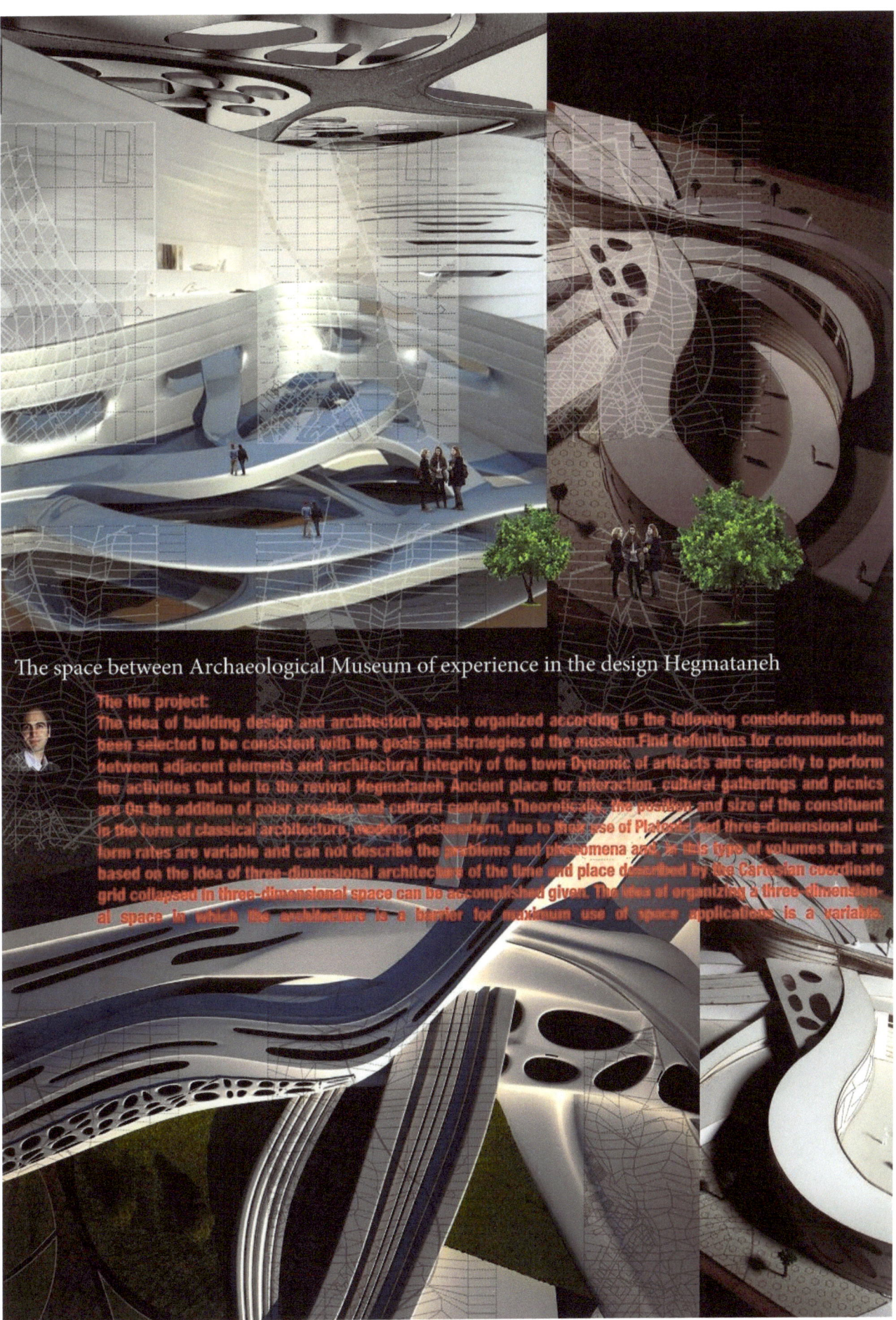

The space between Archaeological Museum of experience in the design Hegmataneh

The the project:
The idea of building design and architectural space organized according to the following considerations have been selected to be consistent with the goals and strategies of the museum. Find definitions for communication between adjacent elements and architectural integrity of the town Dynamic of artifacts and capacity to perform the activities that led to the revival Hegmataneh Ancient place for interaction, cultural gatherings and picnics are On the addition of polar creative and cultural contents Theoretically, the position and size of the constituent in the form of classical architecture, modern, postmodern, due to the use of Platonic and three-dimensional uniform rates are variable and can not describe the problems and phenomena and, in this type of volumes that are based on the idea of three-dimensional architecture of the time and place described by the Cartesian coordinate grid collapsed in three-dimensional space can be accomplished given. The idea at organizing a three-dimensional space in which the architecture is a barrier for maximum use of space applications is a variable.

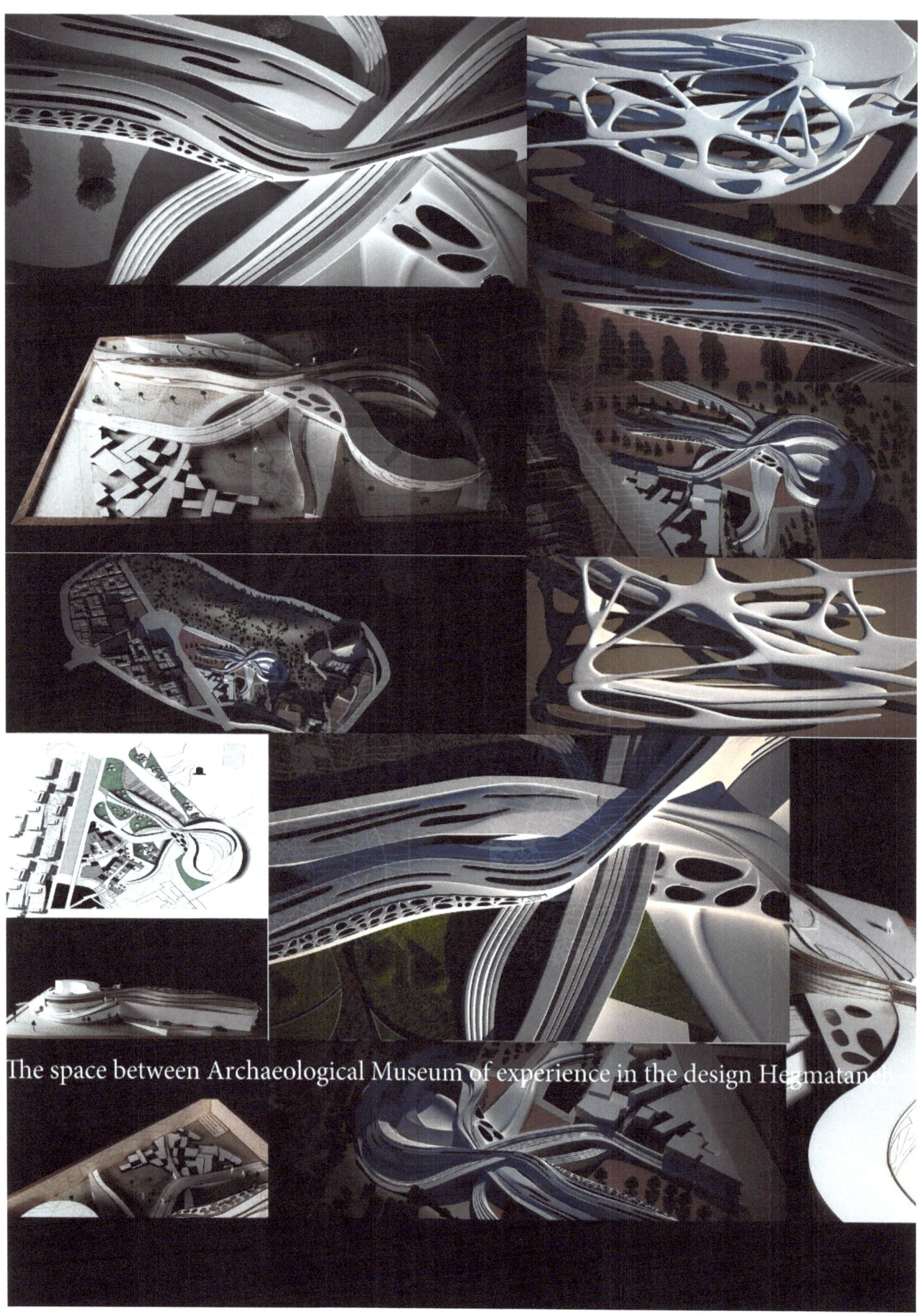

The space between Archaeological Museum of experience in the design Hegmataneh

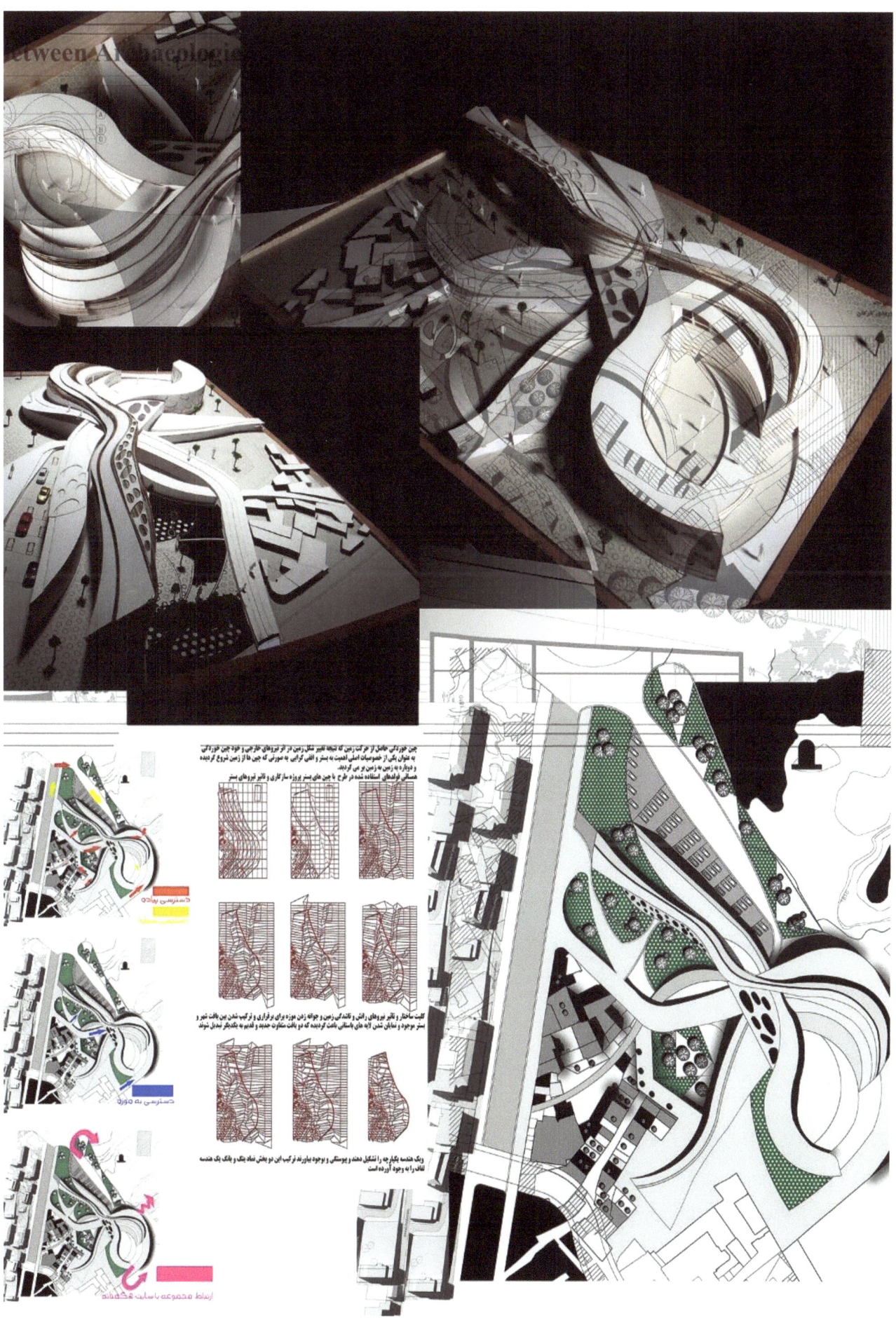

Tabriz Music Museum

Amir Navadeye Shahla

Master of Architecture

Project design process

To design music museum in Tabriz, sol key was used as an ideal form during initial stages of the design process. The key may create one of the best forms for the museum because of its fluid and dynamic form. Appropriate circulation is one of the factors which should be considered in museum design. The circulation created an appropriate and fine form for the museum due to dynamic nature of sol key and its relation with music.

Sol key is a sign found at the beginning of left hand of the staff and indicates to location of the sol note on the second line of the staff. The other notes are recognized or named based on sol key.

Location of sol key on staff:

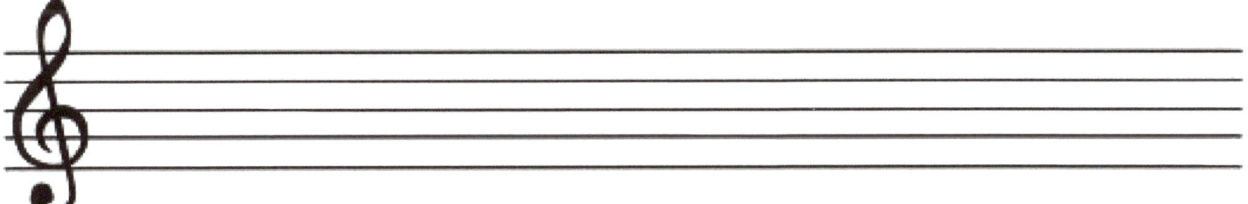

Once the sol key was used as the ideal form, the design was begun with the first sketch.

After the first sketch, primary etude is used for main parts of the sketch and following form is

created.

Due to its extension in one story, being very long, and making the addressee bored, this form requires second sketch.

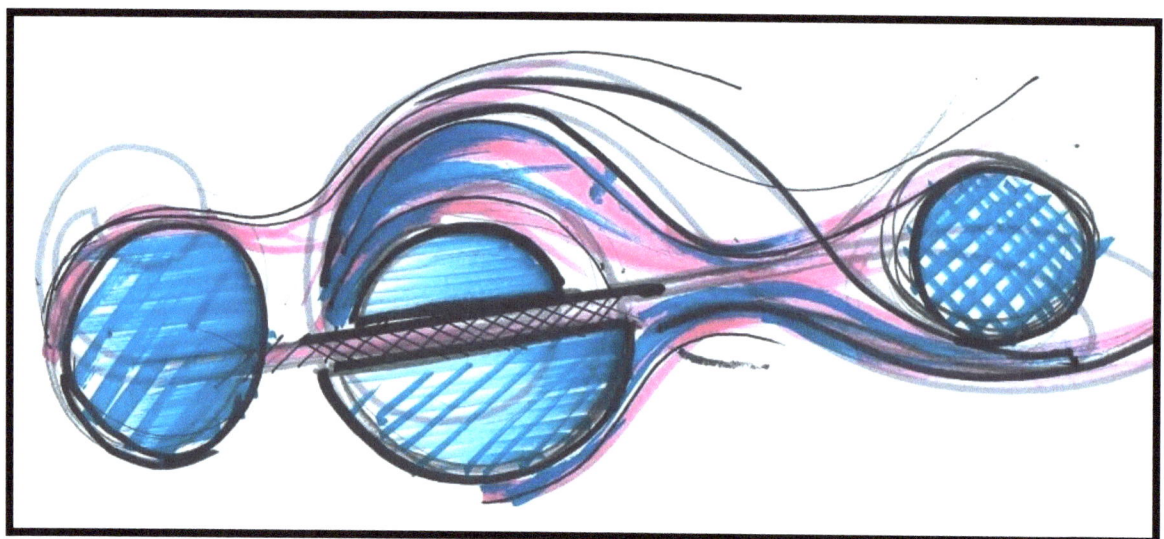

After this sketch, the first section is drawn.

After the first sketch and form, new forms are designed using the second sketch. The following form is created which is different from the first design considering non-extension in one story and locating the spaces in different stories. There is a corridor at the middle part connecting three volumes.

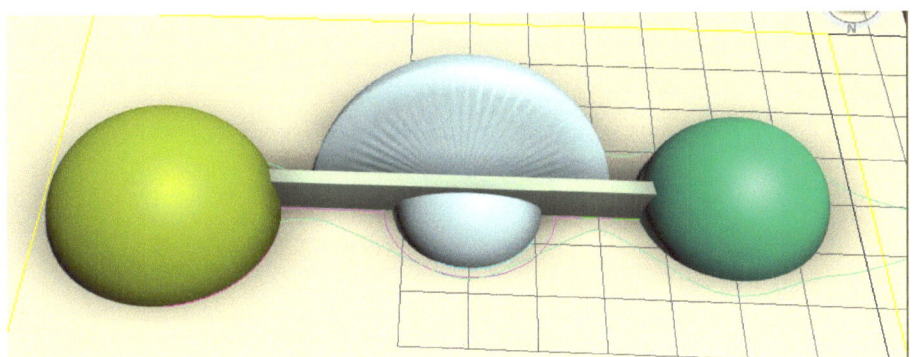

After the first form, the second form is designed where the middle corridor is eliminated and following form is created being inspired from the staff and adding these lines to middle part of the volume.

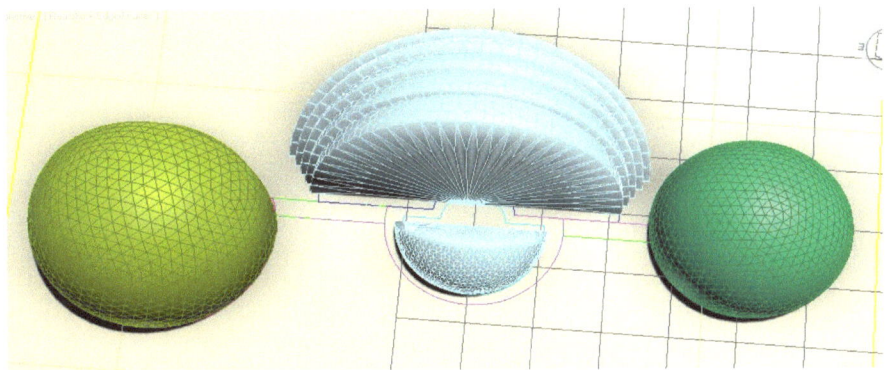

Due to design imperfection, lack of design correlation, and existence of four separate volumes found in the second form, the third form is designed where the staff is separated from the main volume, a communicative corridor is created in all volumes, and an entrance is defined for the building.

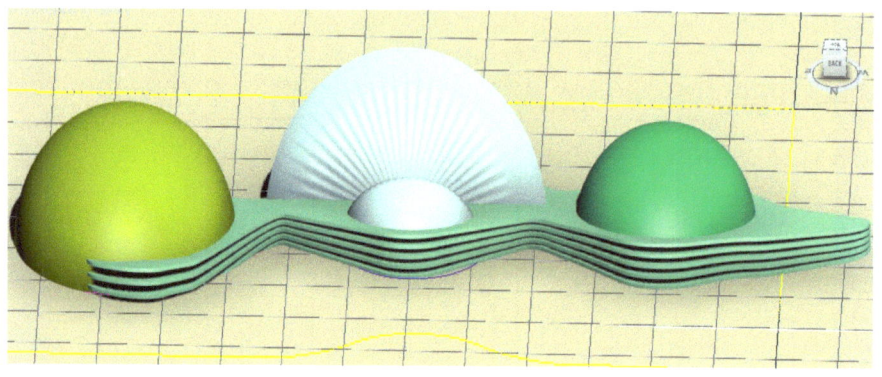

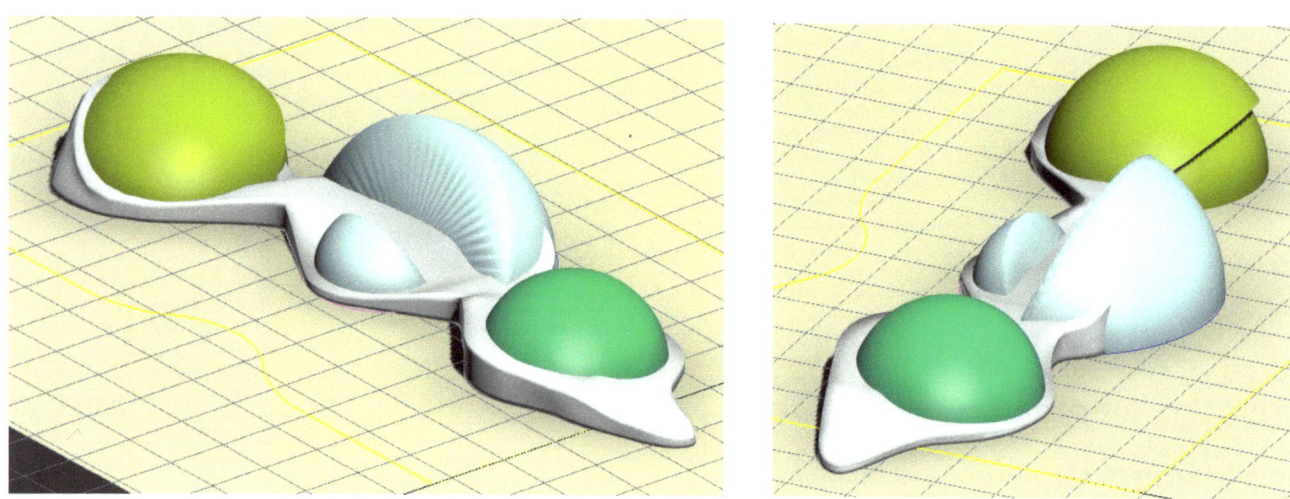

Considering that the third form suffers from some shortcomings such as uniform levels and light capturing problems, the fourth form is designed through eliminating of the staff and making some variations such as slope at corridor part of the volume. Thus, the volume is made less uniform and simple and the following form is created.

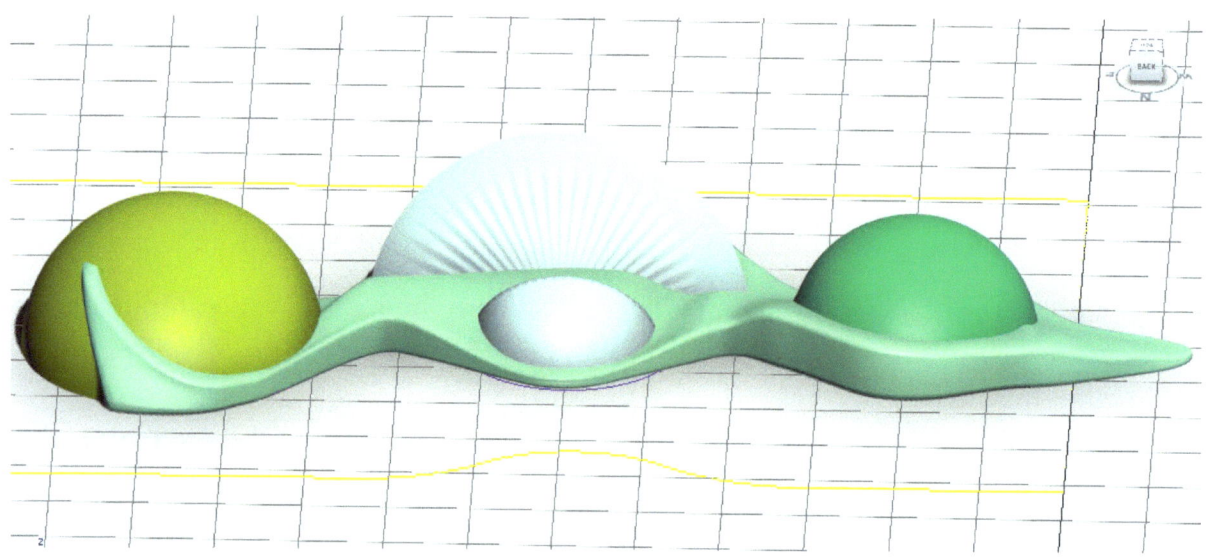

Once the fourth form is designed, some changes are imposed at two middle parts of the volume because of cold and mountainous climate of Tabriz and weak light radiation during year. In the first four volumes, the light conditions of Tabriz climate was not considered in design. Opening the two middle parts and shifting the angle, conditions for appropriate light capturing are provided for this volume.

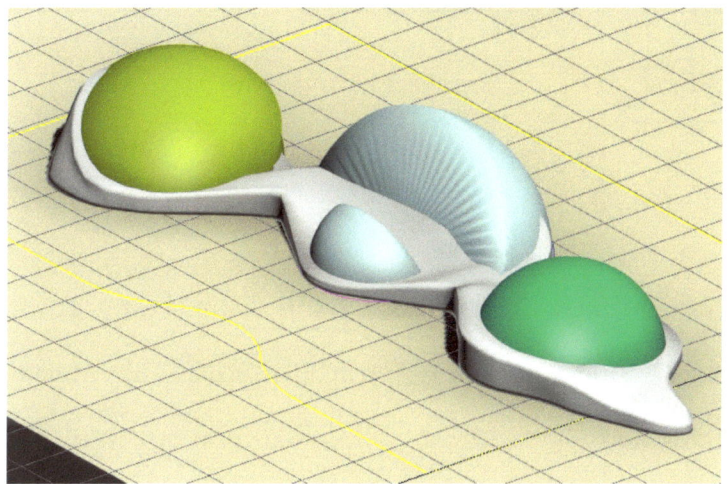
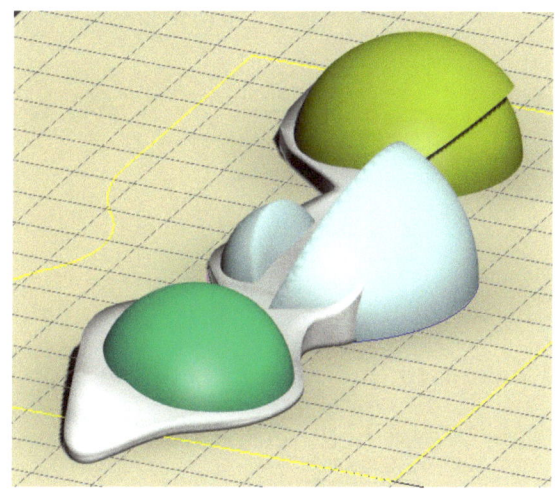

A new etude was drawn and the sixth form was designed due to shortcomings of the fifth form such as simplicity and light capturing problem of some parts of the design. Here, corridor-connecting part of the volumes and consisting of some parts of the design- is designed based on Islamic patterns through adding the staff and creating rhythms by inspiring of music and making some variations in light capturing nature of the middle parts.

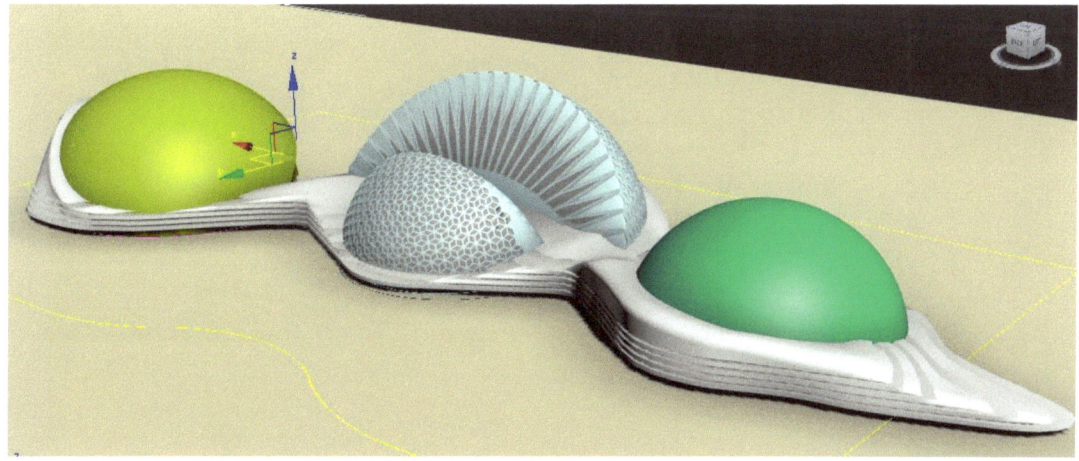

Following form is created by eliminating some parts of the building behind, changing color and façade of the building, adding brown color to its body being inspired of traditional context of Tabriz and body color of most musical instruments which are made from wood and are brown, and integrating it with a modern building.

The final form is designed through adding sunshade to entrance and increasing light capturing of the administrative sector.

Plans Descriptions

Total area of the museum: 7110m^2

Area of the superstructure: 4330m^2

Site plan

Site plan of the complex (located at Aref St., Valiasr) was consisted of spaces such as access route for pedestrian, access route for vehicles, two parking lots (one for employees located at the building behind and the other for clients located at the building front (left hand)), mosque for clients and employees, outdoor amphitheater for live plays, park and green spaces for the addresses.

Plan of the basement

Basement plan which is under the administrative sector consists of mechanical and electrical installations, and a big warehouse. Ventilators of the museum are located at the mechanical installations sector. According to the studies, ventilators are the best cool and warm air conditioners for museum because it has no piping and there is not any risk of pipe break. Electrical installations are a place for generators to automatically supply the required electricity of the complex when the power goes off. Other parts related to electricity are also located in this sector. The big warehouse is a room to keep extra equipment of the museum.

Plan of the ground floor

It consists of several parts such as entrance, parcels room, watchman room, shops, WC, some galleries, administrative sector, amphitheater, and restaurant which are briefly described as follows:

- Shop: There are five shops located at east and west side of the entrance to sell cultural products, music instruments, music specialized books, and etc.
- Galleries: There are seven galleries located at middle of the ground floor. They are designed being inspired by seven music notes. Out of these, there are five main galleries inspired by five kinds of musical instruments described at theoretical fundamentals of the thesis. They include galleries of wind instruments, stringed instruments, percussion instruments and so. There are two temporary galleries, too. The ground floor of the complex welcomes three galleries.

- Training sector: It is located at west side of the complex and upper of the administrative sector and includes specialized music library, three audiovisual rooms with different numbers of chairs, music archive, music training center including six rooms for those interested in music, and WC for men and women.
- Galleries: There are two galleries located at middle of the complex and upper of galleries of the first floor, Similar to three galleries of the first floor, these are also regarded as main galleries.

Structure

The museum structure was designed with cooperation and consultation of structure engineer considering the design, seismicity of Tabriz, dome-shaped structure of parts of museum such as amphitheater and galleries where the spatial structure was used as the roof structure considering its advantages such as more attractiveness and fineness in architecture, high speed in producing and executing the plan because of its pre-fabricated nature, very light weight of elements in comparison with other structures, high safety coefficient against earthquake, storm, and fire, possibility of executing of kinds of opaque, semi-transparent, and transparent covers, possibility of designing and executing of structures with high spans without central pillar. To pass the light, glass or ETFE was used for glassy parts. ETFE (Ethylene Tetra Fluoro Ethylene) is a polymer resin obtained from recycled minerals and has advantages like very low dead load, capability of covering big spans in different forms, extraordinary durability, remaining intact against atmospheric pollution, self-cleaning, and so. Pre-stressed concrete was used for ceiling of the administrative sectors and galleries. It has advantages such as execution of bigger span, possibility of making big and irregular windows on roof, less thick slabs, eliminating of pillars, possibility of using pillars at irregular distances, decreasing the building weight, and improving seismological function. Generally, the structure designed for music museum consists of pre-stressed concrete, spatial structure, and modern materials such as ETFE.

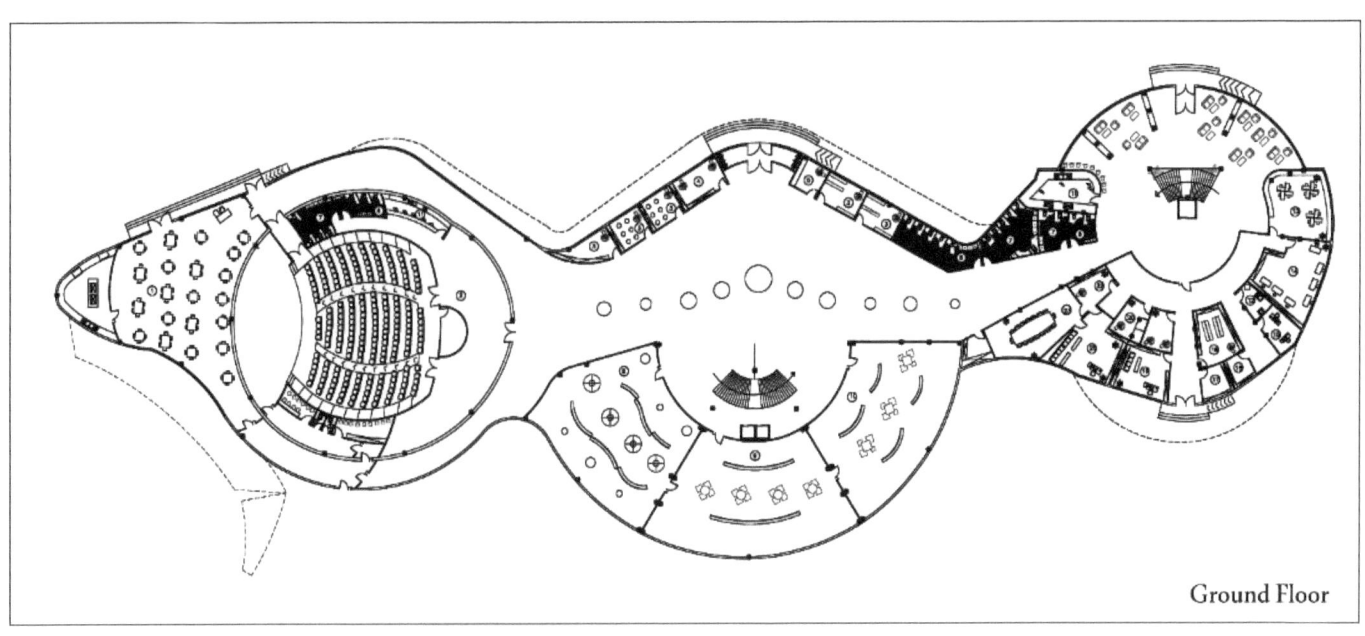

Ground Floor

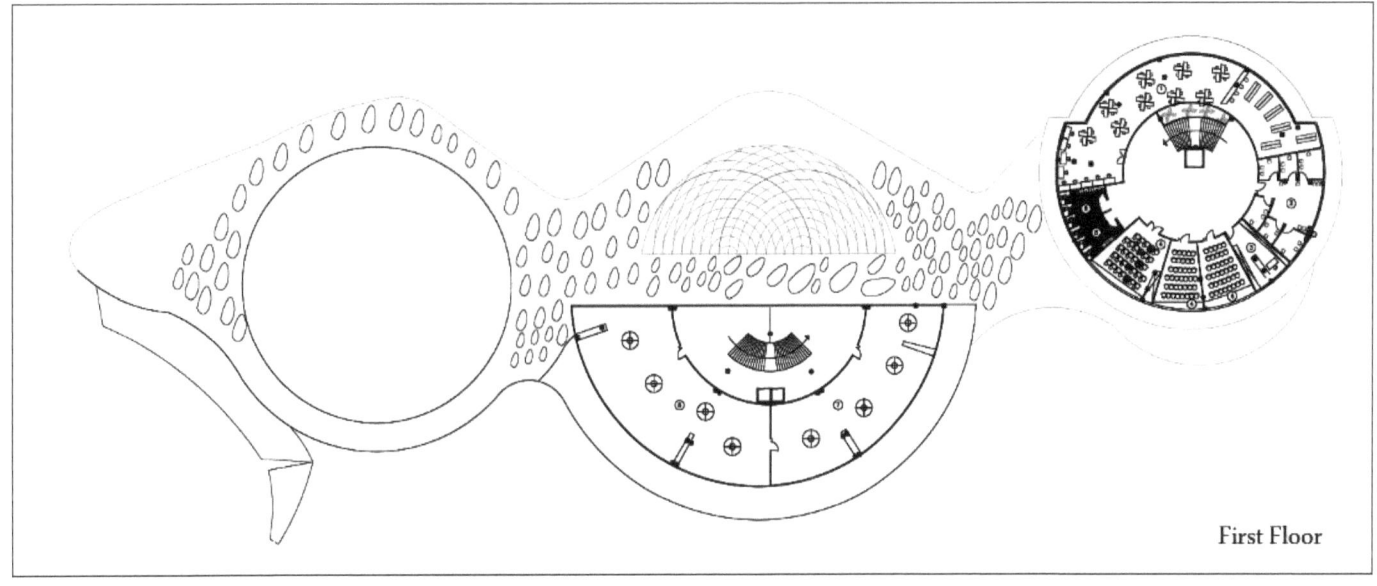

First Floor

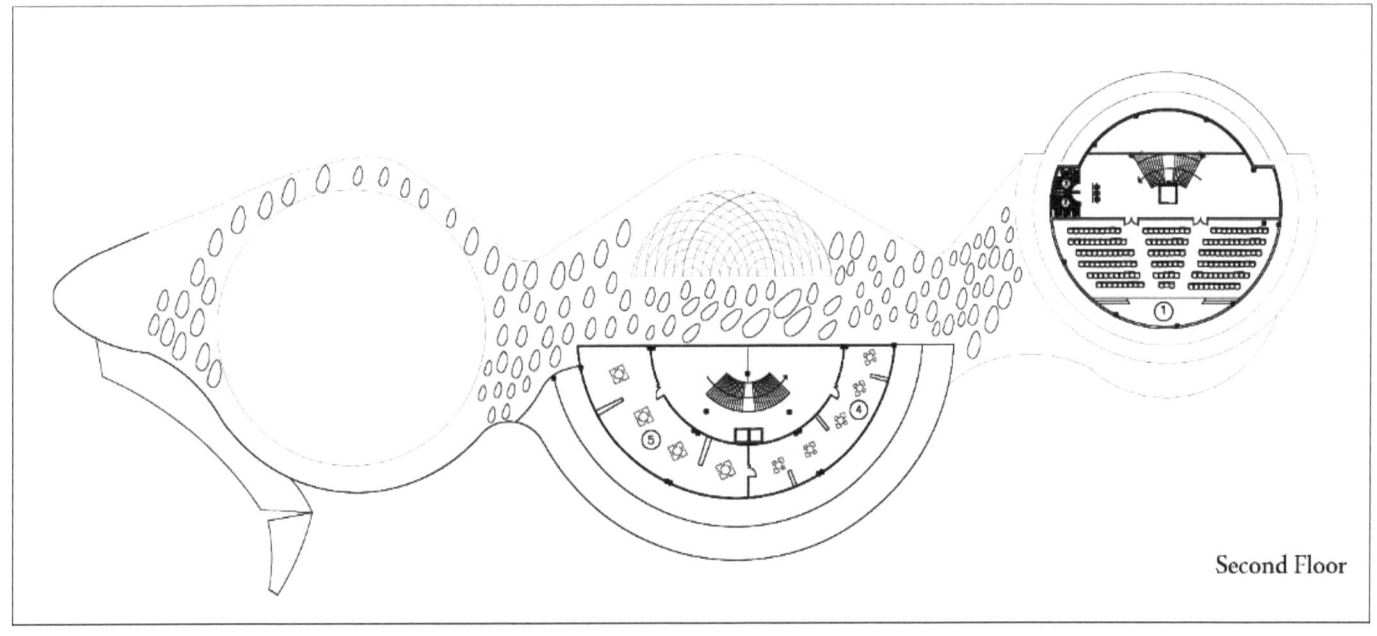

Second Floor

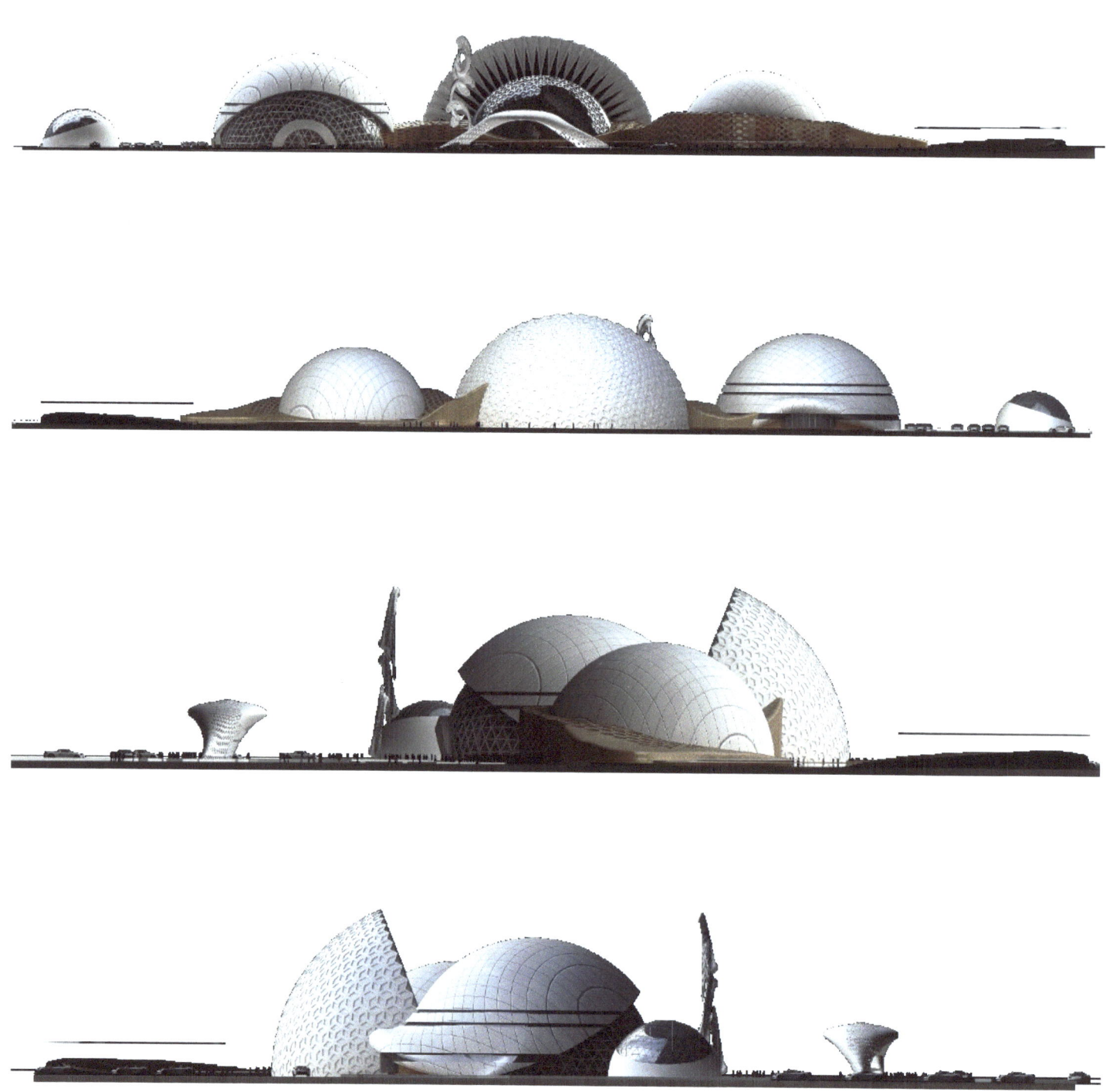

Elevations

Tabriz Digital Museum

Mitra Dolatshahi

Master of Architecture

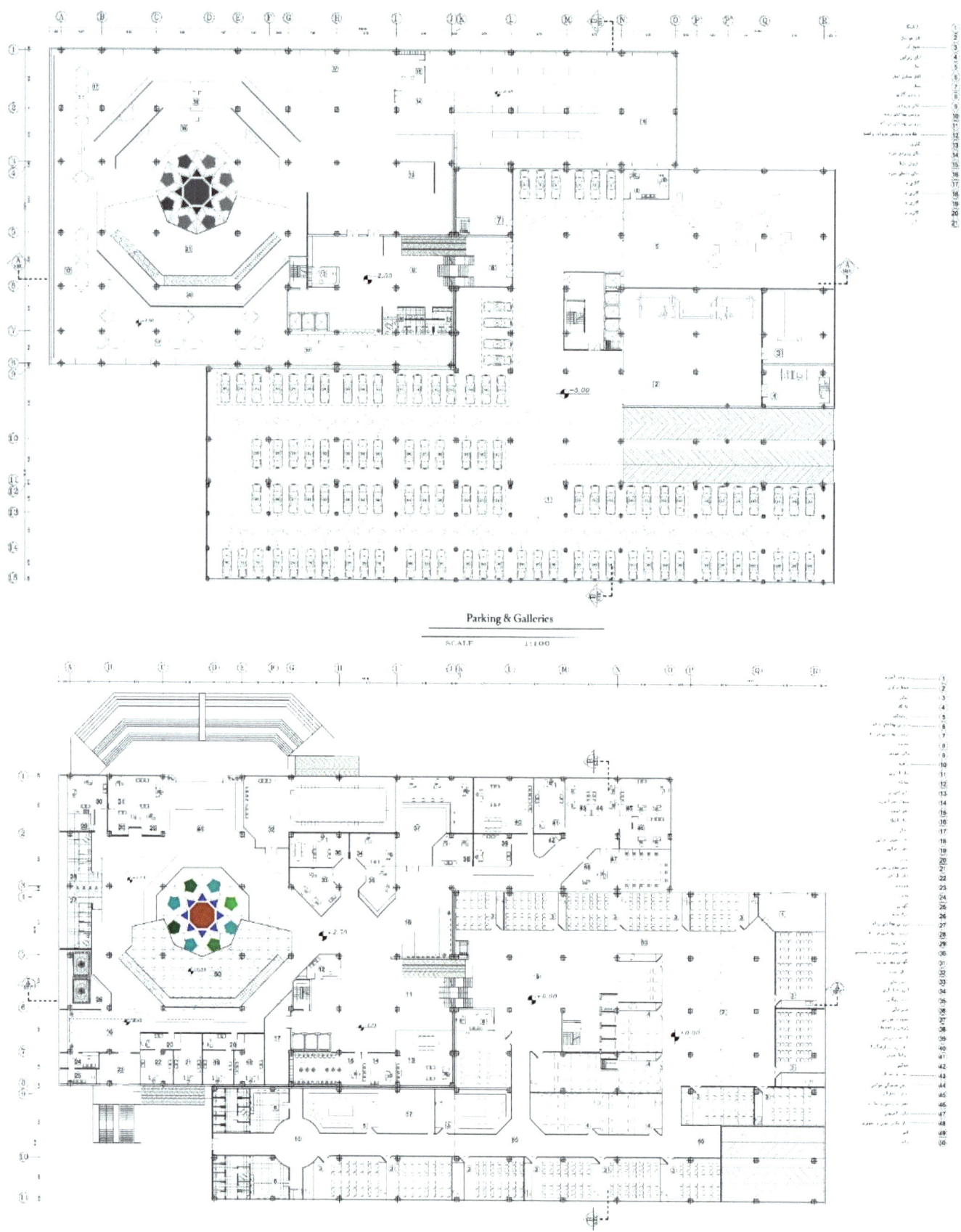

Parking & Galleries
SCALE 1:100

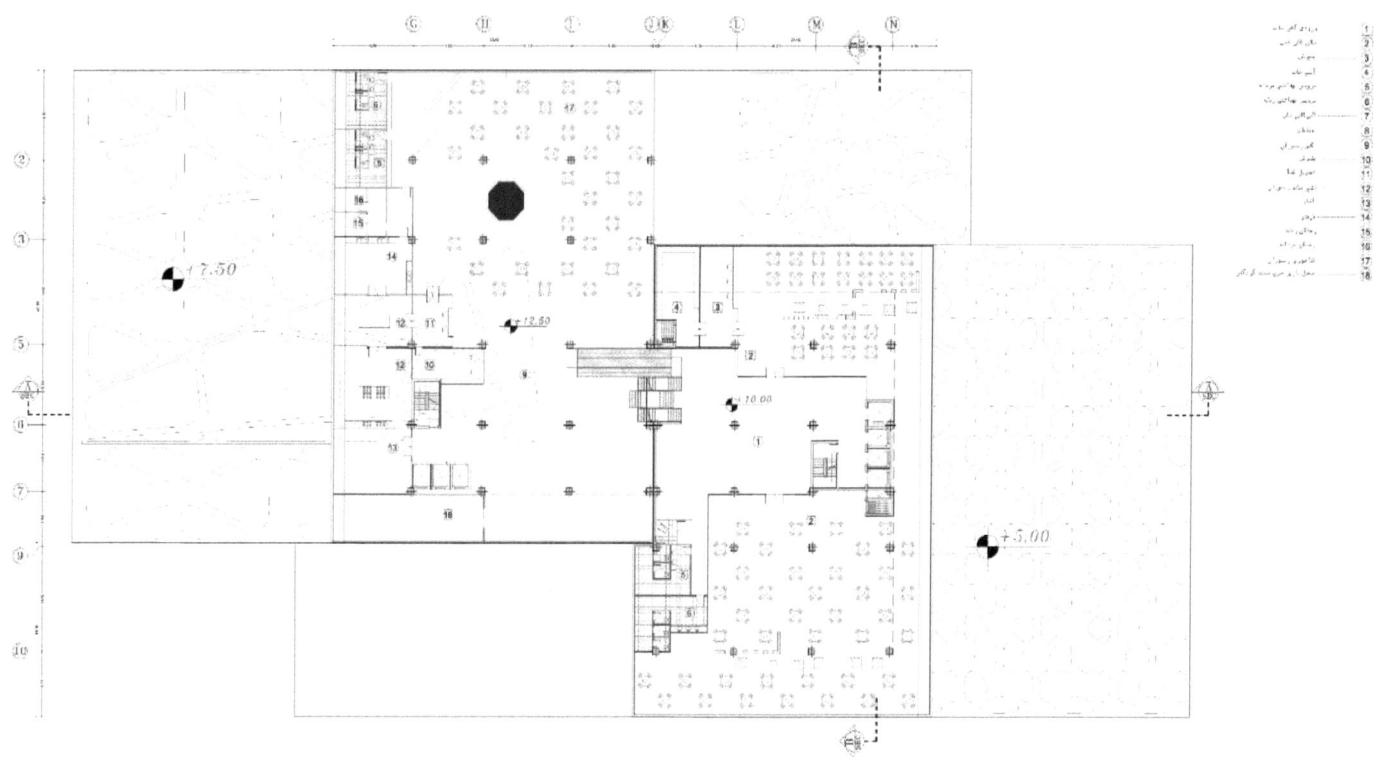
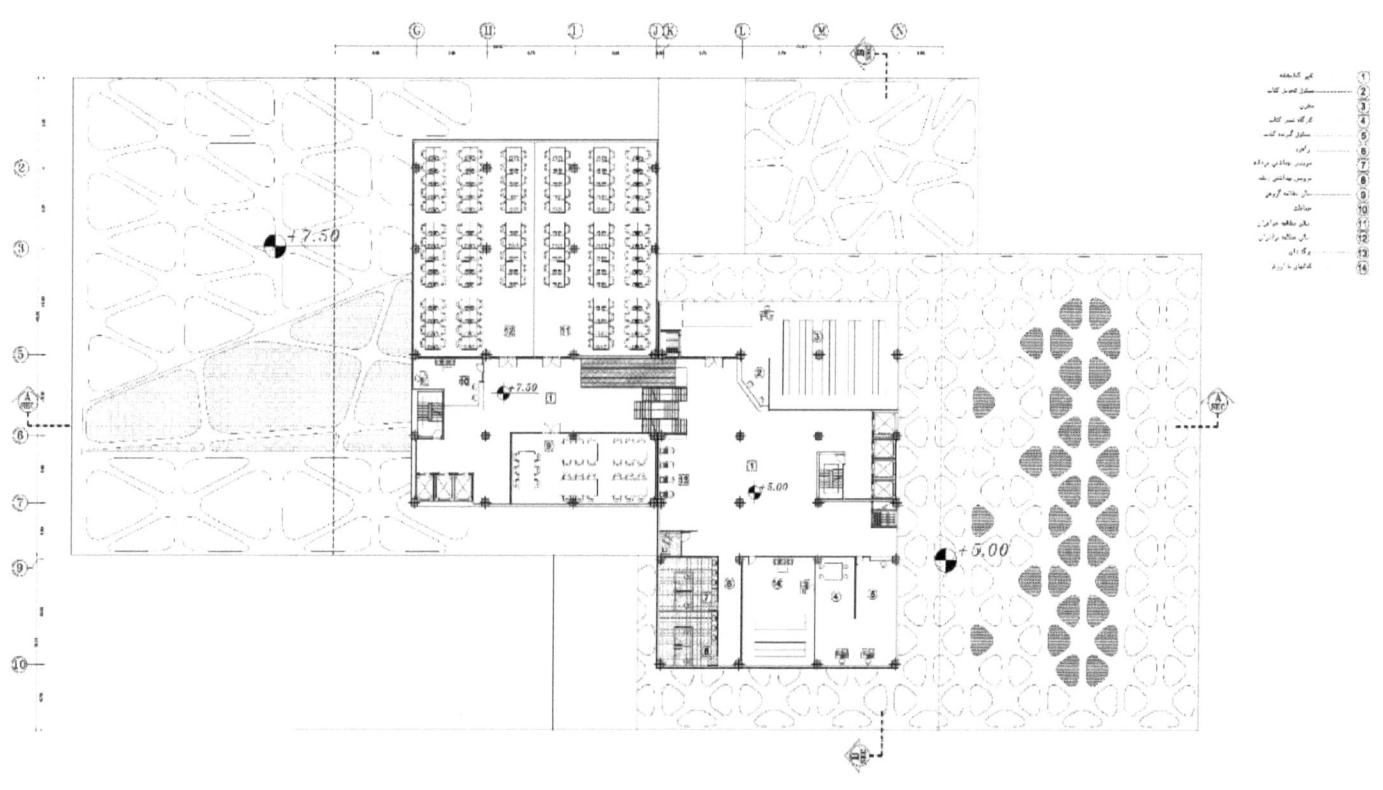

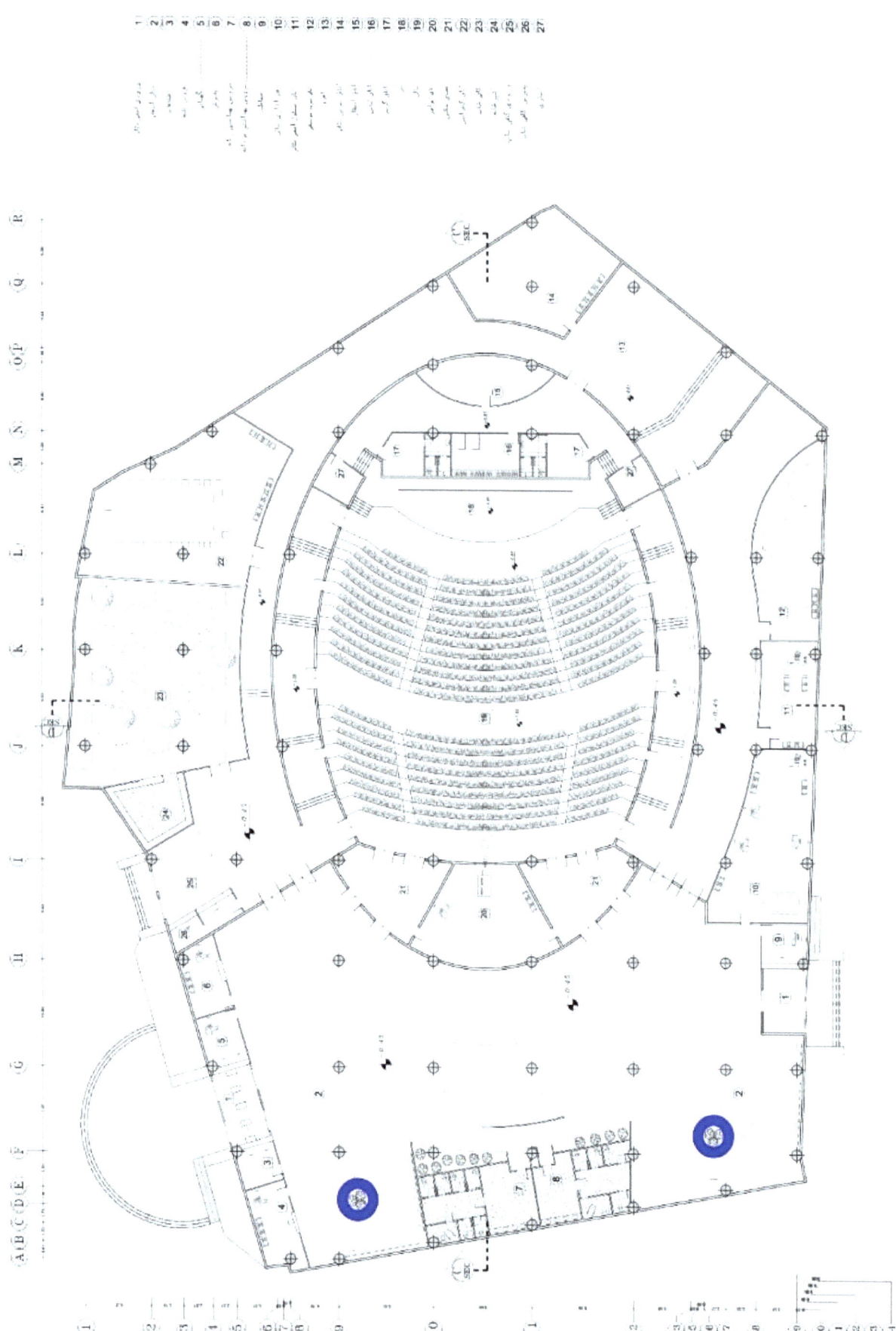

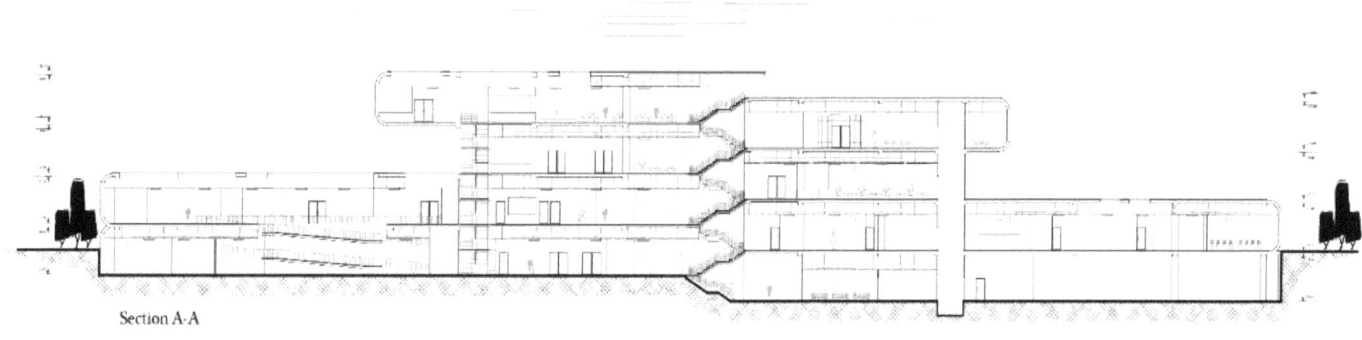
Section A-A

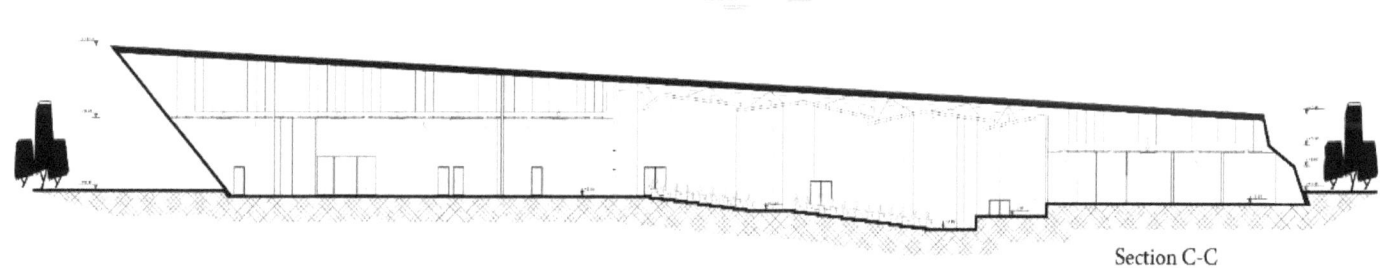
Section C-C

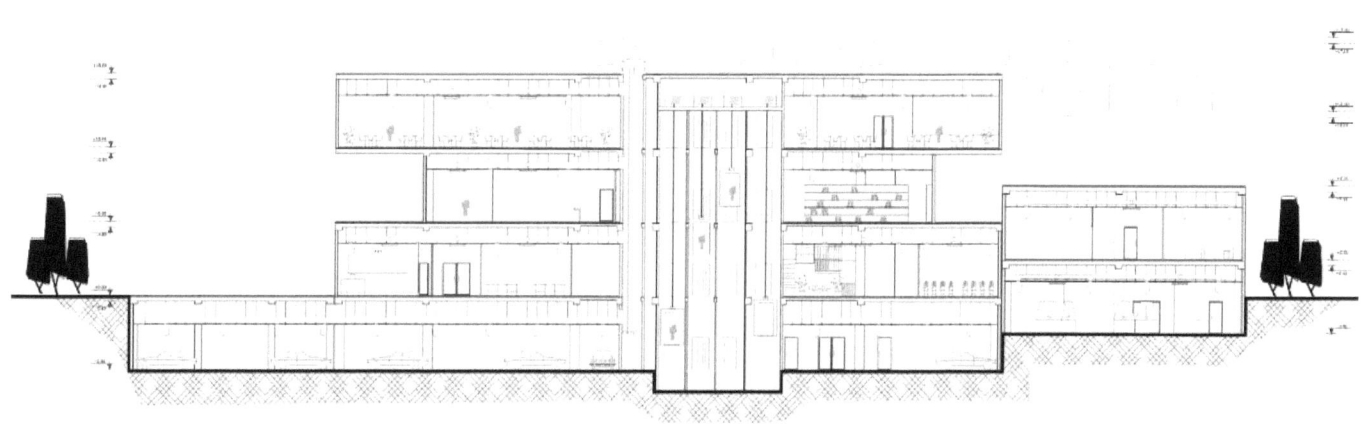
Section B-B

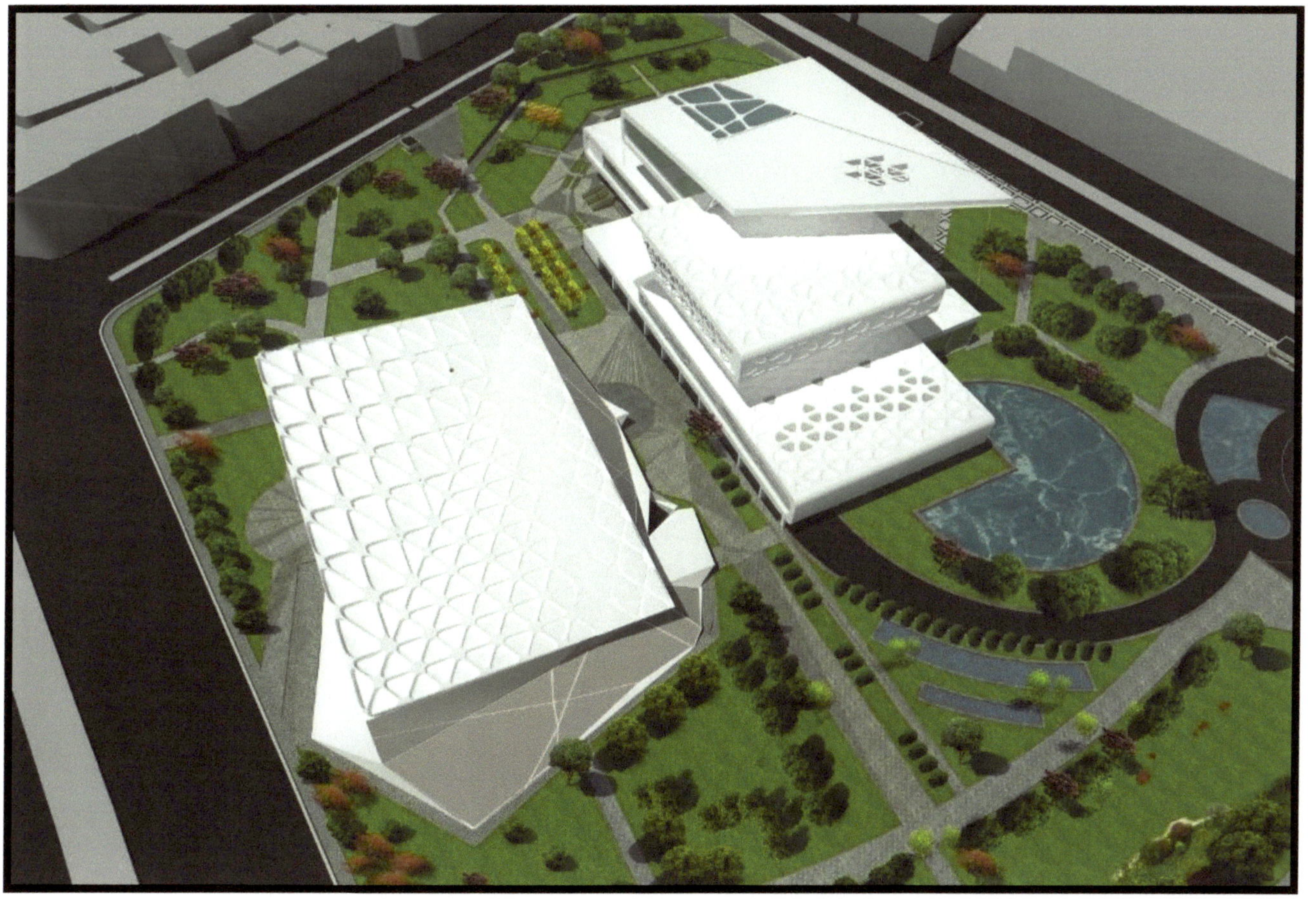

Tabriz Children's Garden Museum

Afsaneh Fardyar

Master of Architecture

During their childhood, all children foster hope of a more pure world, a world free of life difficulties, a world decorated by a magic, furtive and safe garden full of miracles, and a world to take a walk and watch human and their surrounding world. Considering their mental and physical restrictions in comparison with adults, children are affected more but, they influence their surrounding less. For this reason, they inevitably follow environmental conditions.

Children are the most sensitive and impressionable age group of societies and need to experience social life in their scale during the most important years of their life, i.e. from beginning of their personal, mental, physical, and social growth until they enter societies. For this purpose, it is necessary to provide a childish, sincere and honest space for them, a space far from uproars of adults' world, a space full of happiness and beautiful colors where children have the opportunity to express new ideas and nourish their talents, a space providing appropriate conditions for the children' creativity.

Sensory perception of children from space

Children should have a feel of convenience, tranquility, and non-anxiety when they encounter volumes and buildings as well as when they communicate or live inside them. Darkness and disproportionate forms frightens children more than any other thing.

Spaces with lively and bright colors and, sometimes, colors with unknown forms (seen in watercolor paintings) induce imaginary and fantasy subjects as well as feelings such as being emotional, friendly, kind, and dreamy in children. Light colors with specific borders, more details in buildings, and smooth curves may be used in designing spaces for older children. It is really difficult to perceive space. Simultaneously, children should both distinguish themselves from the surrounding world and analyze the world. It is realized through identifying objects found around.

Children and architecture

It is necessary to reconcile our industrialized world with ideals of suave people and elements constituting their life space. All people should try to humanize the space. However, it is more important for architects who are responsible to organize the space in a more or less urbanite civilization. Urban developers, planners, contractors, green space experts, artists, and architects are responsible to experience the coordination between human being and its surrounding environment.

The space designed for children should include:

- Nature spaces: tree, water, and alive creatures constituting the most essential and important space for children
- Open spaces: wide spaces where children run and discharge their internal energies
- Road spaces: before allocating of paths and roads for vehicles, they were places for playing of children. They are ways where children meet each other and are networks connecting different spaces.
- Adventure spaces: complex spaces strengthening imagination and visualization power of children
- Hide out spaces: children' independency is formed through these spaces
- Play structure spaces: These spaces are known as playing fields.

Architect is the first instructor of children after their parents. They are educated via the forms made by them and constitute their surrounding environment. For this reason, the relation between children, architecture, and space is regarded as core of humanize the civilization.

Due to being free from ancient traditions, the contemporary children adapt with news or even presumptions of contemporary architecture and urban development easier than adults. They can easily adhere to and inspire new forms. Thus, balance between life spaces of every person and architectural forms of space should be gradually established "to children" and perhaps "by children".

For this purpose, architects should understand children, space, and their demands, know their problems and needs, learn how to solve them, be familiar with living environment of children, and understand it well. Architects should try their best to compete with educationalists, sociologists, physicians, and psychologists who know the children world completely.

Self-recognition and progress are equivalent to space perception and complete it. Through a long-term learning (lasting during childhood), we learn to dominate the space and dominate ourselves, as learned. The learning process depends on our inner balance. Thus, the first experiences of children are very important in this regard. True and successful education without any serious contact should assist them in finding their position in space in order to recognize their centrality there. The space does not mean a lifeless geometrical limit; rather it should be an active and influential space with security and freedom. Our surrounding space plays a significant role in forming of our personality and protects our privacy. Size of the space varies considering each person or different life stages.

The person can easily find him/herself in this space which varies in size considering his/her actions. Thus, space is not an ordinary environment; rather it is a dynamic psychological reality. The space shall not impose itself on us; rather it should form in accordance with our personality.

In this regard, however, our industrialized era makes the problem more complicated. Since beginning of the present century, space-constituting elements have encountered profound evolutions. Our ancestors lived in a space with human scale but the contemporary space has different dimensions and has changed significantly. Appearing of big cities with gigantic buildings, considerable density of population, more vehicles, and public use of Mass Medias have created a modern environment for the contemporary human. However, not only he has not get accustomed to it completely, he could not find the opportunity required to get accustomed to it because of continuous technological evolutions and permanent variations of spaces.

Children & colors

Colors significantly affect human, especially children, personality and result in emotional experiences such as happiness, laugh, sorrow, grief, tranquility, incitation, calmness, and excitement. The qualities are intensified in children. Considering their happy, pure, friendly, and fresh soul, children prefer lively colors combined appropriately. It should be taken into account in design, decoration, and coloration of indoor spaces and appropriate colorful combinations of natural spaces. Using different colors, size and weight of a specific object may be increased or decreased. Essentially, warm and bright colors extend the objects while objects are seemed smaller than their real sizes in dark and cold colors.

Children and colors psychology

Colors are classified into three groups:

- Primary colors: red, blue, and yellow
- Secondary colors (obtained through combination of three primary colors): green, orange, violet
- Tertiary colors (obtained from combination of primary and secondary colors): greenish yellow, greenish blue, and etc.

Colors are used in two ways:

- Objective and natural modeling: for example, sea and lawn are drawn in blue and green colors, respectively
- Colors unconsciously occurs to mind without any special rule

Artistically, color is a strong tool to express deep internal states. Children' drawings are an evident example of presenting variable colors at a wide range. Lack of colors in all or part of children' drawings indicates to emotional void or, sometimes, their antisocial tendencies. Compatible children use five colors in their drawings while isolated children or those who do not like to communicate with the outer world do use only one or two colors.

Warm and stimulating colors inspire brightness, make life happy and create mobility and encourage children to be active and lively. On contrary, cold colors lead to passive states, immobility, and inspire sorrow and grief. Warm colors increases heart rate and are used in exciting spaces. Among warm colors, red is so influential and fast-moving which catches the eye before any other color.

Effect of environmental conditions

1. Light and brightness: Light is an architectural essential in supplying visual convenience of space and leaves different mental effects on humans. According to the studies, natural and bright light positively affect children senses and they consider these spaces as friendly and joyful. Sufficient light and lighting of spaces increase tendency of children.

2. Precision and mindfulness are increased, eye health and sight are secured, and mental tiredness is prevented.

3. It results in variety and spatial emphasize.

Since children cannot tolerate tension and fatigue, sharp contrasts lighting, whether natural or artificial, should be prevented.

Soft and mild light seems appropriate for children spaces except when spatial emphasize is considered through using variable lighting.

Noise: Children like sounds and background gentle sounds are useful for their imagination and connect them to the outer life. Some noises such as that of traffic, commercial applications, and industrial workshops are regarded as undesirable sounds of children spaces. The spaces should not be dead acoustically.

Ventilation: It is necessary to have appropriate ventilation systems in educational spaces, especially classrooms, to work with minimum fatigue and provide children health.

1. Accurately locating the vents considering wind direction

2. Using appropriate materials in walls

3. Using plants and trees to naturally ventilate the surrounding environment

Design Process

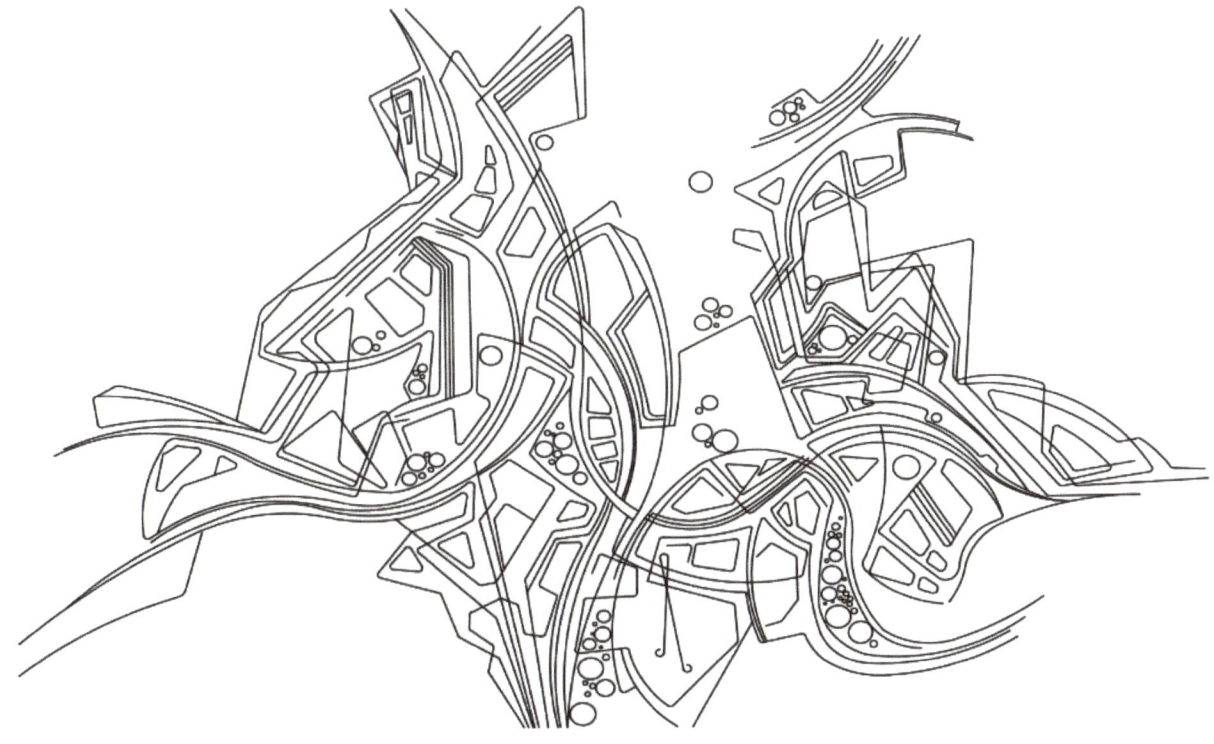

Conceptual sketch of Project

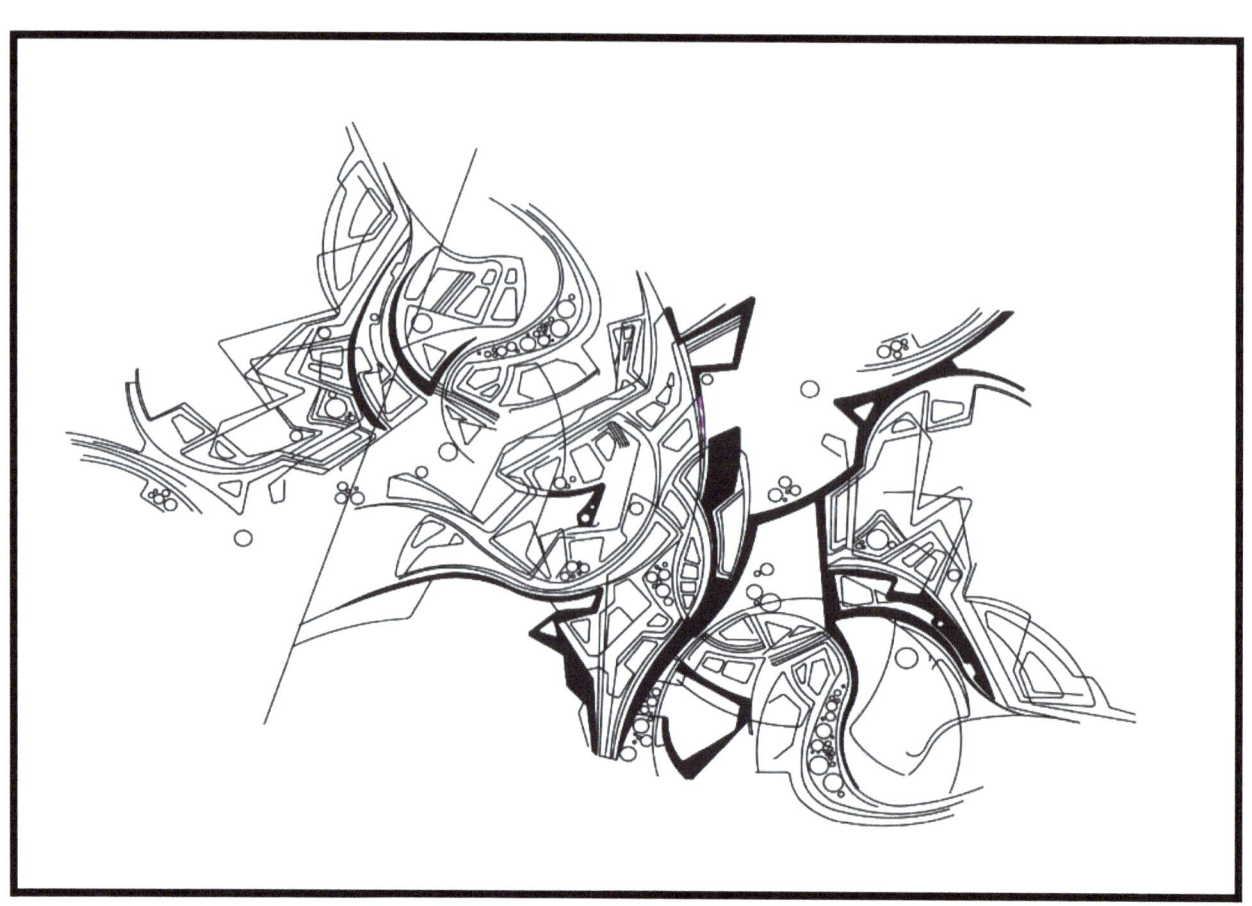

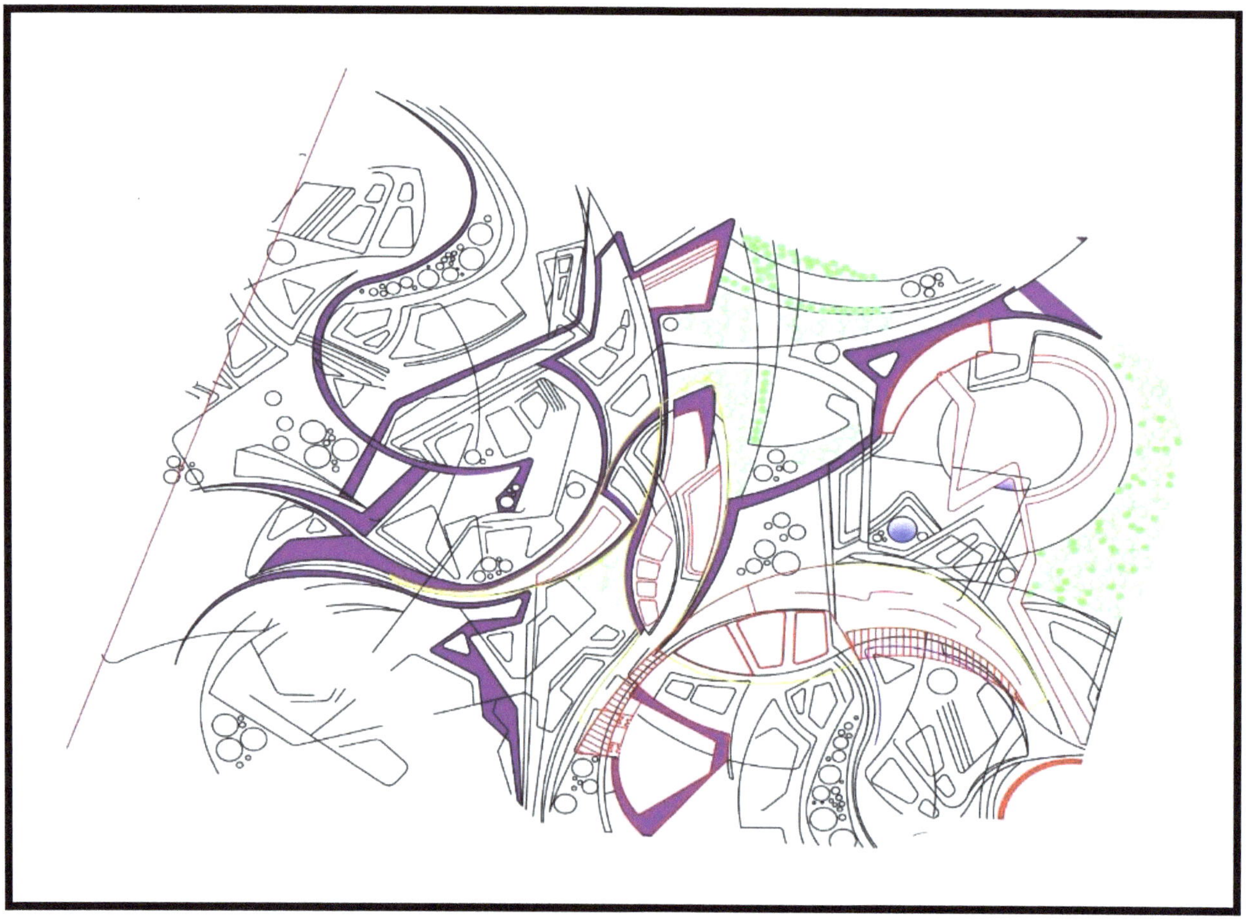

81

Amphitheater

84

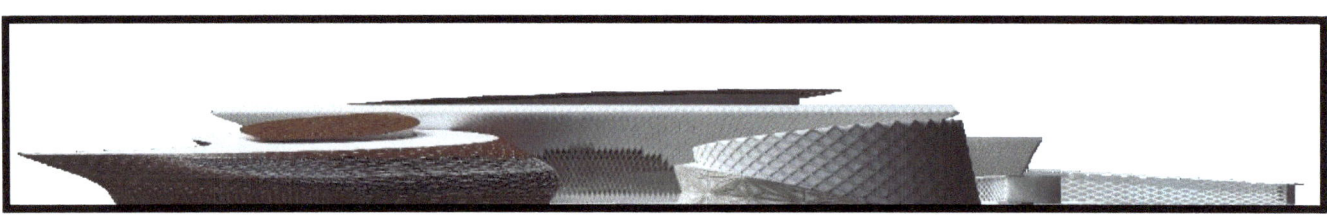

Elevations

Tabriz Theater

Elmira Amiri

Master of architecture

Theater is not merely a place to go there; rather it is a place to makes us experienced. A theater lets an ordinary gathering become an identified society. It may be a circular space for people need to speak, hear, and enjoy their time. I tried to create such a space in my design. This oval space represents purposeful gathering considering its concept in architecture. According to a concept derived from theater, however, it may be defined as a space where viewers sit together to watch an important event. Circle is of the main social symbols of human.

Theater stands as a symbol of a city or even a continent. Comparing with museums, theaters were mainly designed as functional buildings for a long time and their appearance was determined considering their function. Theaters are now built in the form of interesting urban elements and create a symbol relying on their buildings with statue features. Some designs restrain themselves with a merely formal gesture. Theater begins with look where two people meet each other. If one stands up and the other looks at him/her, it will certainly be the beginning point. A third person is required to have a progress and create a contact. Then, the life controls affairs and progresses. But, these three elements are essential. Play occurs where the actor faces viewer whether in a city square or a street and platform in a market or teashop. Theater does not make sense without architecture.

Scene is the most evident symbol of theater. The building of theater- as a place where human exhibits the most popular perceptions of life and their relations- may enjoy the piety belonging to a symbolic architecture although every architectural work is regarded a symbolic work by itself. To find an appropriate context to their activity, theater styles required some form of architecture due to their structures during different times. Now, this shell-like building at seashore may create an artistic and fantastic space for artists of theater and music as well as the viewers along with descriptions of the hall because of its excellent acoustic system and new perspective in downtown.

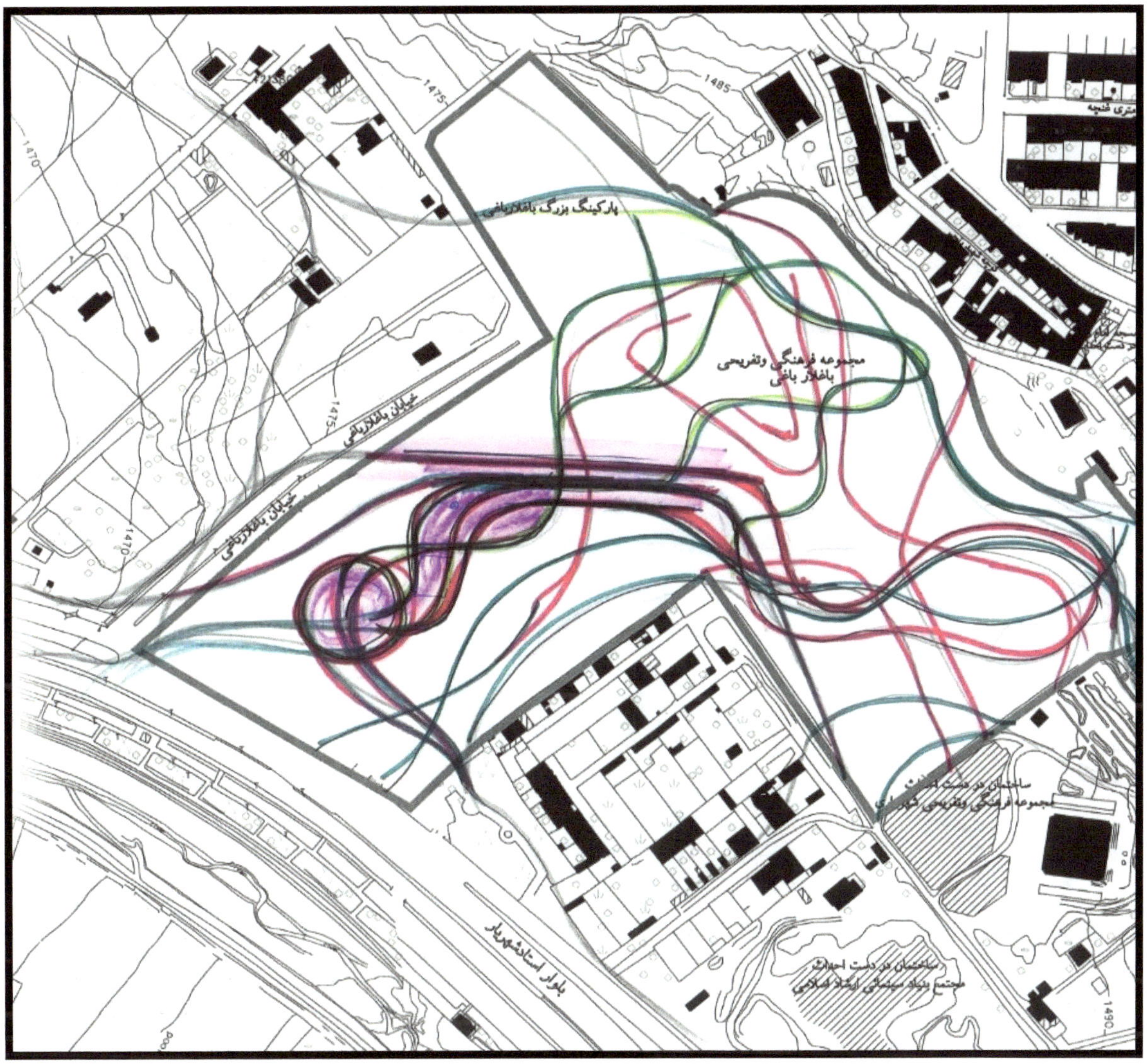

1475
1485
1470
پارکینگ بزرگ باغلارباغی
مجموعه فرهنگی وتفریحی
باغلار باغی
خیابان باغلارباغی
1490

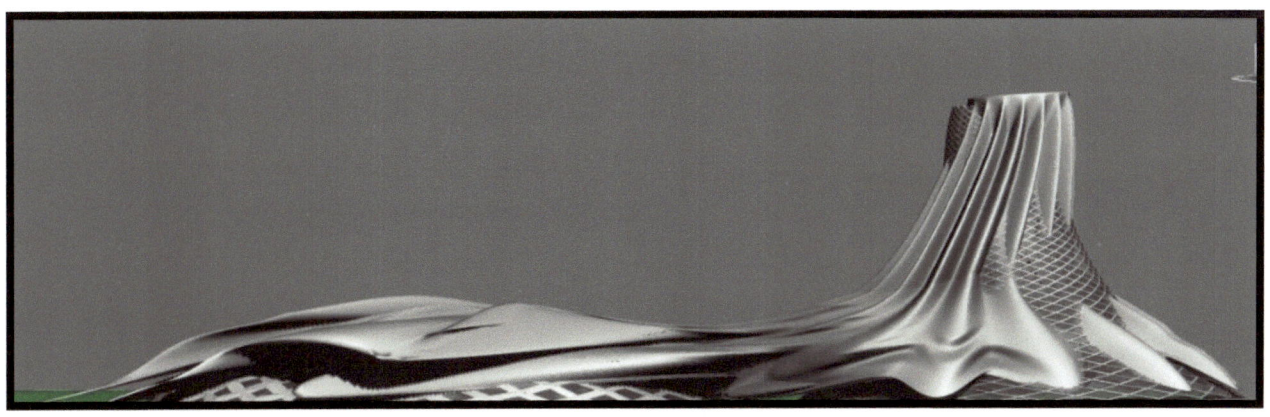

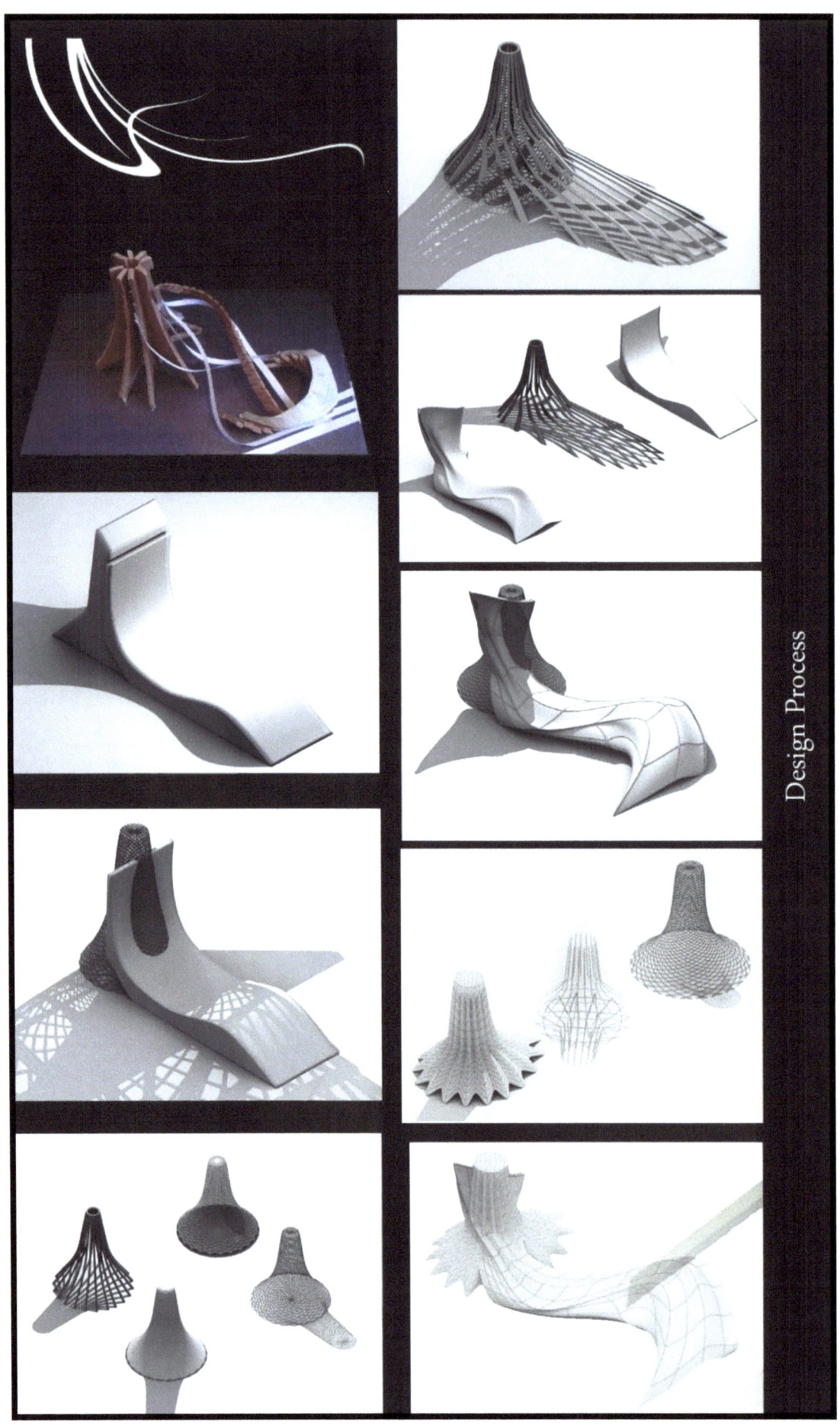

Design Process

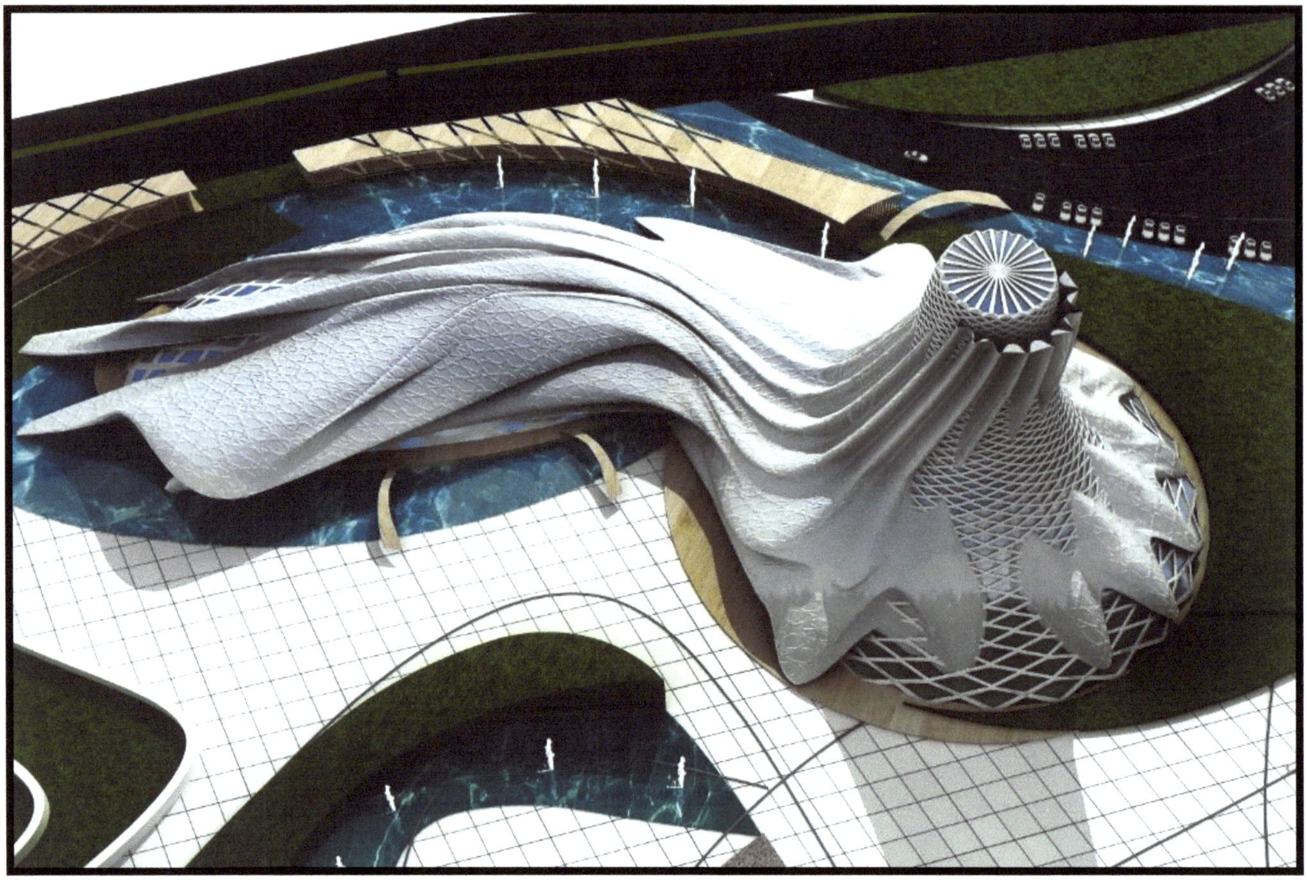

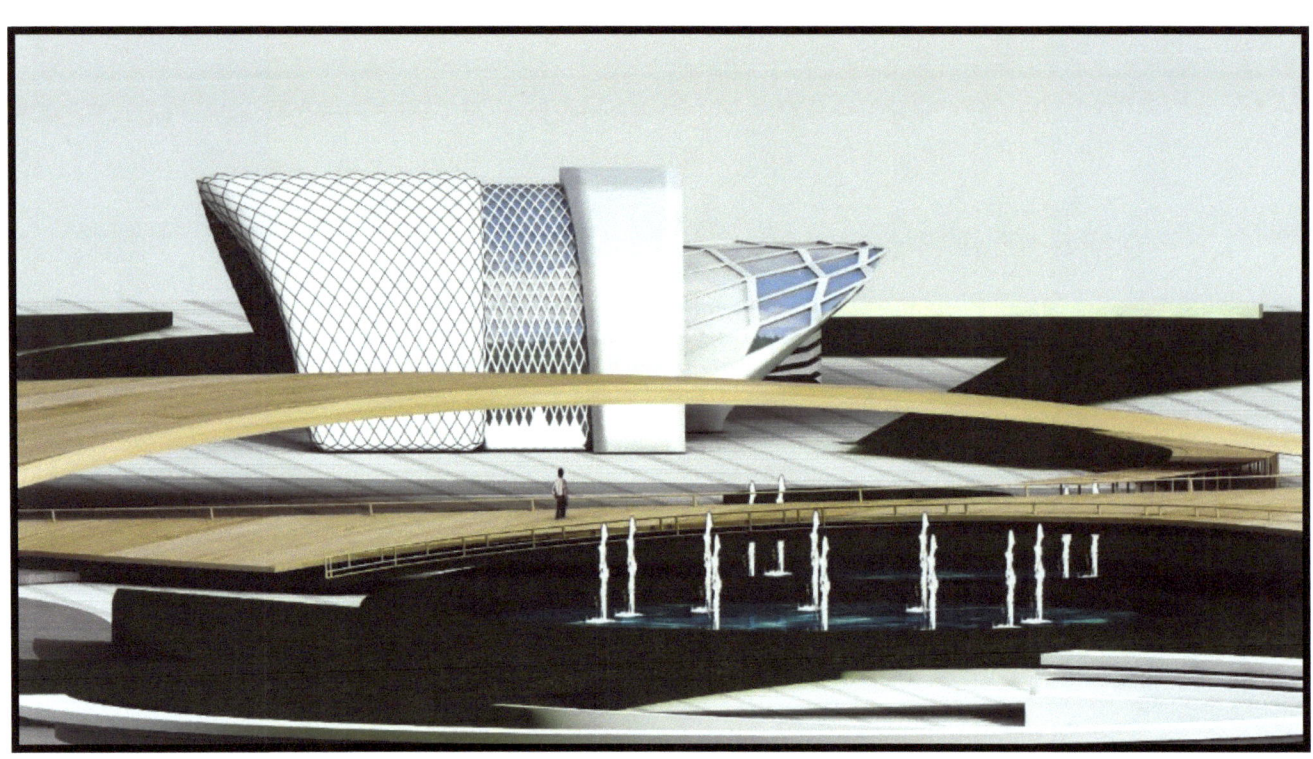

Women Cultural Center of Tabriz

Nasim Tabrizi

Master of architecture

Mehdi Bahari

Bachelor of architecture

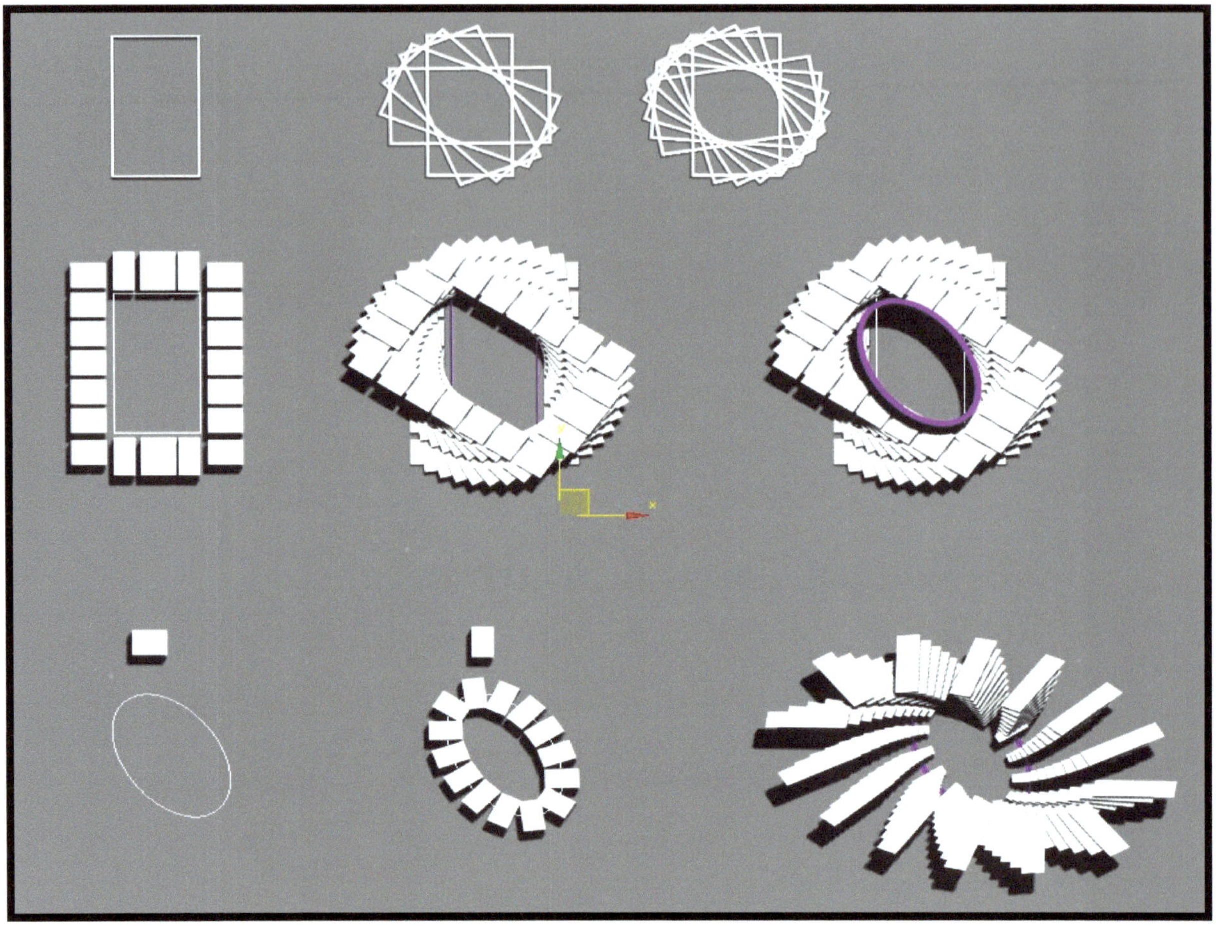

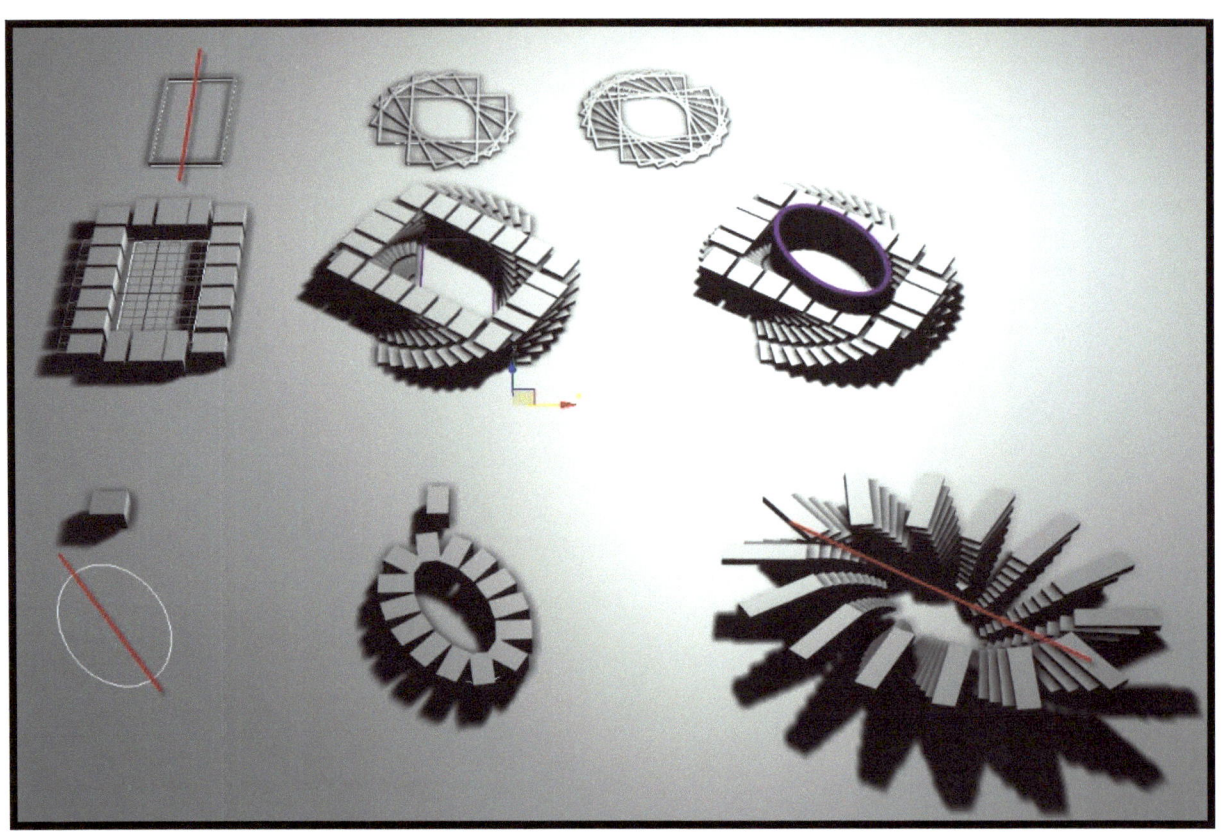

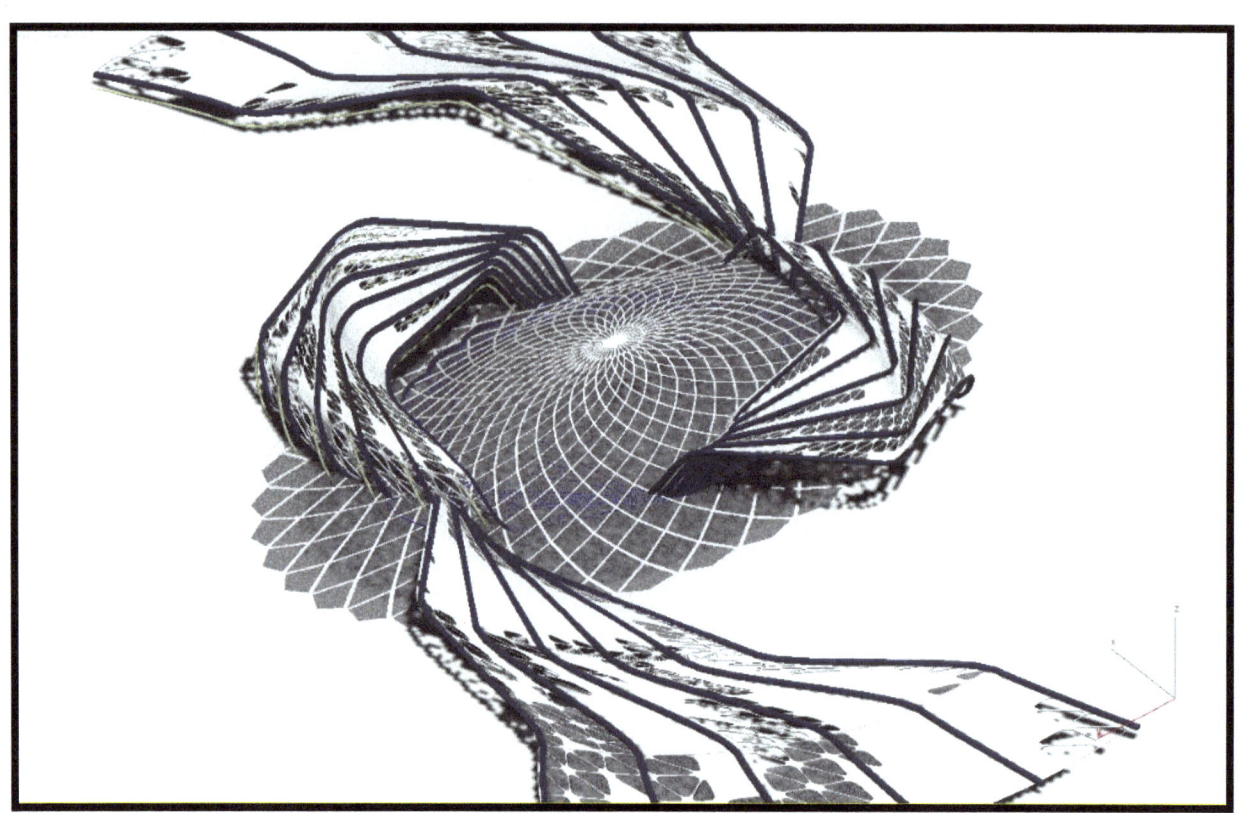
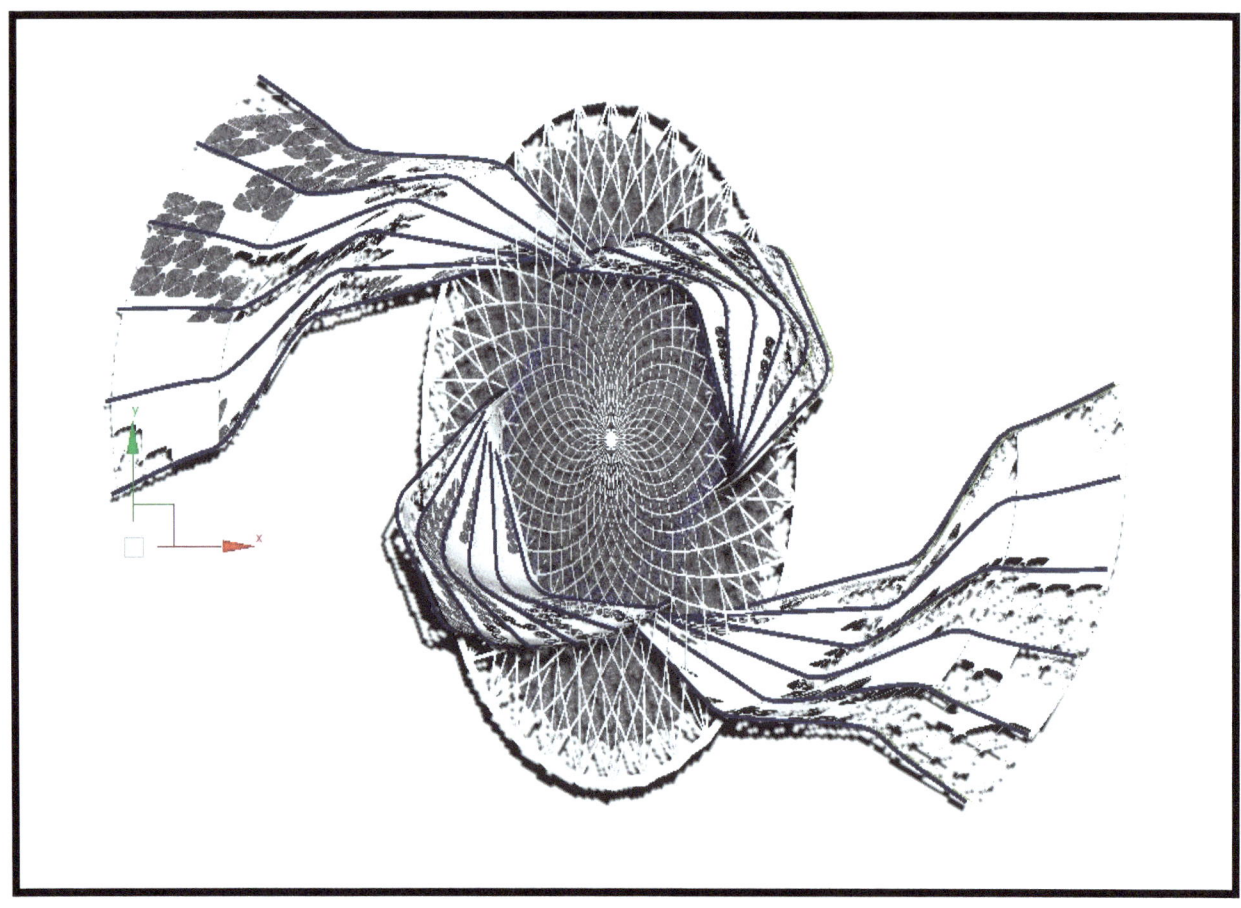

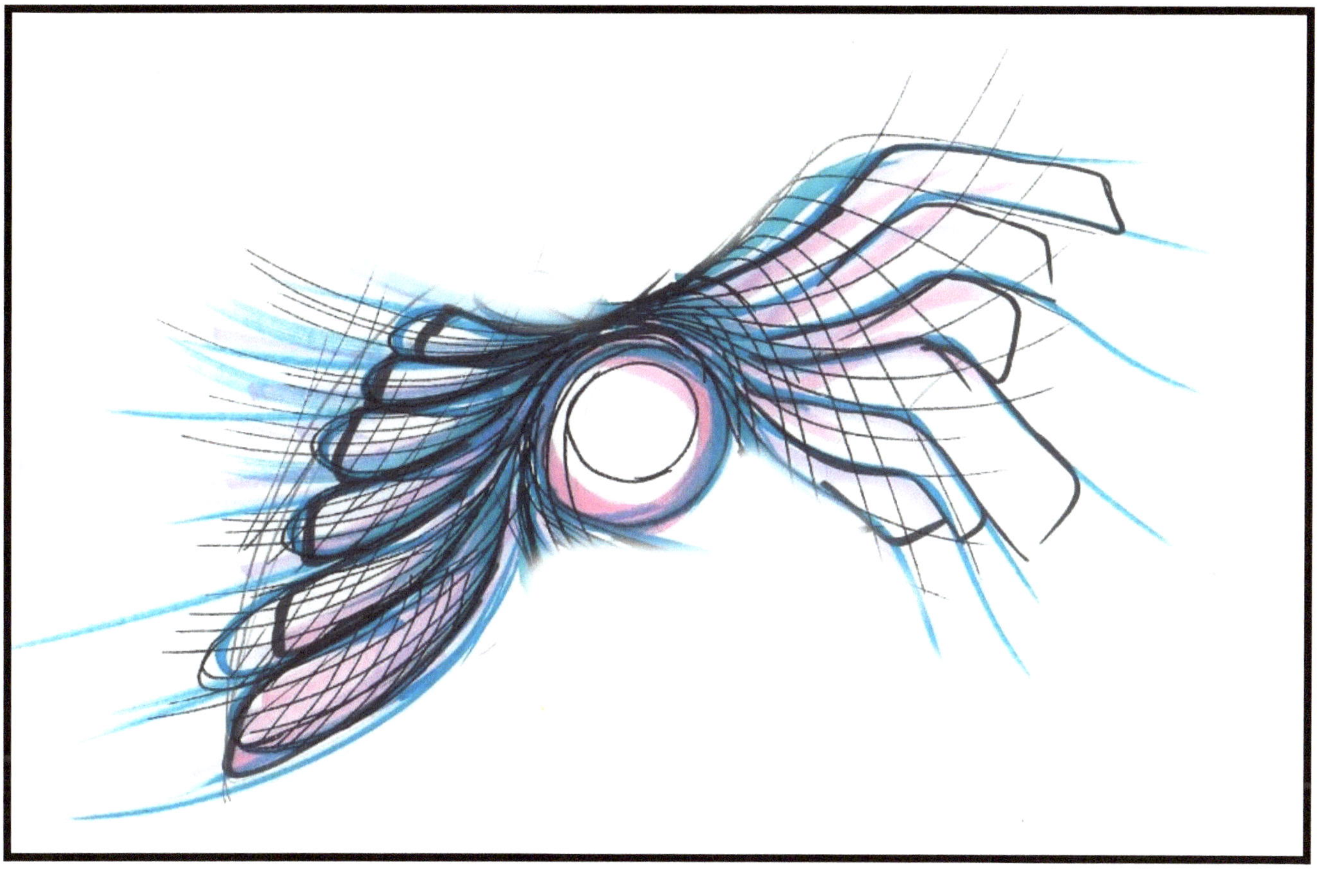

Lobby

Coffee Shop

Parametric Art Museum

Ali Khiabanian

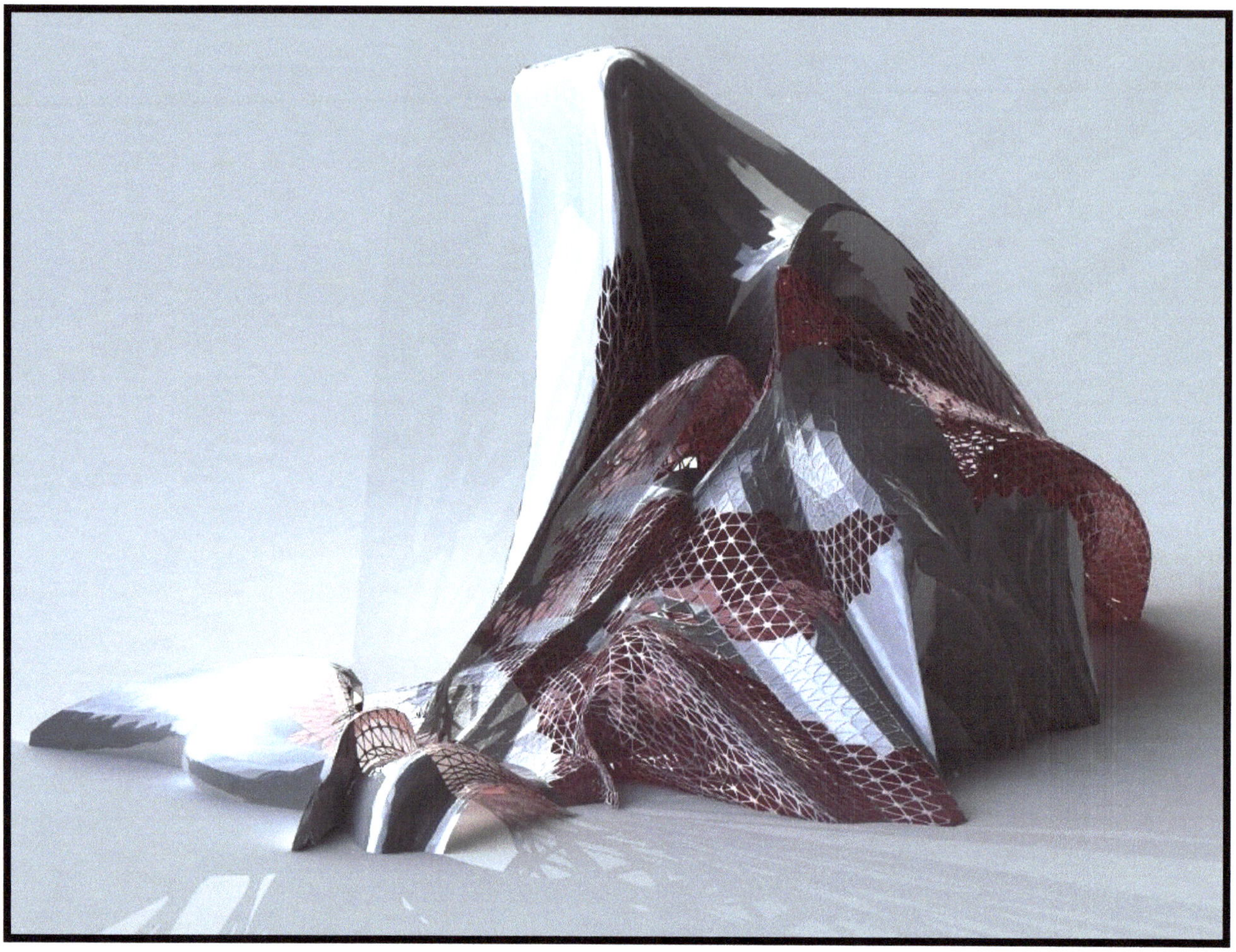

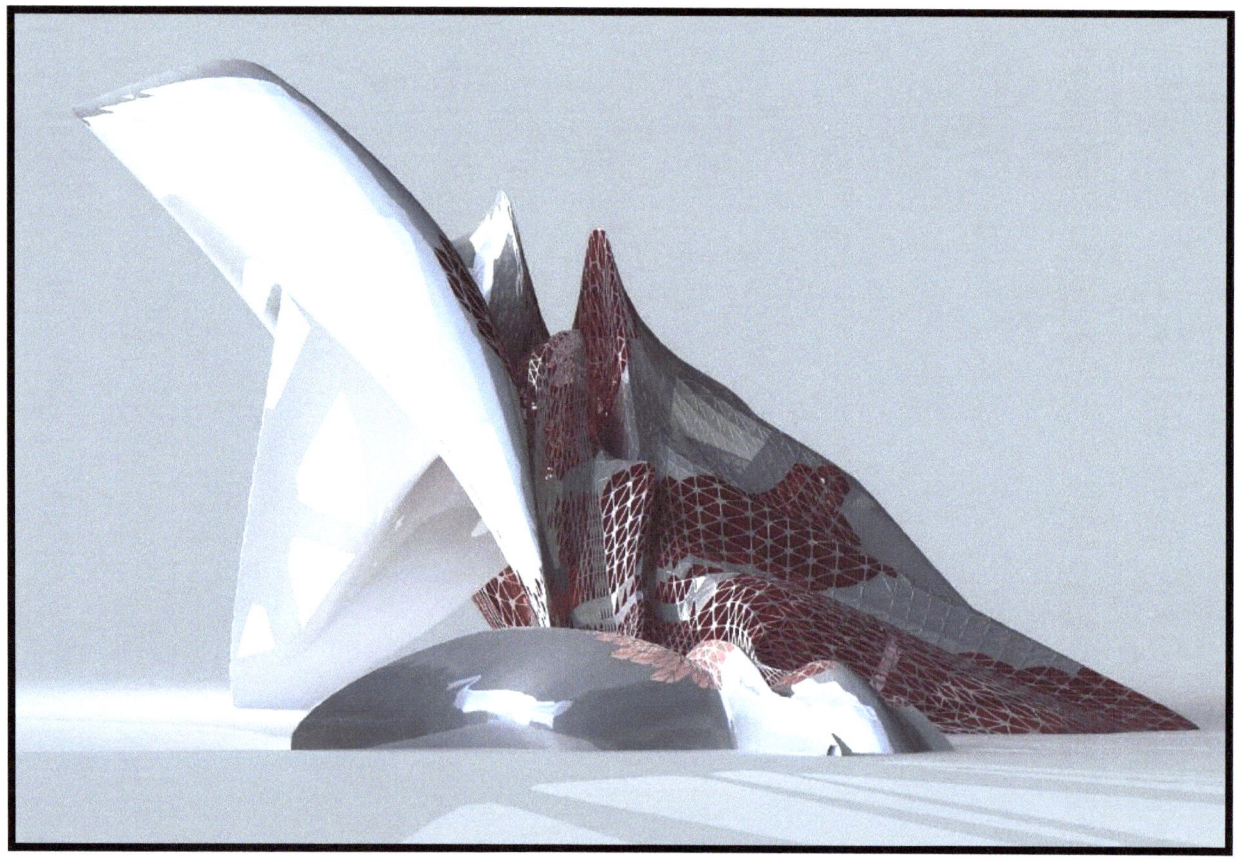

Graphite Modeling Tools
Freeform
Selection
Object Paint
Polygon Modeling
0 / 100

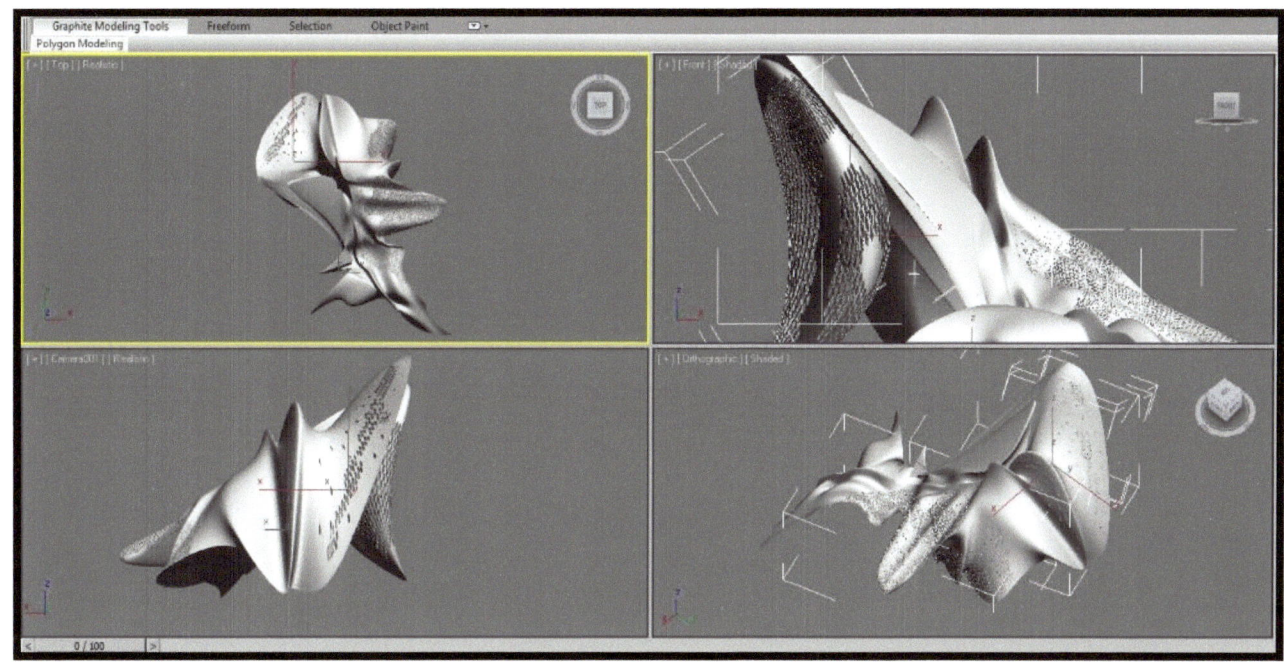

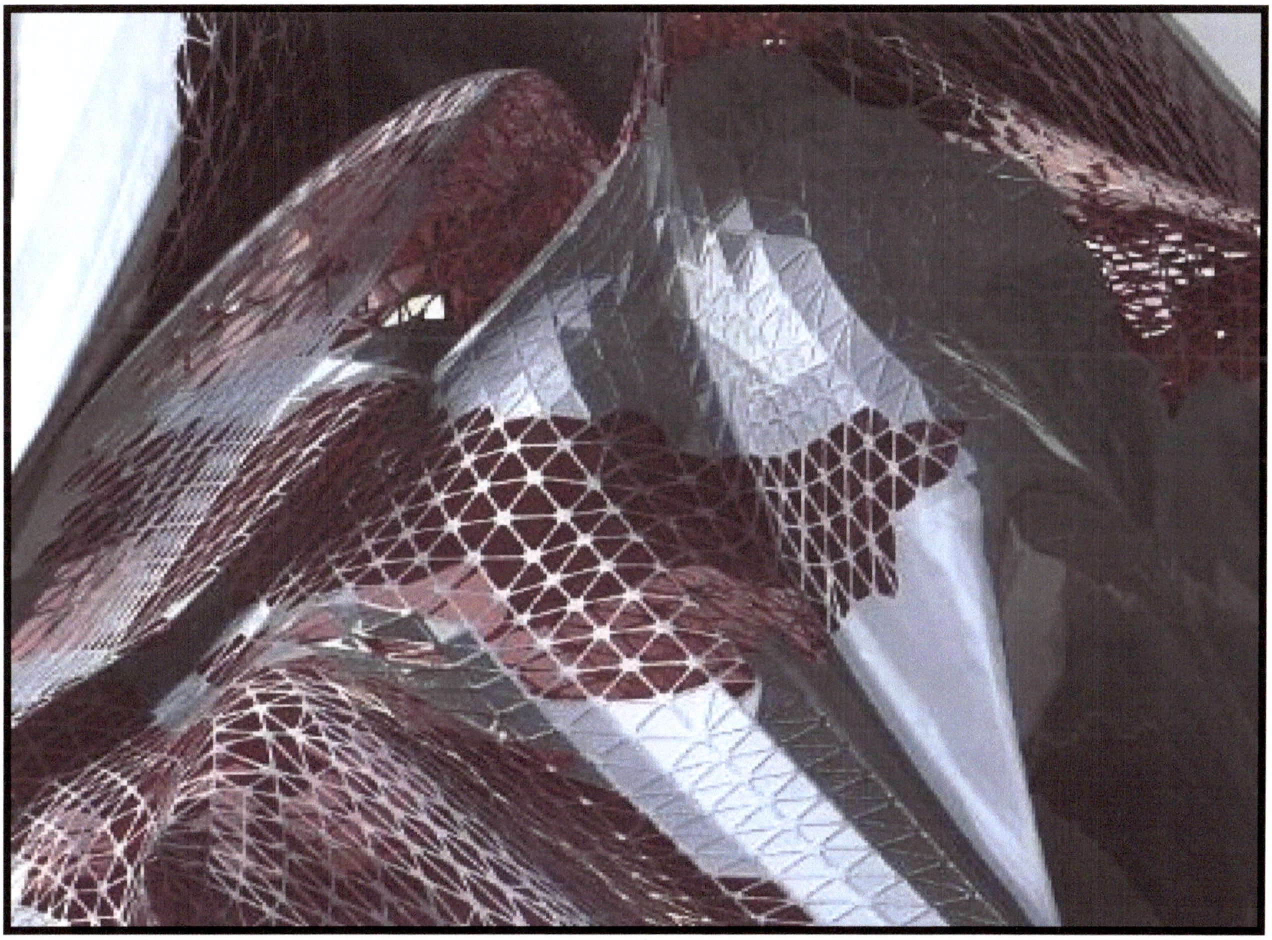

Parasite Brighton pier- Parasite Millennium Bridge London
Negin Hosseinalizadeh Alamdari

Negin is currently a graduate student in architecture at the University of Brighton in England. She did her BS at Azad University of Tabriz in Iran in architecture. Her main research interest is in the area of sustainable architectural design and that is what she is working on, as her Master's Thesis under the supervision of Frank O'Sullivun. The projects presented afterwards are samples of projects done in architecture department in 2014-2015.

Parasite pier Brighton

The major aim of the proposed project was to examine the student's ability of designing structures, which can improve the functionality of the pier, with the least possible damage to the existing structure of the pier. Parasite can be defined as "An adaptable, transient and exploitive form of architecture that forces relationships with host buildings in order to complete themselves. Parasites cannot sustain their own existence without siphoning energy from the surplus supply demonstrated in host buildings."[1] In this project, after series of investigations in terms of the geography, history and the users and operators of the area, we come up with the idea of an engaging and user-friendly structure, which can be represented both on and underneath of the pier, supported by beams that were embedded deep in ooze.in term of the materiality the structure is consist of materials such as mirrors, ETEF cushions, waterproof metals. (fig.1)

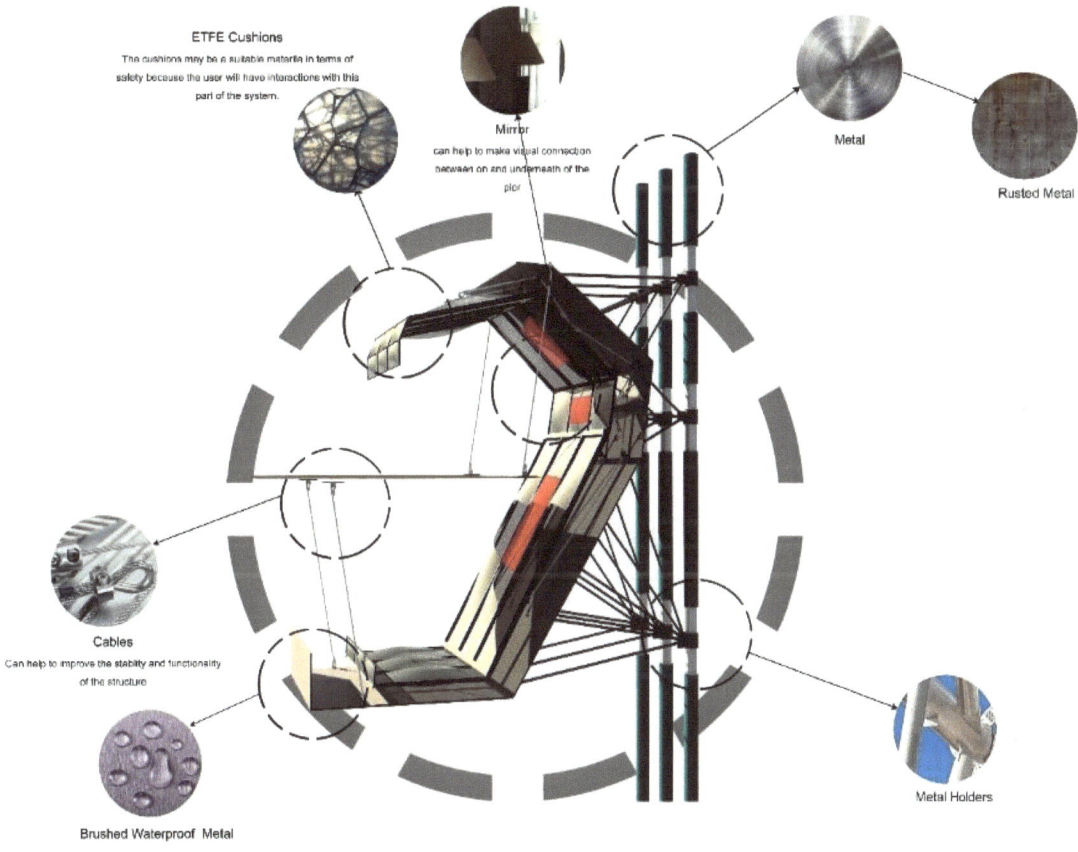

Fig.1. Materiality of the structure

The mechanism of the designed parasite structure leads it to do series of movements very the first moment that it is occupied with the help of series of spools and cables embedded between the two cores, the hard shell acting as protector and the ETEF cushions as shown in diagram below.

---

[1] http://buildinganddecor.co.za/walls/walls-categories/international-projects/616-trend-alert-parasitic-architecture.html

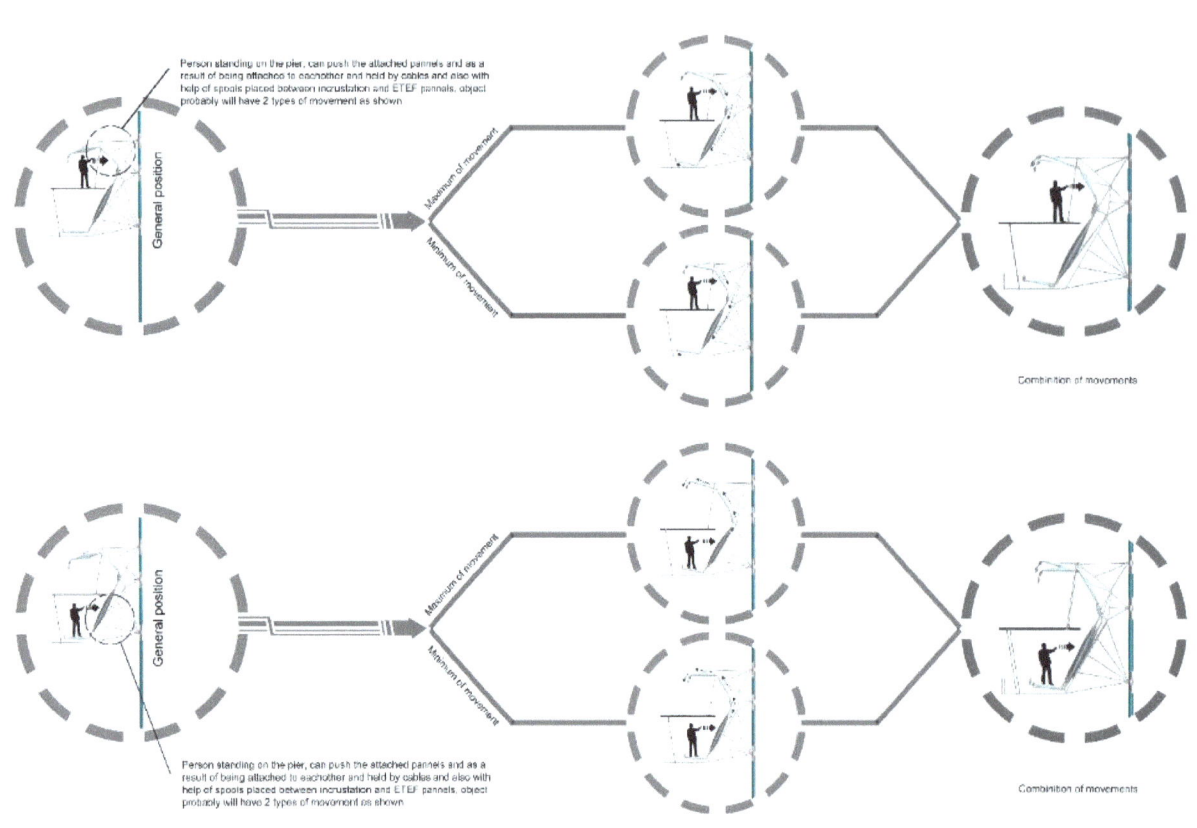

Diagram 1. Analyze of possible movements of structure while it is occupied

Therefore if a person on top of the pier touches or pushes the ETEF cushions in neither of the places, thee energy or movement will be transferred thorough the panels and this continues up until impacting the position of the second occupier without being present there.(fig2-3)

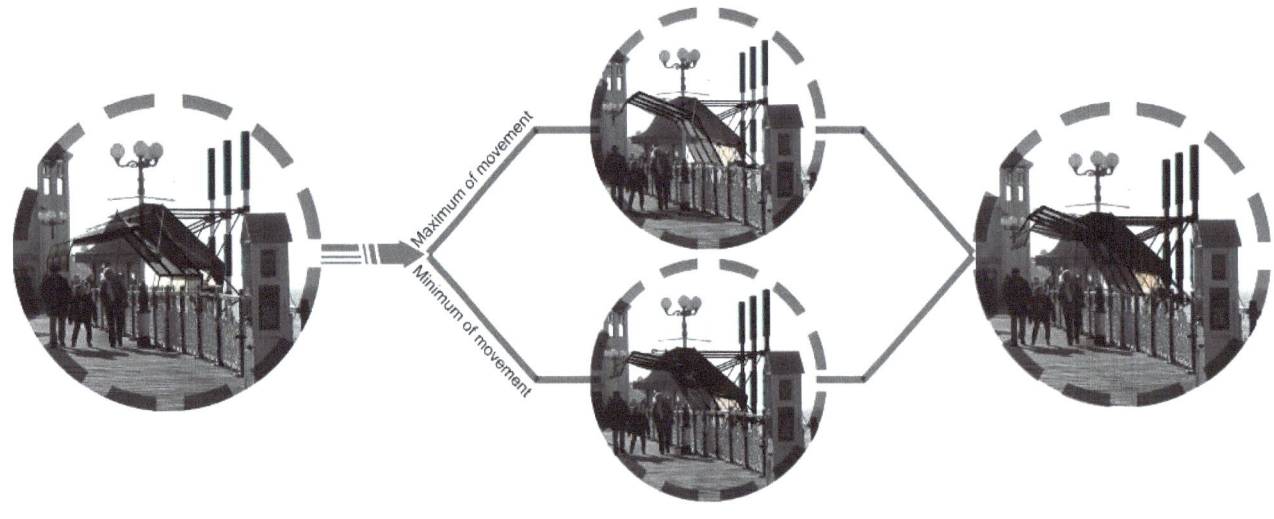

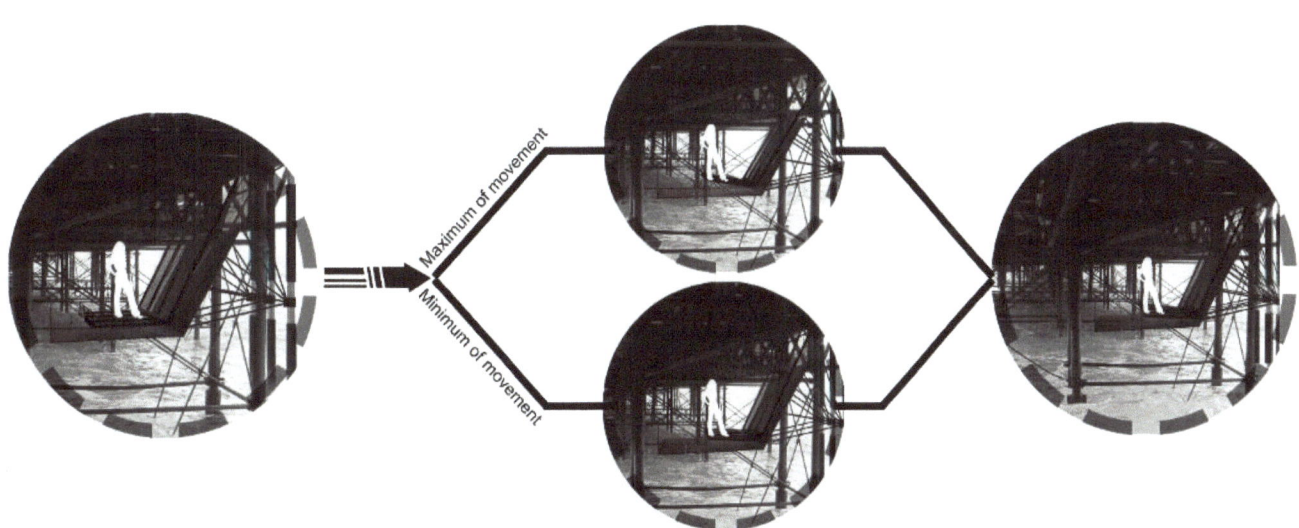

Fig.2. perspective and analyse of movements on top of the pier

Fig.3. perspective and analyse of movements on top of the pier

Parasite Millennium Bridge (London)

As a part of attached parasite projects, in this project students were asked to design a structure, mainly inspired from the parasite Brighton pier structure, which not only was supported by the Millennium Bridge as a host, but also contained features of the parasite pier project that best suits the Millennium Bridge. Alike the parasite pier project, series of investigations took place in terms of the location and surroundings, history and the users. Combination of information gained from investigations and useful pieces related to pervious project, in first step, led us to come up with an initial idea of a modern wireframe - technology base structure, which was represented on and underneath of the bridge. As shown in (diagram.1) users can change the appearance of the sphere by pulling or moving.

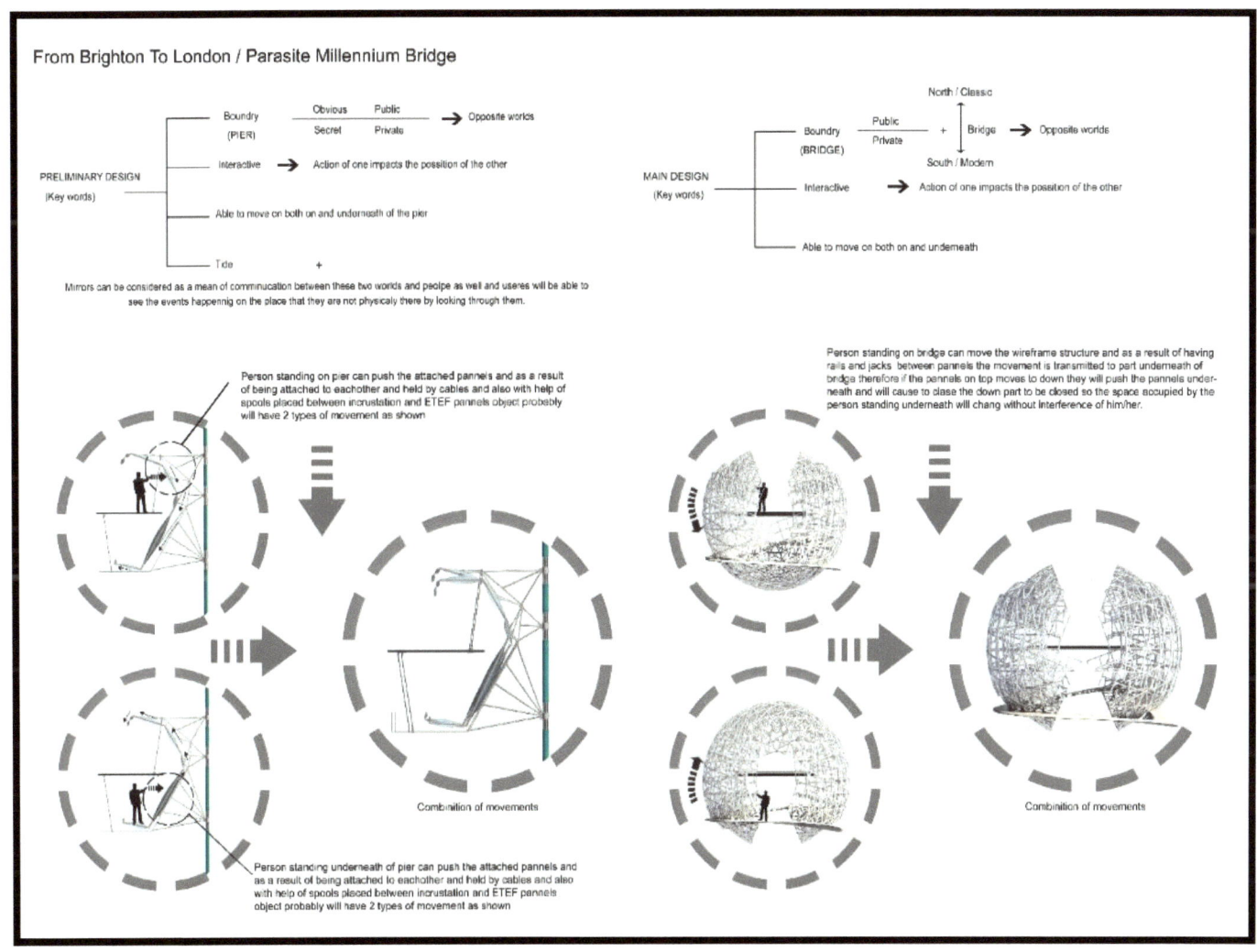

Diagram 1. Analyze of possible movements of structure while it is occupied

While designing and looking through different ideas and concepts, finally we decided to develop the idea of a modern structure which not only can do series of movements inspired from previous design, but also a space to step out of the routine functionality of bridge such as connecting the southern and northern London. Alike the parasite pier design, in order to make communication between the users, we decided to create wireframe structure that people can attach padlocks as symbol of their presence on bridge (fig.1) inspired from a common tradition of attachin wishes to wishing trees in china, Dakhil-Bastan tradition in Iran and the Pont de Arts Bridge in France. (fig.2)

Fig.1. padlocks attached to wireframe structure

Fig.2. Up left: attaching wishes to wishing trees tradition in china

Up right: tradition of Dakhil- Bastan in Iran

Below: 'love padlocks' attached to a fence of the Pont de Arts Bridge over the Seine River in Paris

The change in appearance of the structure is not specifically related to users. The colorful glass, inspired from Nasir Al- Mulk mosque in Shiraz (fig.3), which has covered top of the sphere creates different shades based on the position of the sun. (fig.4)

Fig.3. Nasir Al- Mulk mosque in Shiraz, known as Pink Mosque

Fig.4. colorful glass and shades on deck of the bridge

As for the part related to the idea of stepping out, the underneath of the bridge and the slope wrapping it, gives the visitor opportunity to experience a moment fully specific and unique. (fig.5)

Fig.5. underneath of the Millennium Bridge

Chapter 2

Conceptual visualization based on parametric design

I think "interactive design" accurately defines digital design where two or more minds try to create a novel phenomenon. It helps interaction and coordination of design and computer as well as better understanding of software. The method which is now used in projects design at Inter-discipline Design Universe, directed us toward another direction or, in better words, a mutation in design, to design merely on computer without any sketch or Marquette. The next chapters exactly support results of interactive design between computer and designer mind where design process is began on computer based on a predetermined concept.

Exhibition spaces design based on Iranians architecture tradition-theories

Leila Manzouri

Bachelor of Architecture
Member of Interdiscipline Design Universe

Bedchamber of Shiraz's Vakil-Mosque (http://dolan.ir/)

West bedchamber of Isfahan's Imam-Mosque (http://shabgar.com)

First Alternative

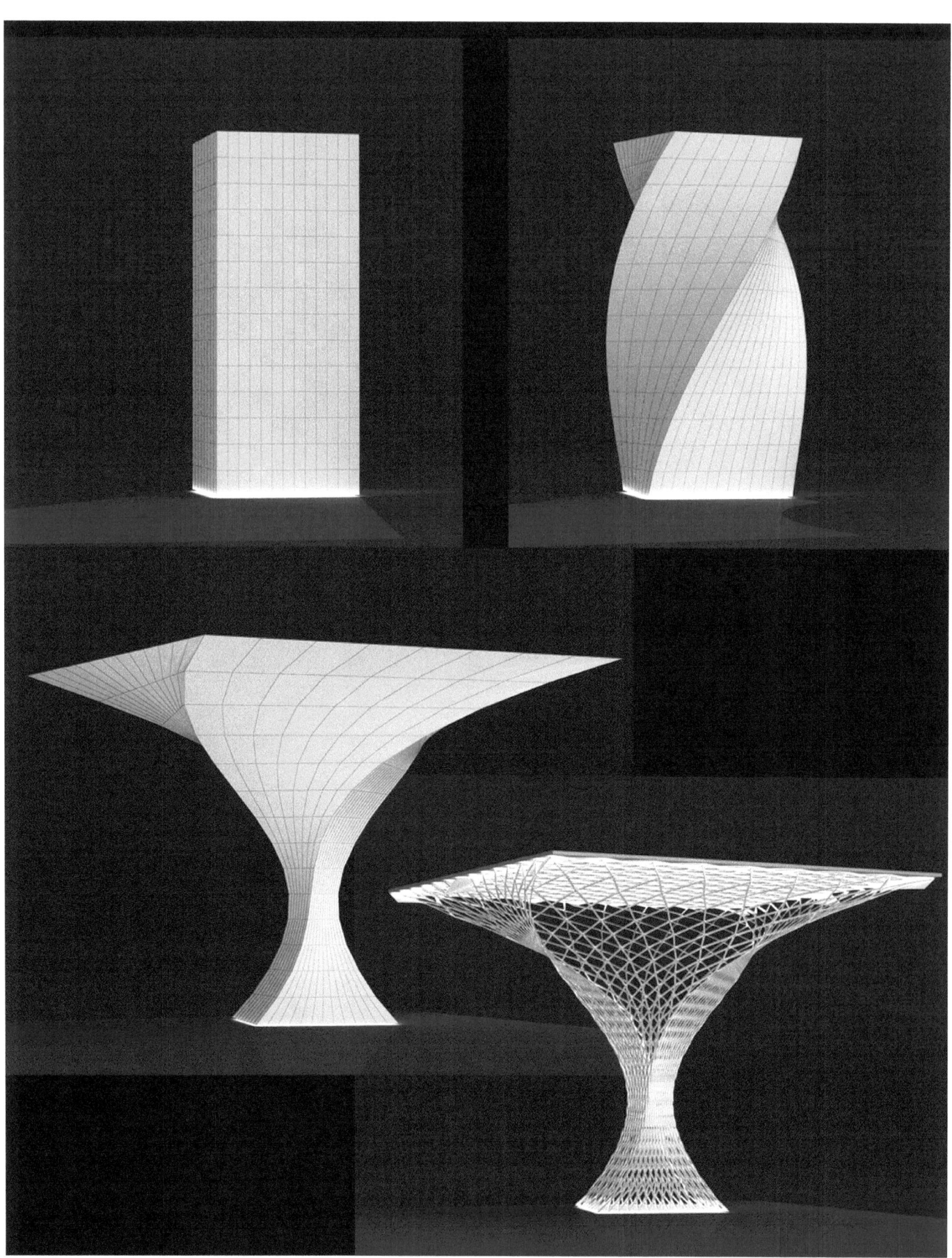

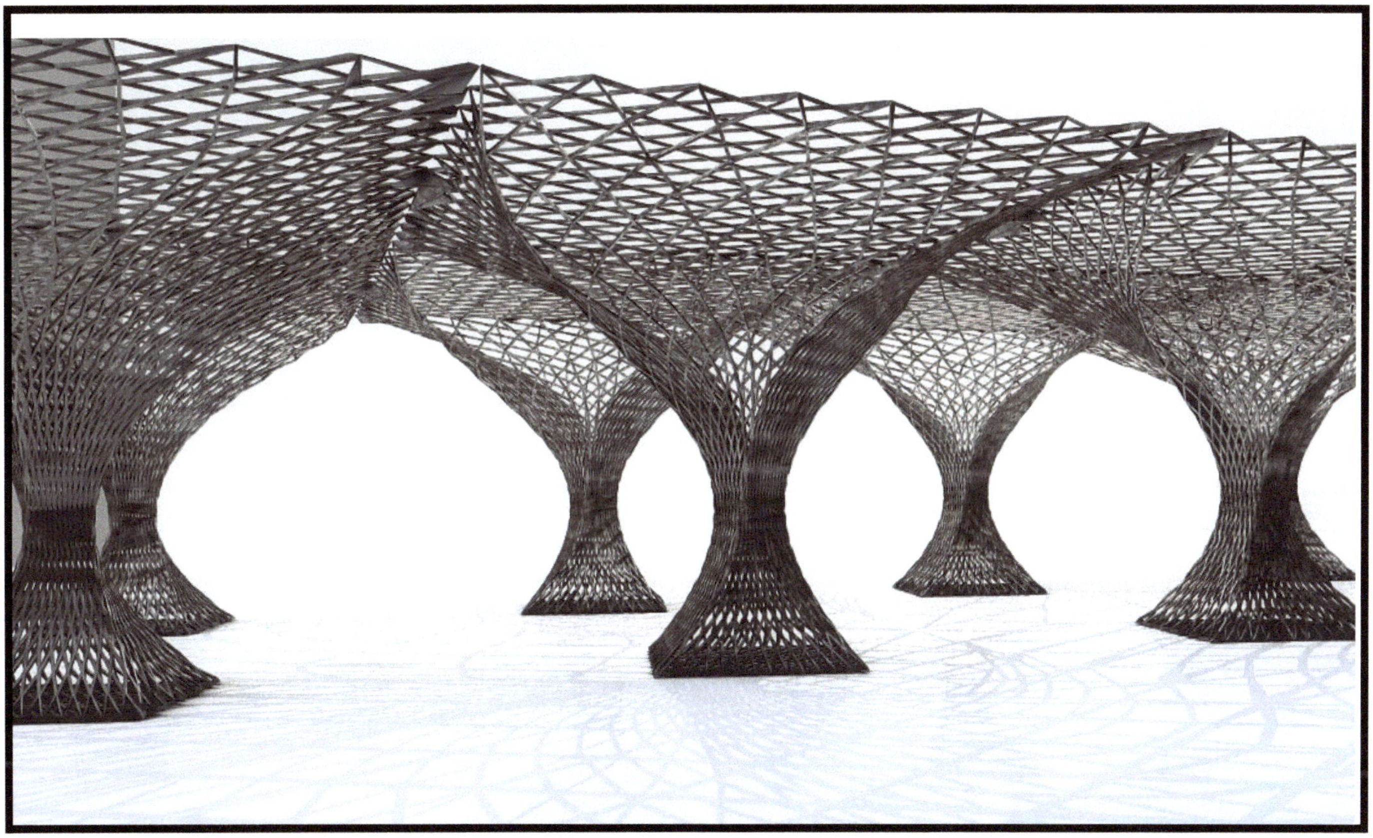

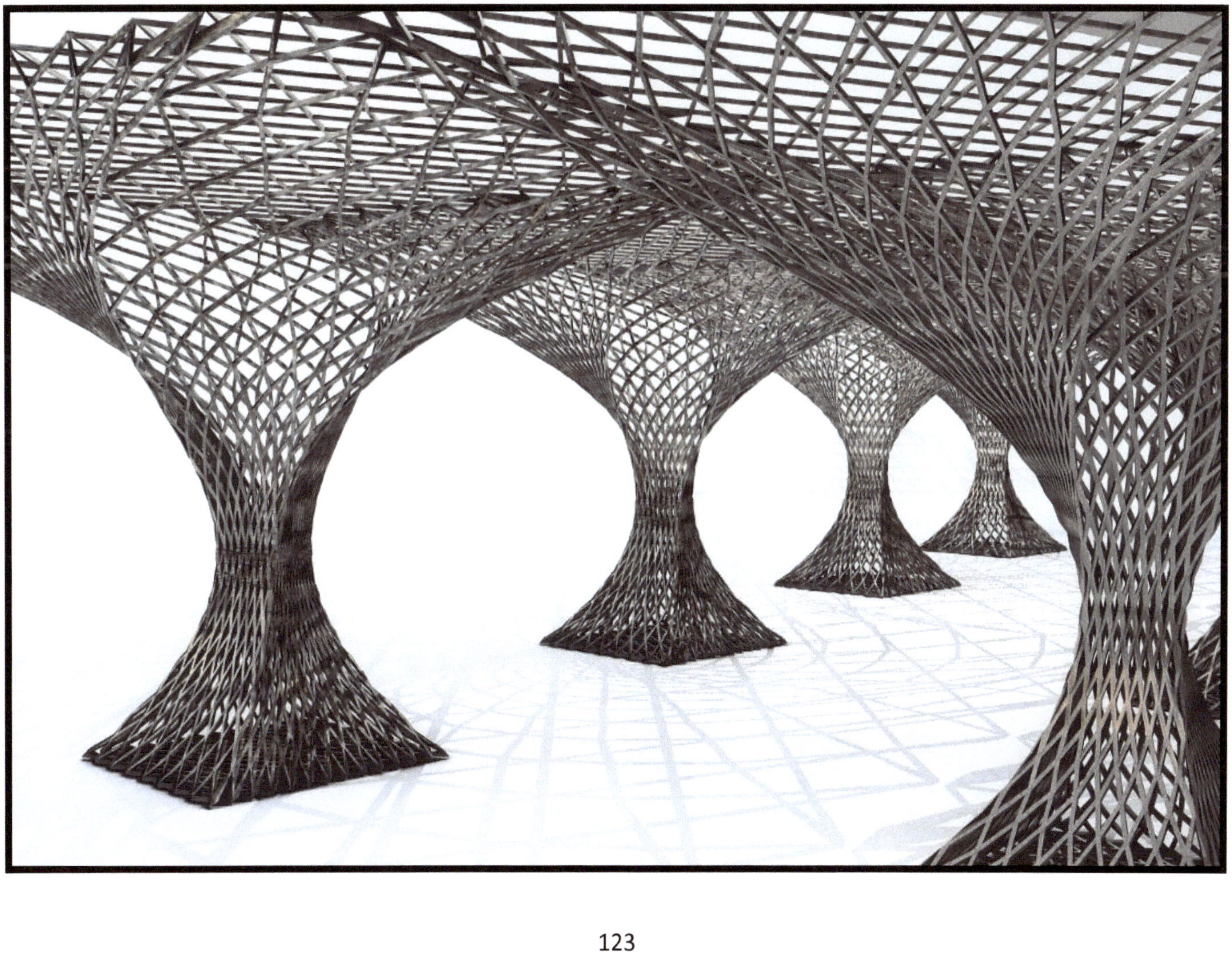

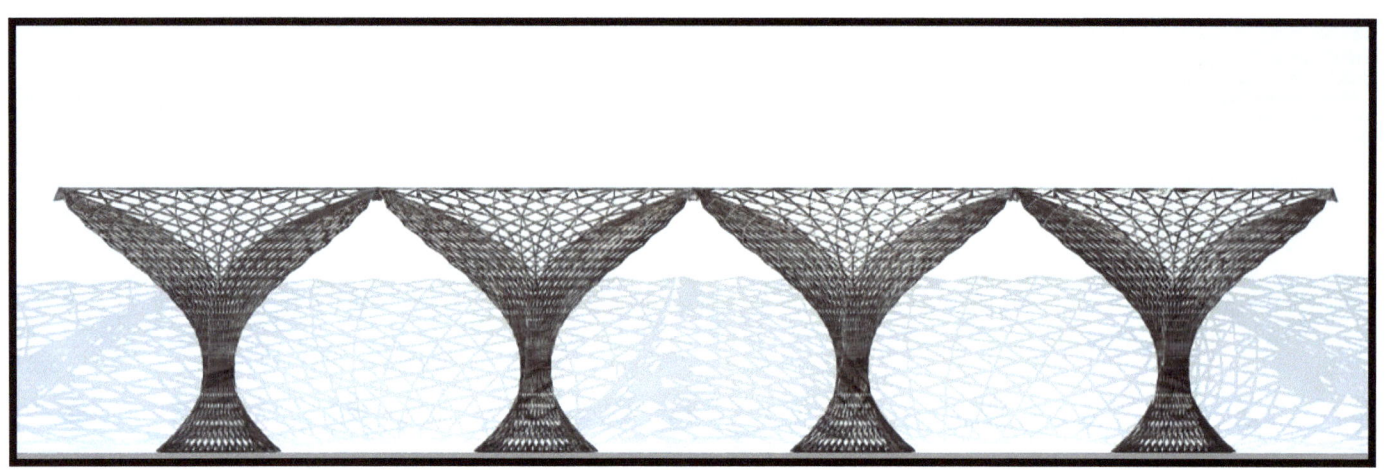

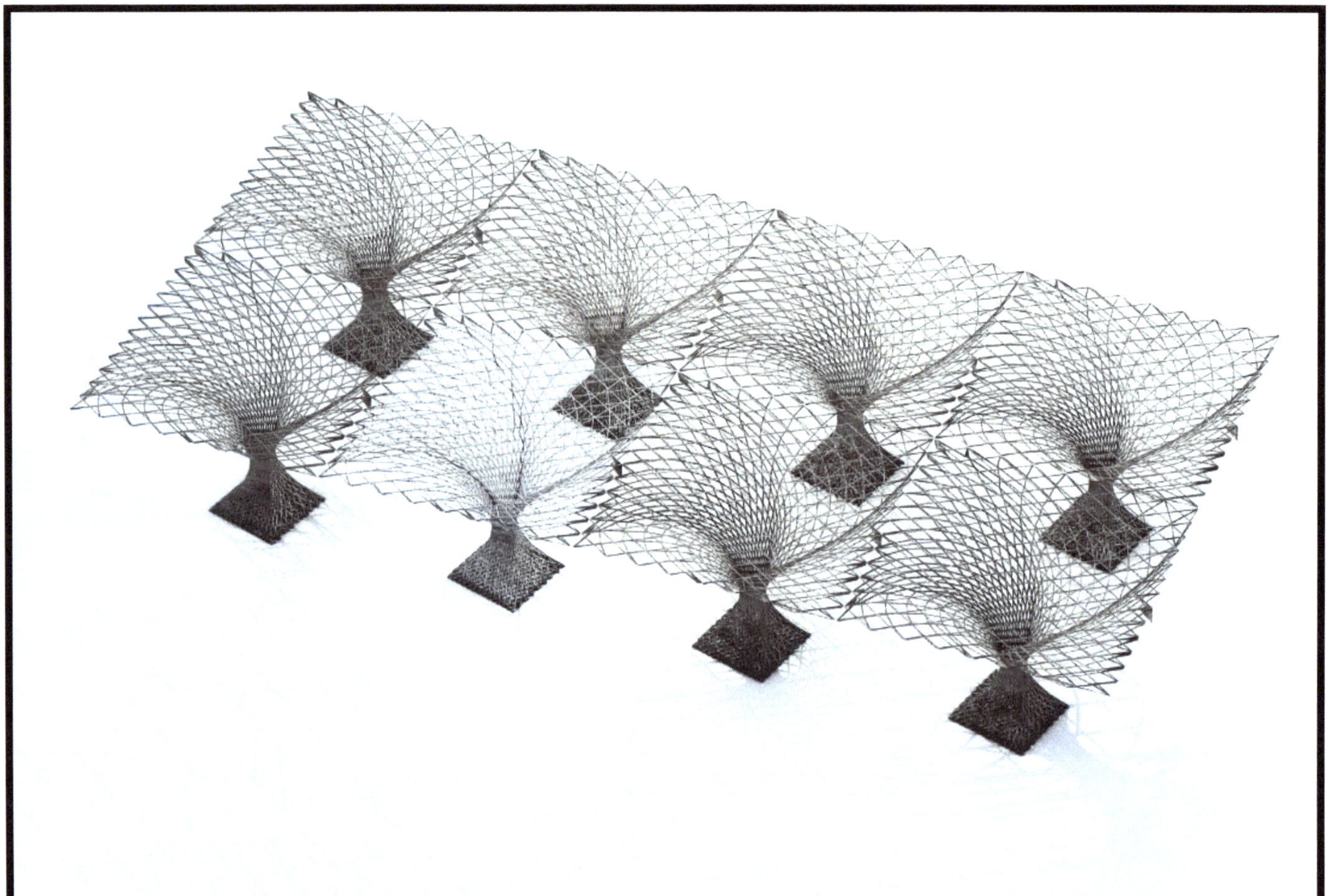

Second Alternative

Parametric Space

Sahand Latifi
Bachelor of Architecture

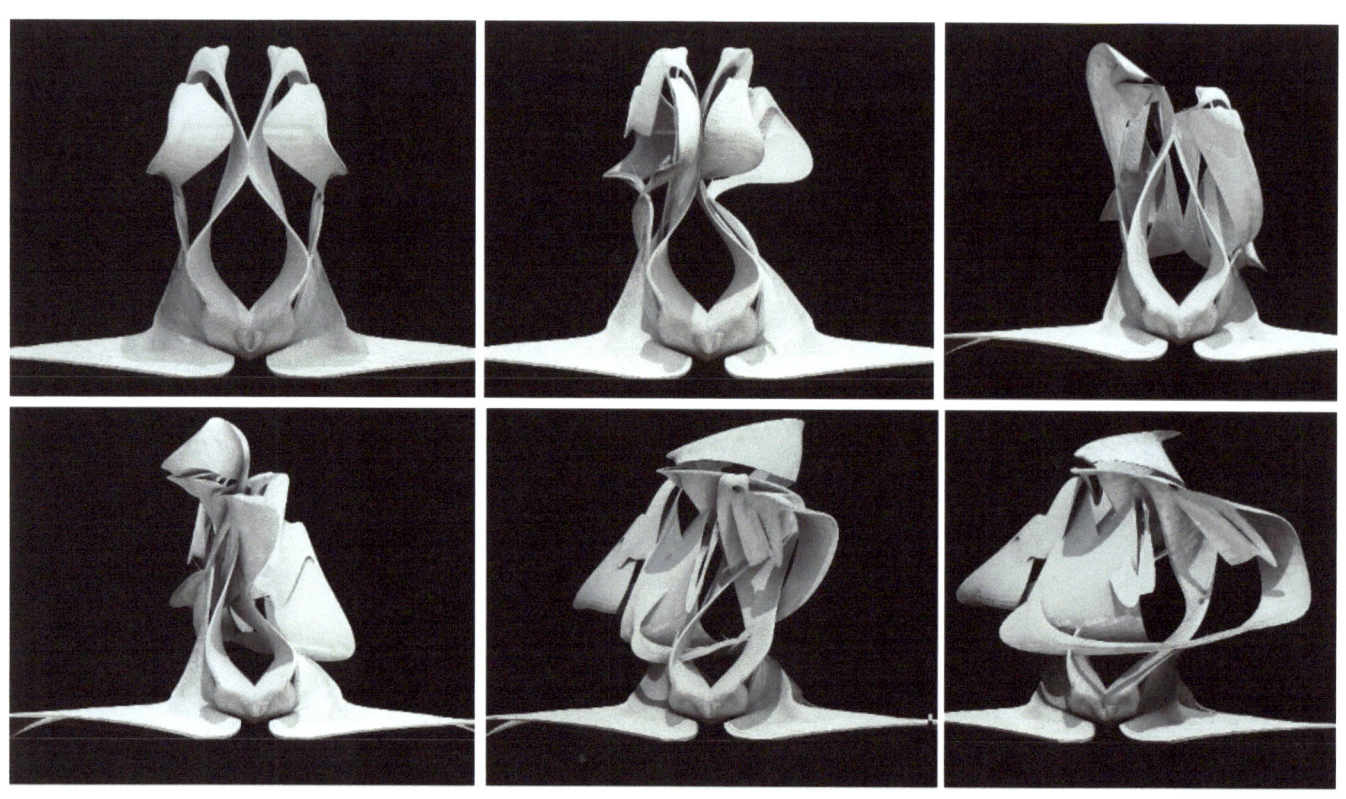

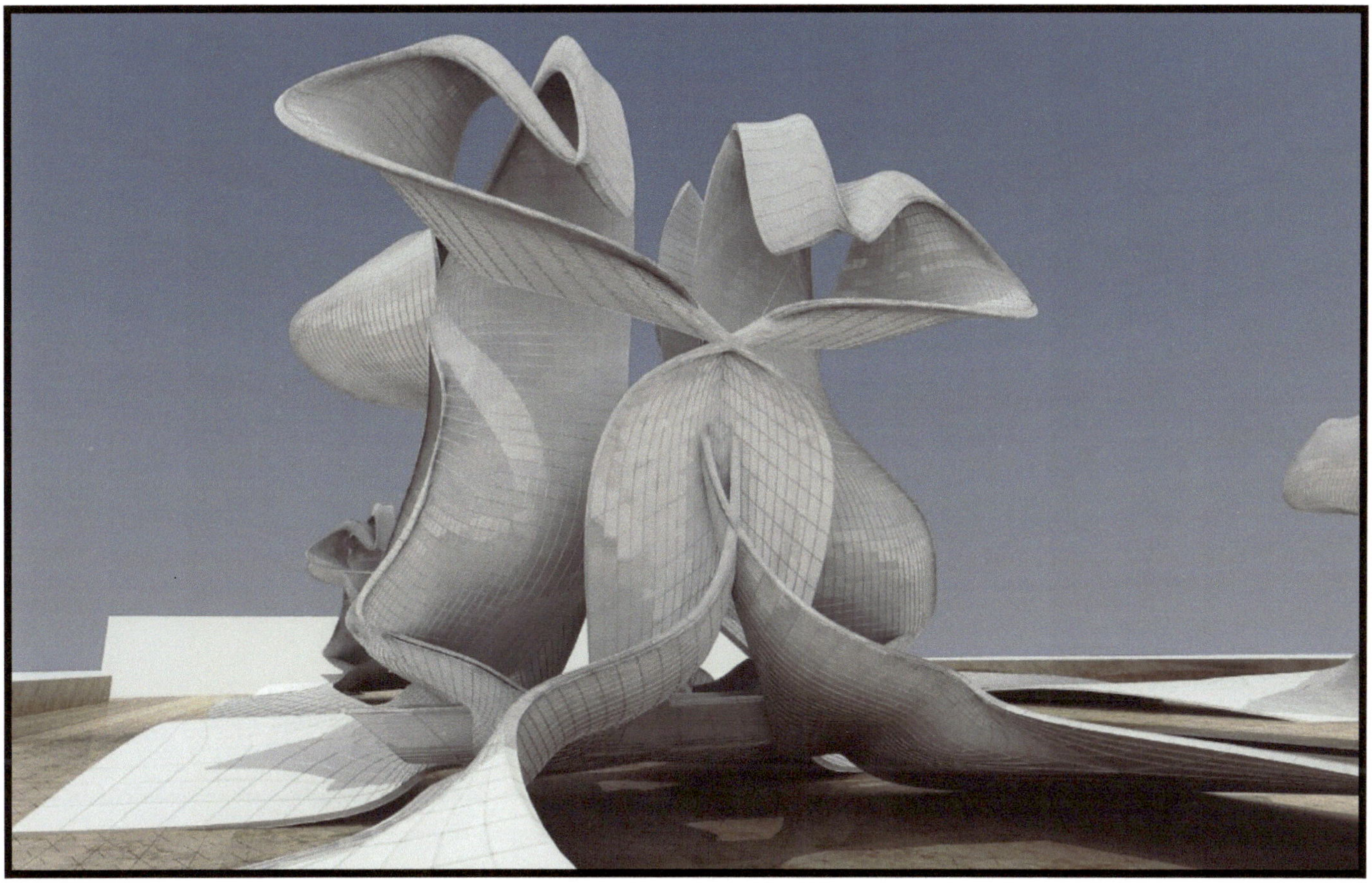

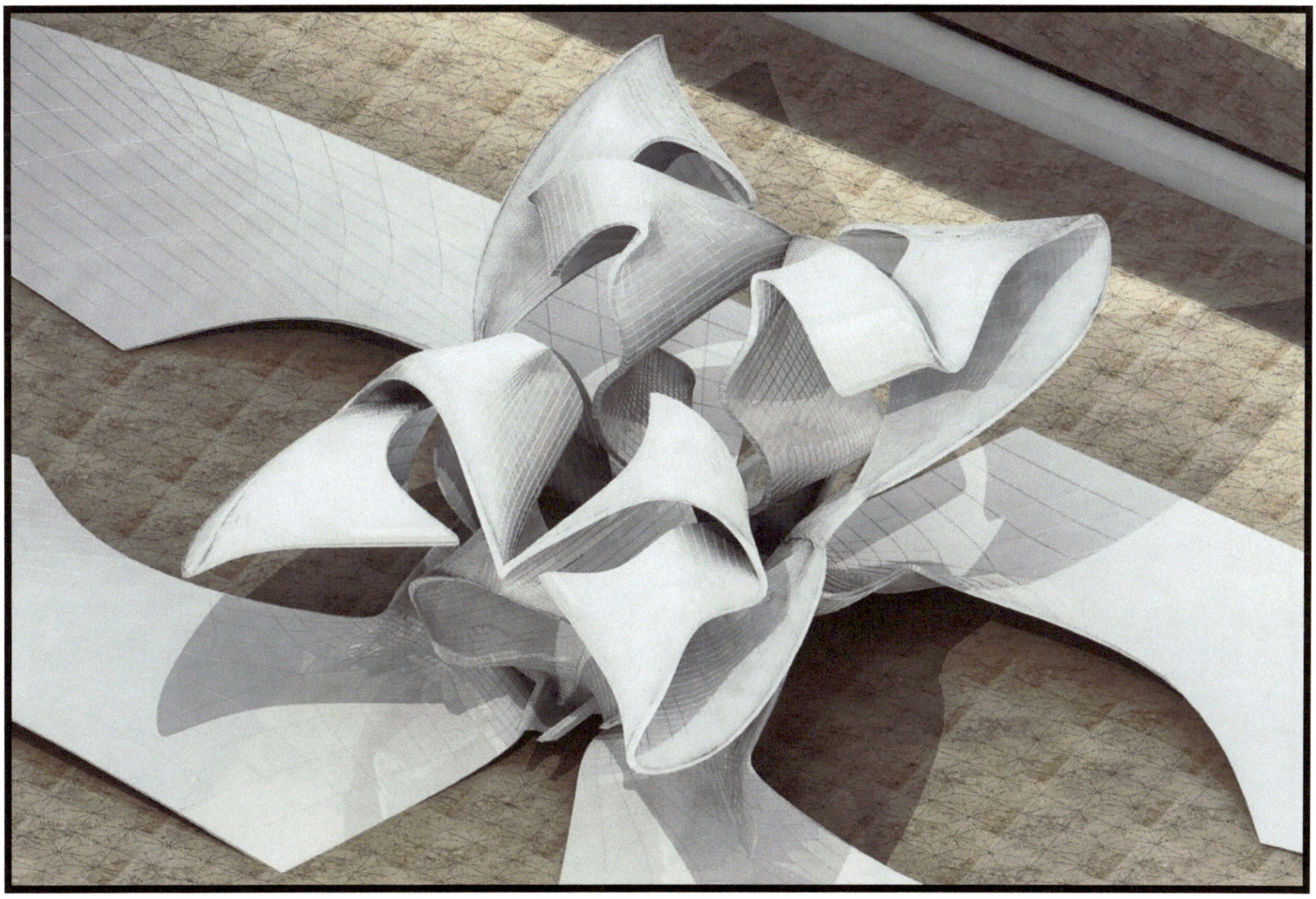

Samples of parametric designs inspired by shell

Pourya Ahmadzadeh
Bachelor of Architecture

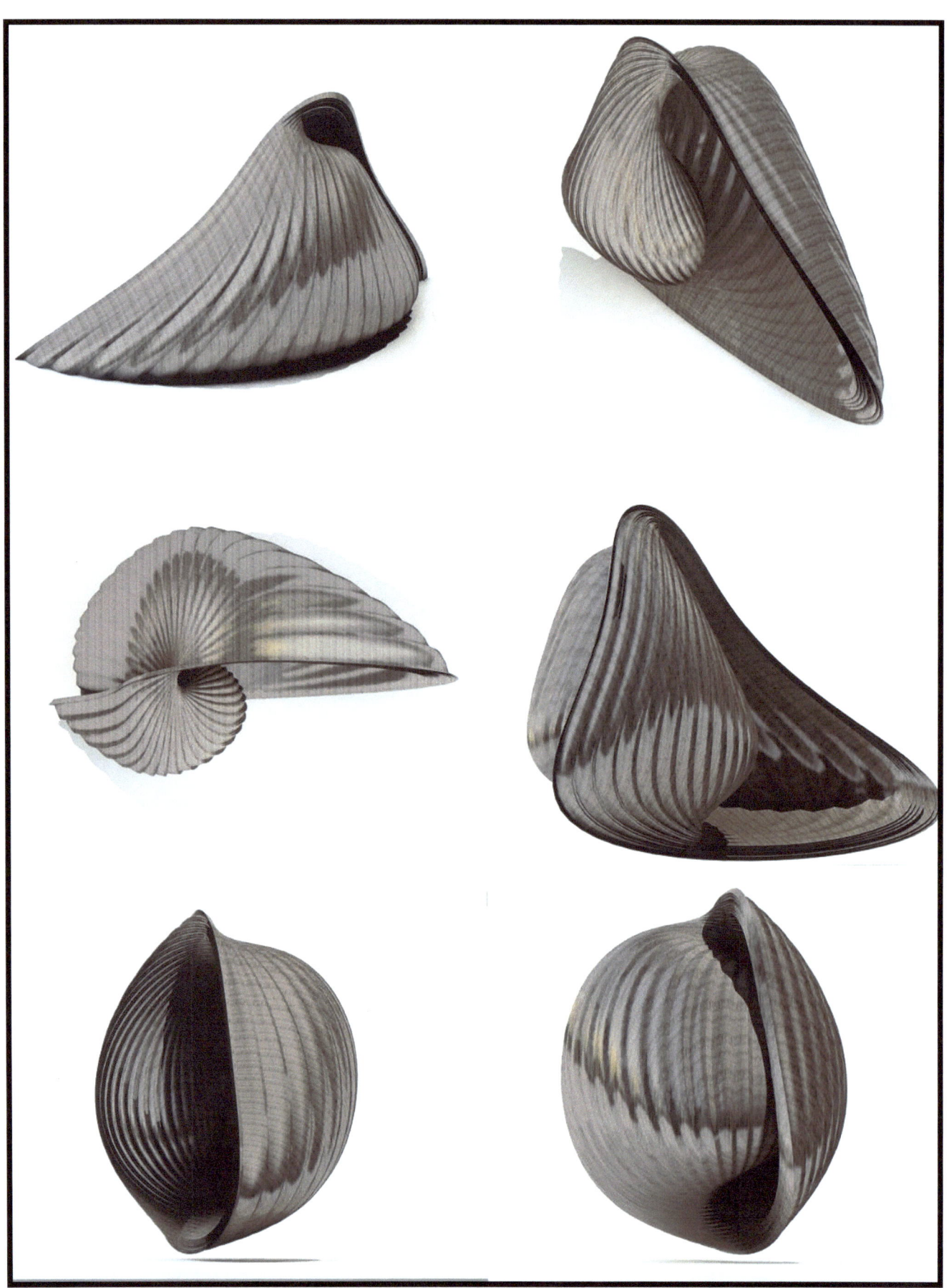

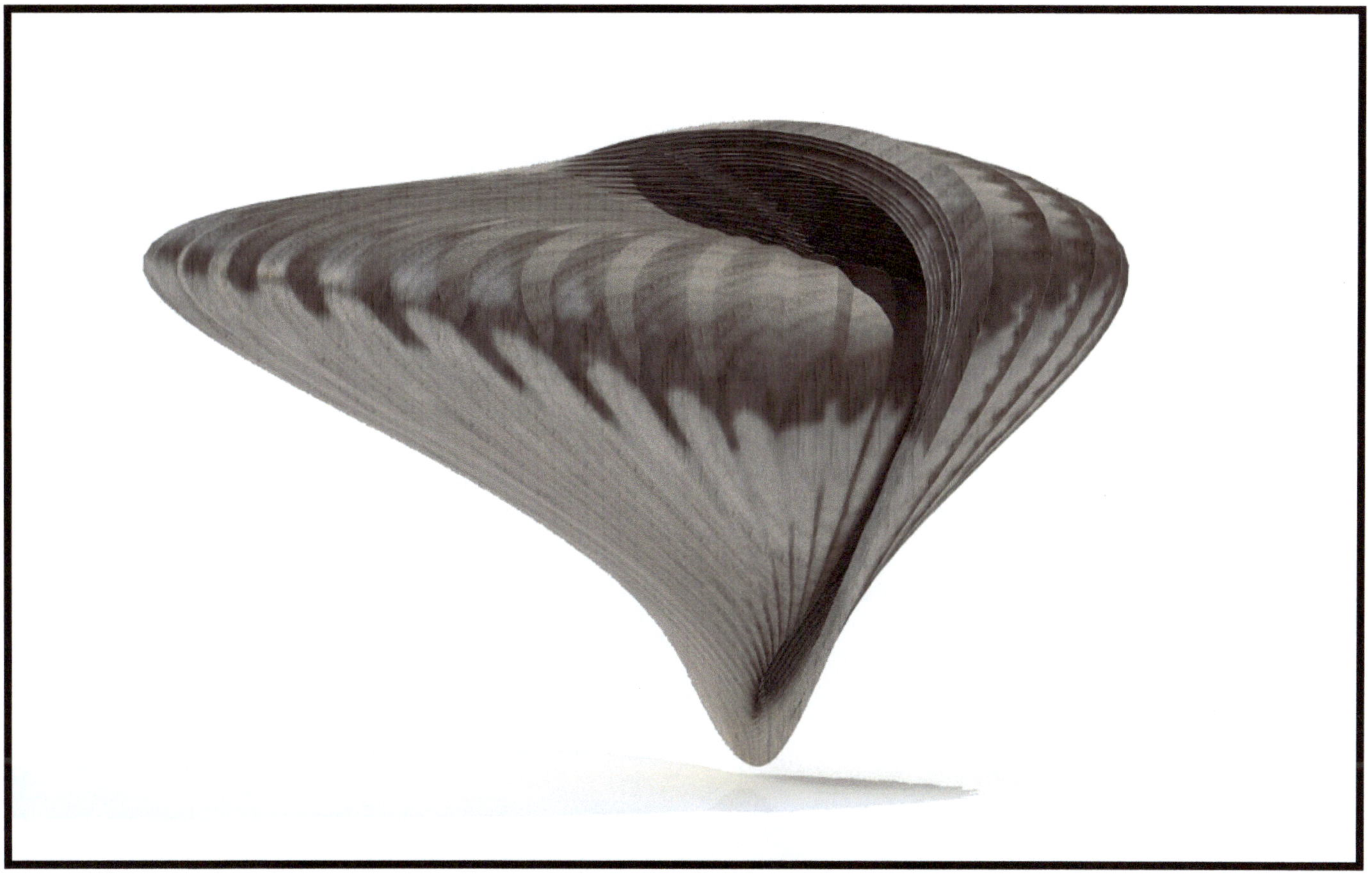

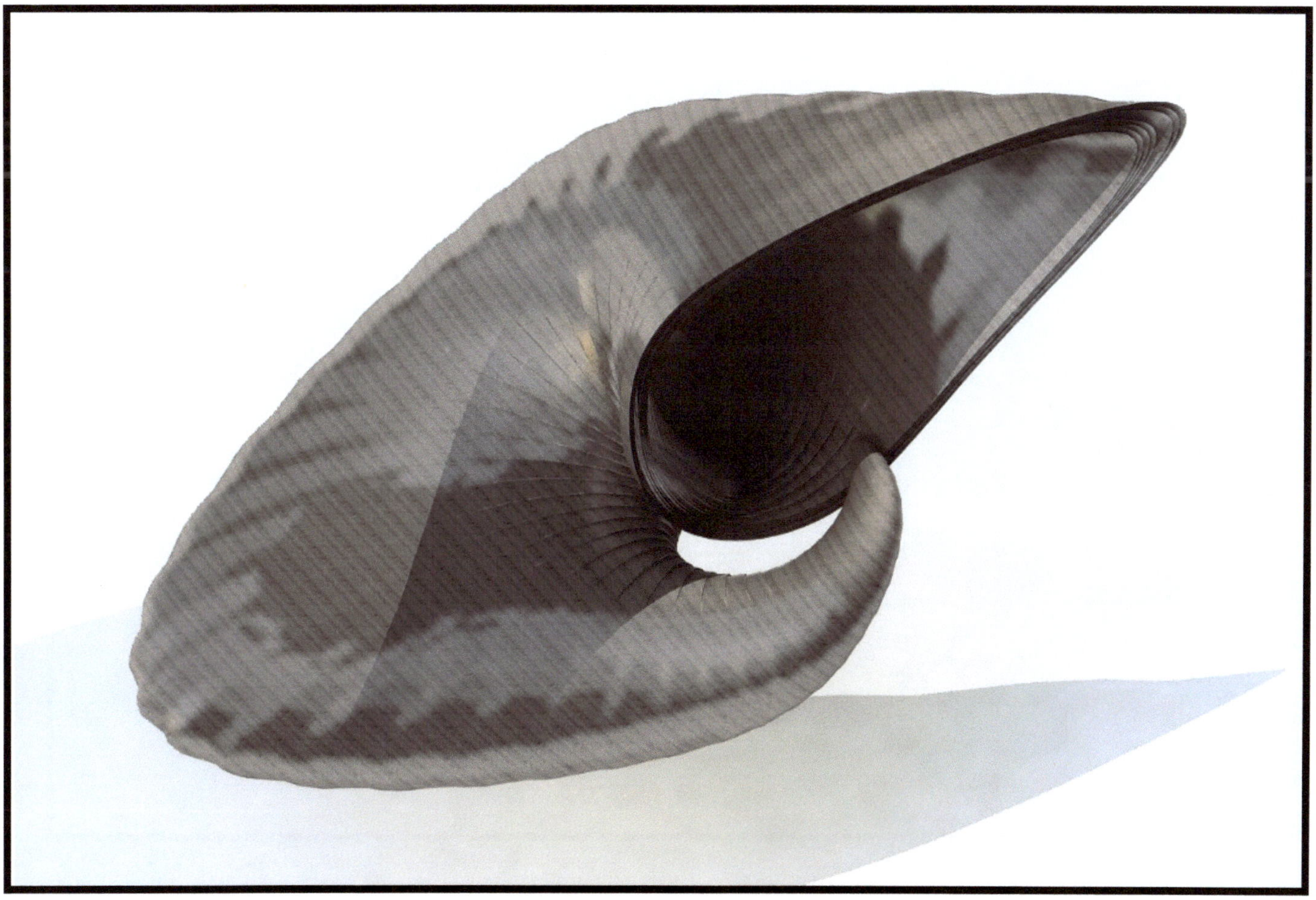

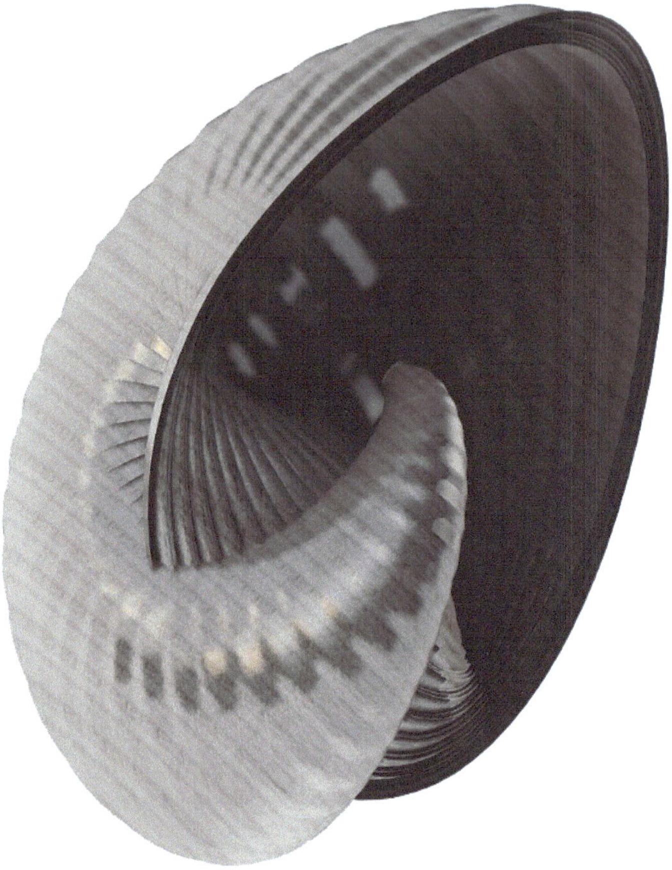

134

Exhibiting spaces design, inspired by snail and the forms created during previous projects

Mahsa Fakhrjahani - Leila Manzouri

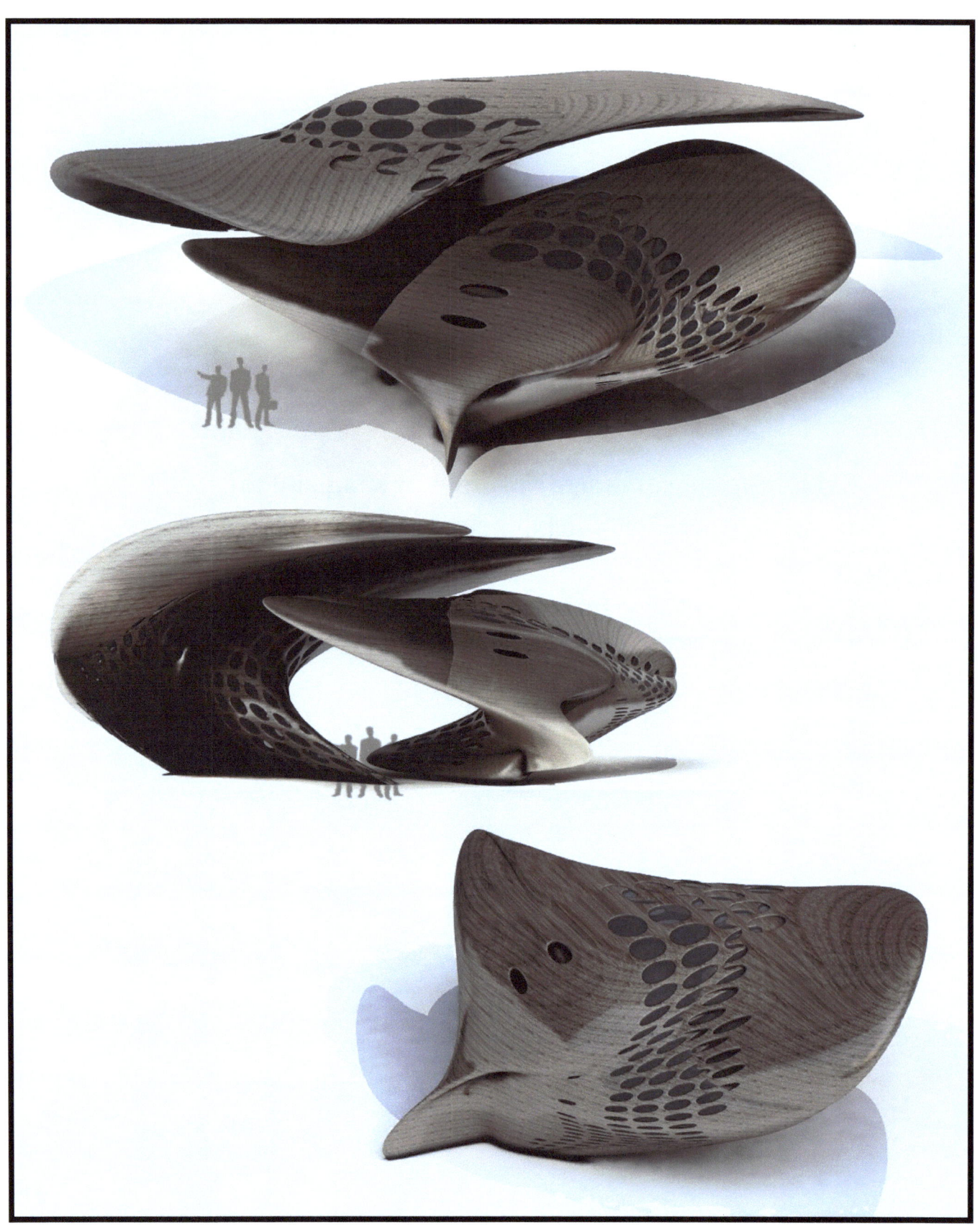

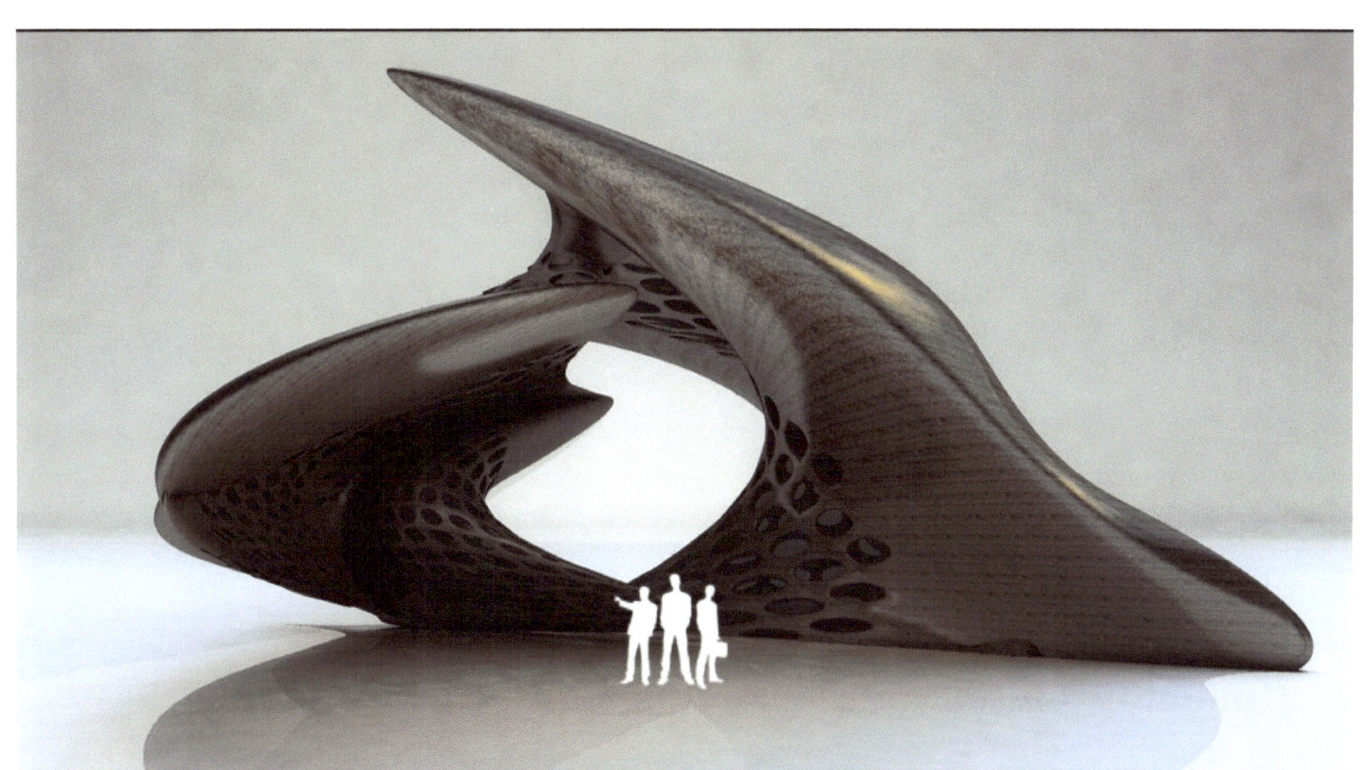

Humanity's history museum design, inspired by human chest

Niloofar Amel
Bachelor of Architecture
Member of Interdiscipline Design Universe

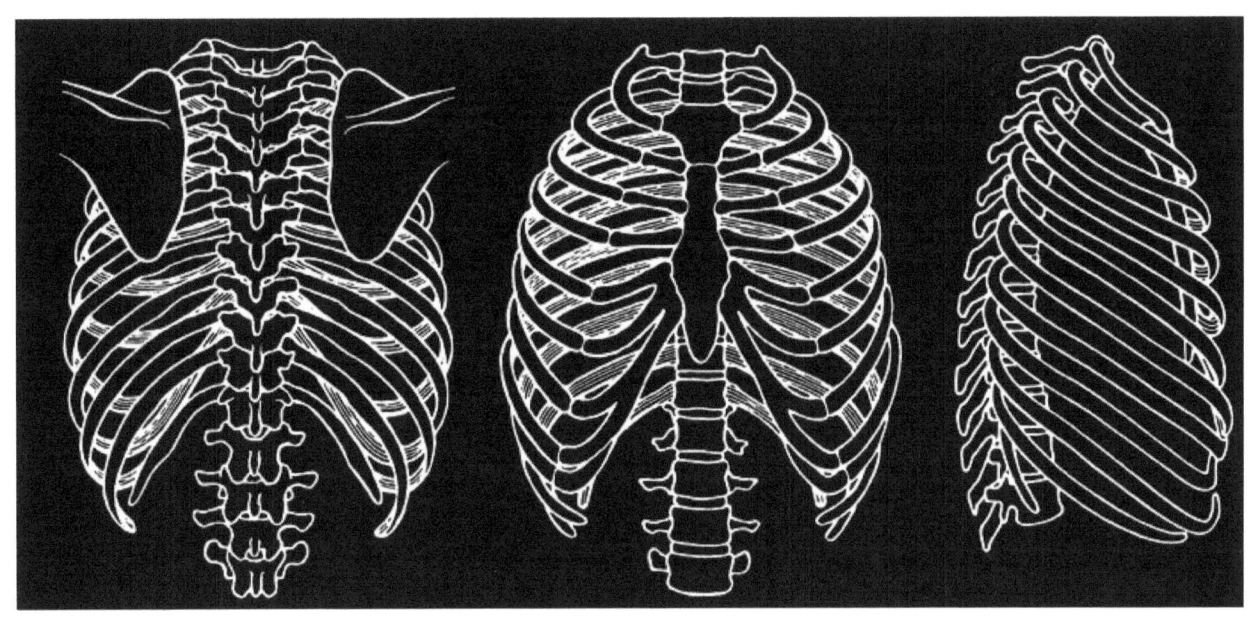

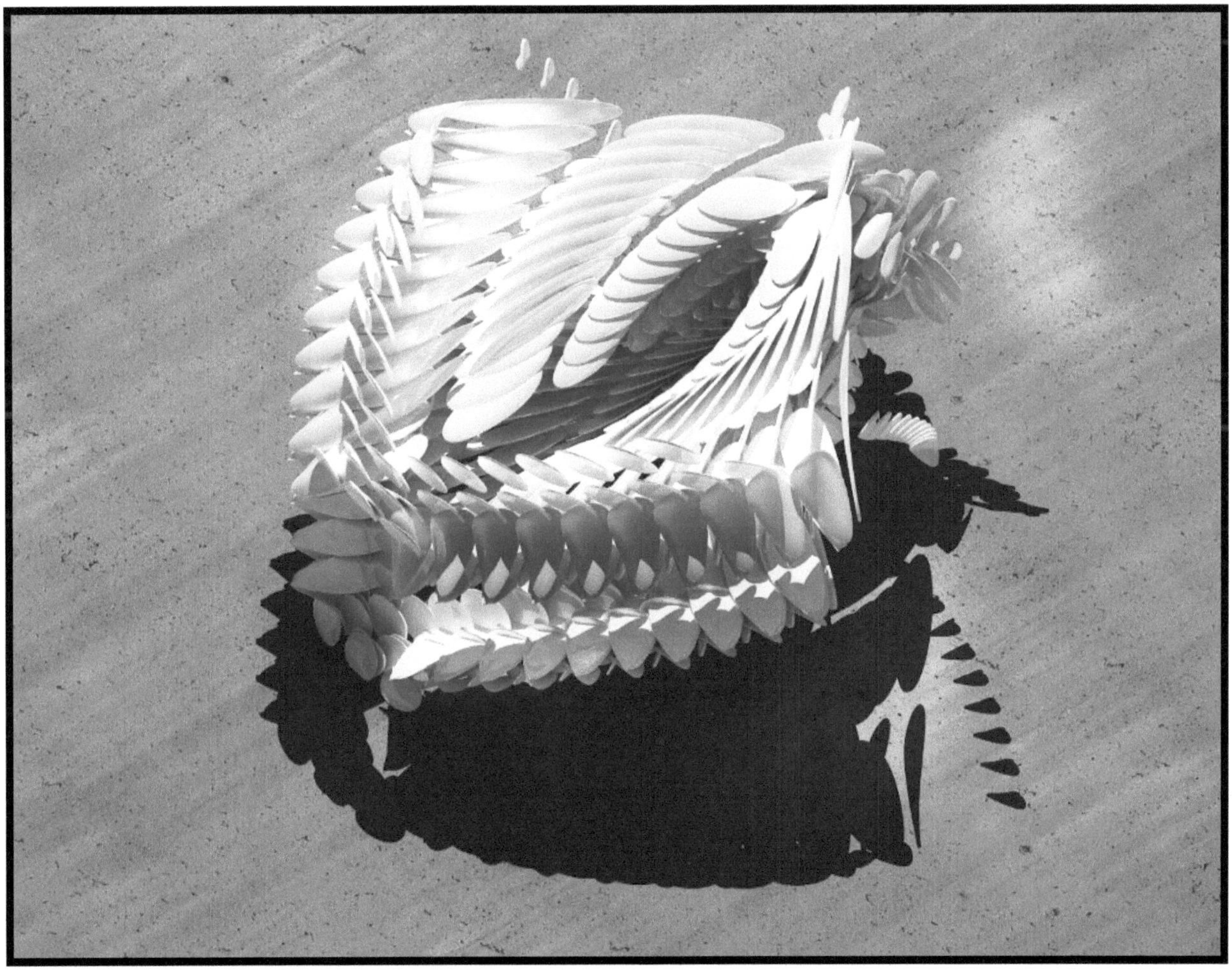

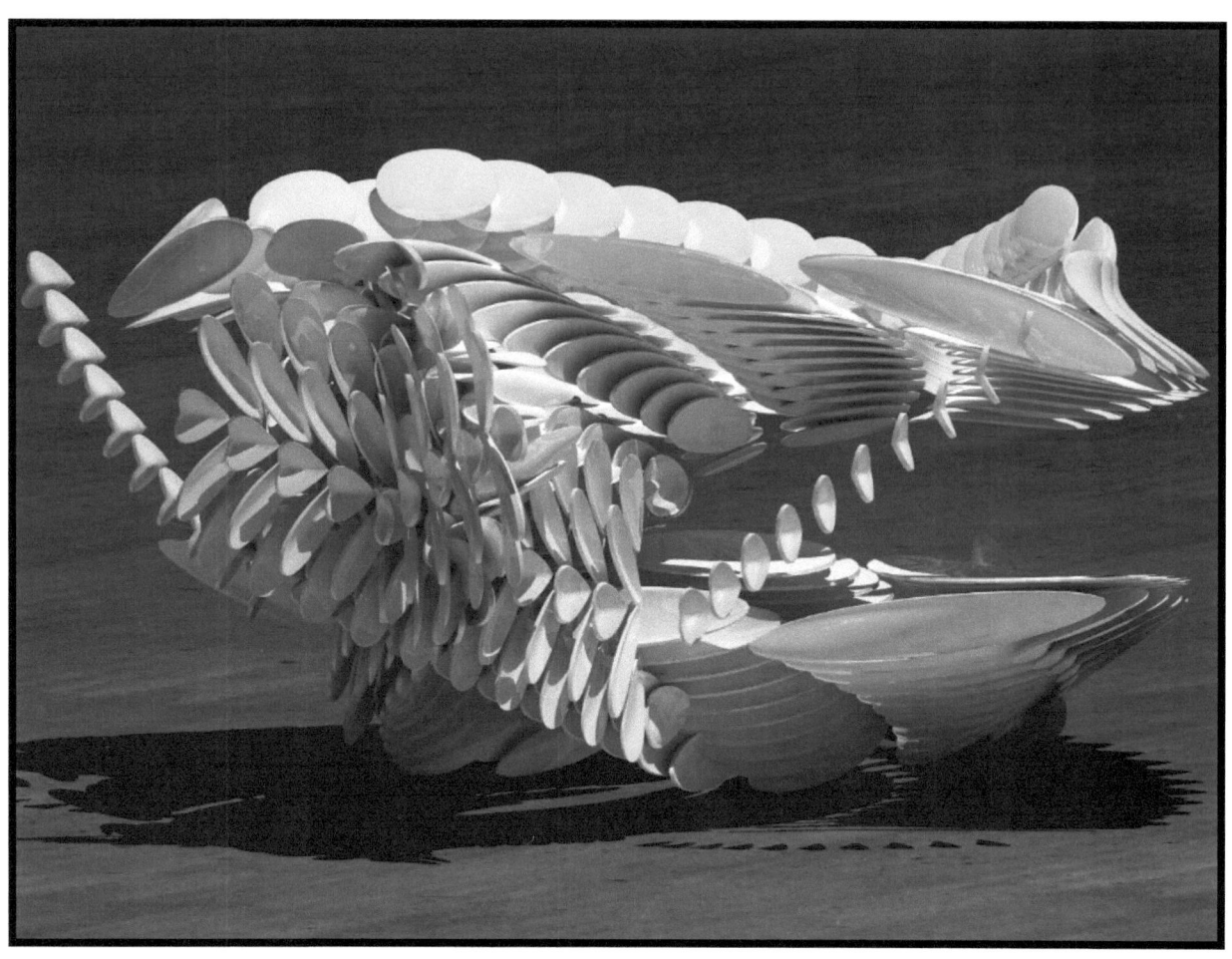

Pelagic animals' museum design inspired by frog skeleton

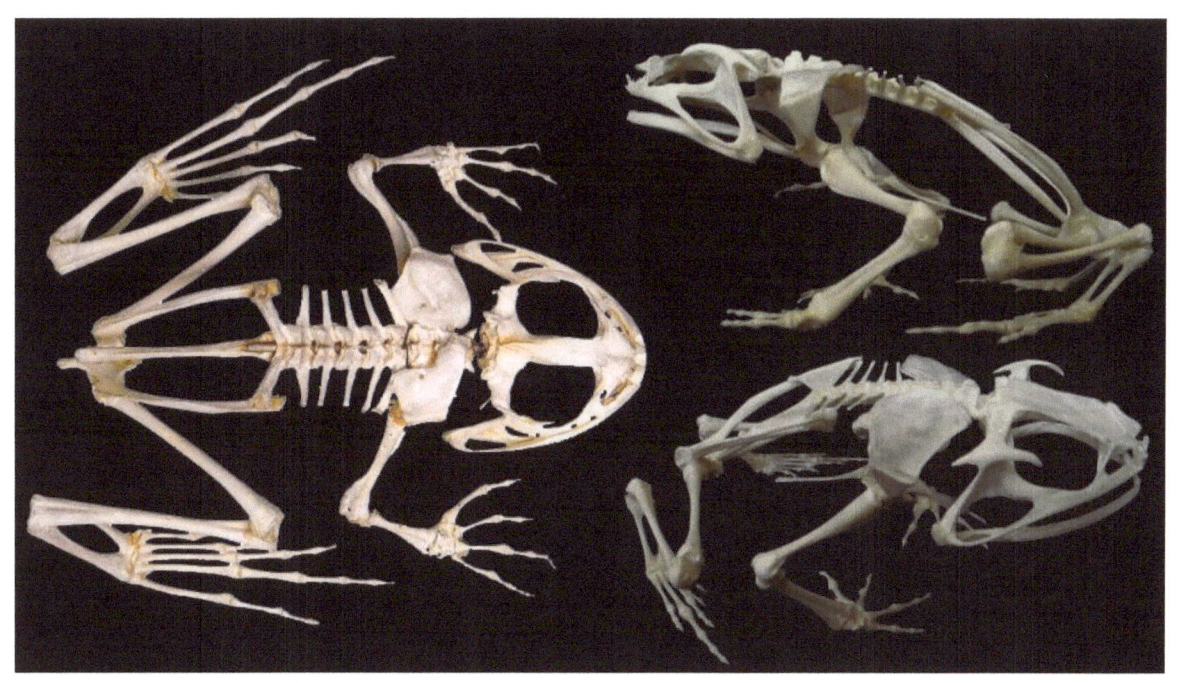

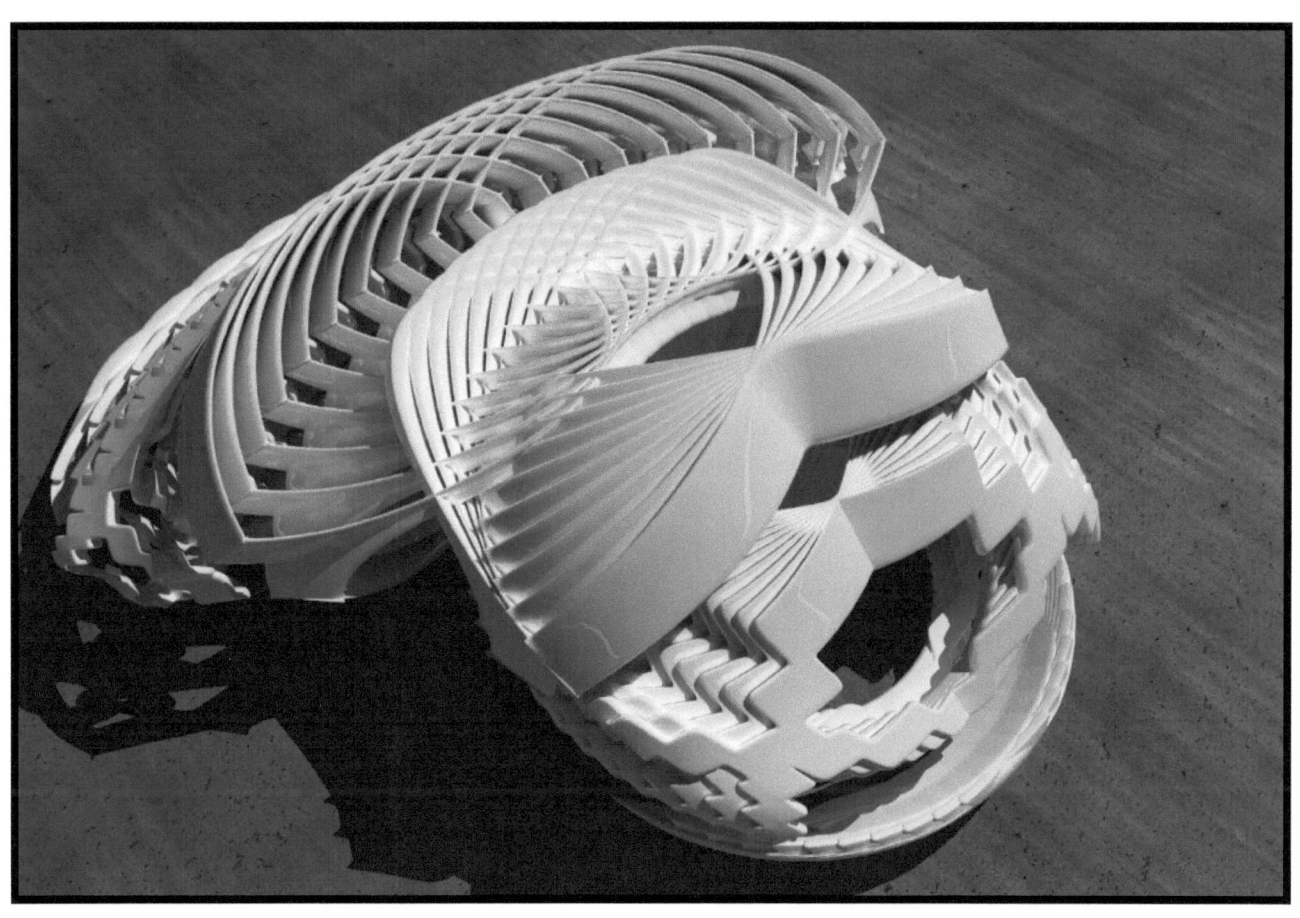

Elevations

Fire temple
"A building inspired by soul of time and worship"

Being excited by intellectual reserves of the environment bringing us, being thoughtful about correspondent agents and phenomena intending to grant a historical aspect to day, being in need to a dignified conversation which was yesterday found in the sense world to create a sumptuous architecture, may force all architects to deliberate before creating their work and to have a fancy to see all sides as far as possible.

Thus, the present article tries to recognize an architectural body of ancient Iran to set foot on a wide and complex way based on the former studies and enthusiasm to know concepts and reserves of the ancient architecture. To arrive the destination, we should turn our face to the heaven, use our hands as a sunshade against the past burning thoughts, watch the sun, inflame our inside fire, begin meditation and purification, appeal to soil holiness, and entrust our inner anguish to it. Here, it will arise, rear its firm pillars, keep the heaven between its hands, and give shelter the fire.

Coincidence of time concept with fire temple architecture

Ancient Iranians who were more engaged in thought and cosmic images in East territories than the West, wanted to see and recognize mysterious world of nature in a way which is still exciting and interesting to hear. Fire temple is one of these spaces and its purist elements, i.e. time and place, were renewed in relation to its main category.

Ancient Iranians believed in relation between place and time: when "Jupiter created the creatures materially" granted it "fire from immense light, wind from fire, water from wind, ground from water, and all material existence of the world". The creator created all in the heaven as a castle and fort, as a house where everything is kept safe. The heaven was formed on six directions:" width of the base equals its length, its length is the same as its height, its height equals its depth, with the same sizes…". The heaven was pattern of the earth and the earth which was appeared after happiness and water was created circular, without ups and downs, with "length and width while the width was the same as the depth" and it was placed "exactly in the middle of the heaven".

According to the data, there was a physical concept for time without passing of day, night, month, and year. It was not understood and defined out of time after the third great creator which was itself born by mysteries of universe.

Ancient Iranians believed in a very eminent concept for time and know it superior than material existence of the world and the soul governing it. For them, time was the most powerful creator. It was time which was given birth to Jupiter.

Ignoring how thought about time and endless time of Zurvan found its way to Zoroastrianism, stayed strongly during changes of Sasanian era, became the main pattern of Manichaeism, lasted by now at least relying on special religious sects such as Dahrieh, and affected Iranian art and literature schools, Zurvanism thoughts both directly and indirectly affected building of fire temples known as Archetype of Iranian architecture. What becomes important with some degree of deliberation is coincidence of concept of time and form in space of such Iranian architecture, i.e. fire temples.

Effect of concept of benediction on concept of space

Iranians who were able to recognize form and applications of place faced with wonderful mysteries in recognizing its transformations and, thus, believed in Zurvan as the most important contributor determining their and material world destiny. Zurvan, the endless time, was known stable from beginning to end of the world. He was the creature of everything including Ahouramazda and Ahriman. He became creature of finite time because when Ahriman went a head of Ahouramazda to his father- Zurvan- contrary to what was asked of him, to take position of his brother, i.e. kingship of the world, which was promised by Zurvan to his well-behaved son and when he could remind Zurvan's promise and ask for kingship of the world, he had no choice except to renew part of the endless time for a specific period of 9000 years and grant this part to them provided that they fight for salvation of Ahouramazda.

Bahram fire temple in Rey, Iran, which has stood since the Sassanid Empire - www.wikipedia.org

Since creation story specially deals with darkness and lightness, night and day, filth and purity, stability and mobility in life space and considers rhythm of time and place variations as deep concepts, it contains points and elements make it possible to understand role of architecture. Recognition of the endless time as an undying force continuously creates based on a specific process and perception of this kind of creation as a matter its final and end point is manifested in eternal being of the endless time necessarily enhances imagination and dream power of Iranians and gradually releases them from fetters of the endless time relying on cosmic, periodical, and natural factors. Bond of faith and destiny was not lost and the purity which was initially found in the insight toward the space made for benediction is ornamented with this new insight. Although the phased-time concept maintains its symbolic and mythic aspects, affects life space development and changes architectural space so far as it relates to space of fire temples or the purist space for benediction. Core of benediction space is not reached directly and its exploitation is regarded as living in such a space. It is based on quality of phases and stages to welcome the desired and is a stage to isolate from the most shining moment of life and pass from it. Passing from phases embodied by a single cover spread by Zurvan all over the way which should be passed leads to creation of an architectural space taking benefit from hierarchies born together with glorification, praise, and sanctification. Open space of nature where the fire temple was located to be seen better is gradually conditioned to stages of being honored and farewell. The yards, entrances, and primary exhibitions are appeared and new ceremonies are celebrated in benediction space. Taking benefit from a dignified and comprehensive unity, the building of fire temple is phased and restricted in some parts and its unity is attributed to God.

Summarizing the mentioned points, it may be stated that time accepts another distinguishing aspect after giving birth to and recognizing of finite time. Whether based on symbolic interpretation or beyond of modern social-cultural relations intended to be developed during Sasanian era, this distinguishing aspect of time takes a physical shape in three stages and is reflected in quality of fire temples.

Fire temple was built as a public space especially before God and fire which was regarded as the most valuable life symbols (worldly & heavenly) of human- fortune (Eghbal) connected Houshang to eternity of sun and depth of the earth to the highest point of the heaven dome- and was placed at its center, its flames-which should not never went out- were toward the heaven along with its elevation. The ever-shining sun was resembled to the worldly life scale of human and eternity was a symbol indicating to piety of human life on earth. Also, primary and genuine cosmologic thoughts of ancient Iranians, in their life domain and during an era where there was not any mental connection with other nations and peoples, resulted in innovation of a really conceptual building. The fire temple has four angles to demonstrate the furthest and unavailable points of the earth surface in the frame of tangible world in a tangible infinity, to find four geographical directions in junction of two earth axis, and know the sun as an element proclaiming whiteness and blackness, day and night, good and bad, brightness and darkness, and shadow during human life and their comprehensive reality and gives a new form to benediction and its space. Cosmic directions with their symbolic concepts find their way into the architectural space and all six affect the fire temples. Fire is replaced in the fire temple relying on its piety originating from ancient fictions- reminding Houshang- and its new role in resistance of fight in favor of brightness and goodness.

Placement of fire between the earth and heaven (in axis of a building toward the heaven) and building fire place in outdoor space, under dome of the fire temple in a way that can be seen from far away and four directions of north, east, south, and west, indicates to realization of a deep thought.

Non-recurring pattern

Considering what was mentioned by now, the space was built by hands of ancient Iranians where to worship, generalize, and practice these concepts, individually or collectively, using their mental and cosmic data and findings, was a compiled and symbolic figure since all its evolutionary elements were created with a mental and thoughtful background. Human space, the space (architectural space of fire temples) built in any way and structure, takes benefit of a main and substantial turning point: Fire and its location.

To access the analysis and assessment recognizing human in its materials and spiritual relations with natural environment, the most important and comprehensive product of human- its architecture- was introduced. Fire temple, the most important and attractive prototype of Iranian architecture, welcomes a four-arch in itself, takes benefit of it as a public space with a fixed concept, transforms it although it is driven from local variables (whether ecological, geographical, cultural, and civil), and may apply their patterns for long times even after that main intrinsic reasons of fire temples are lost.

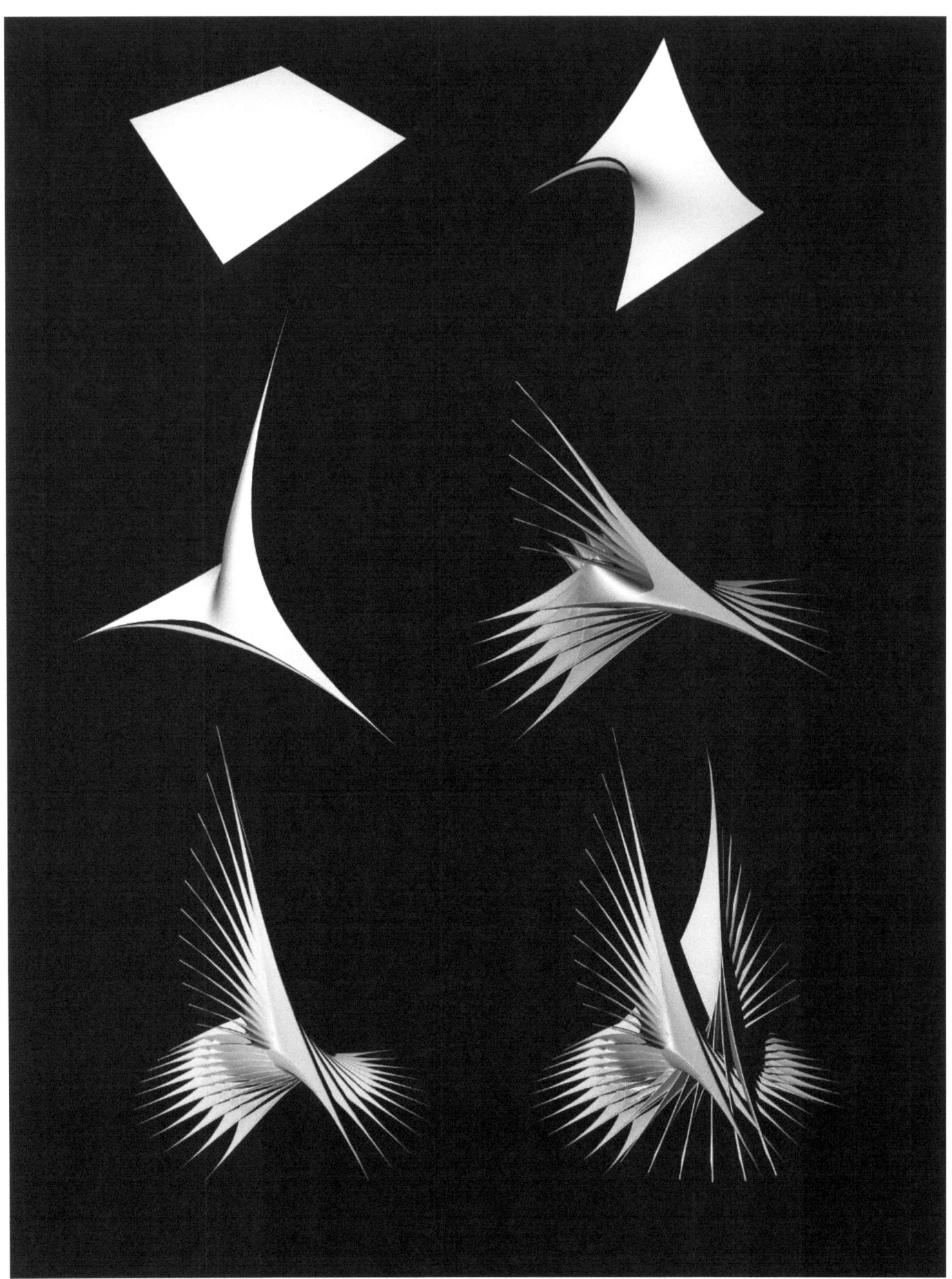

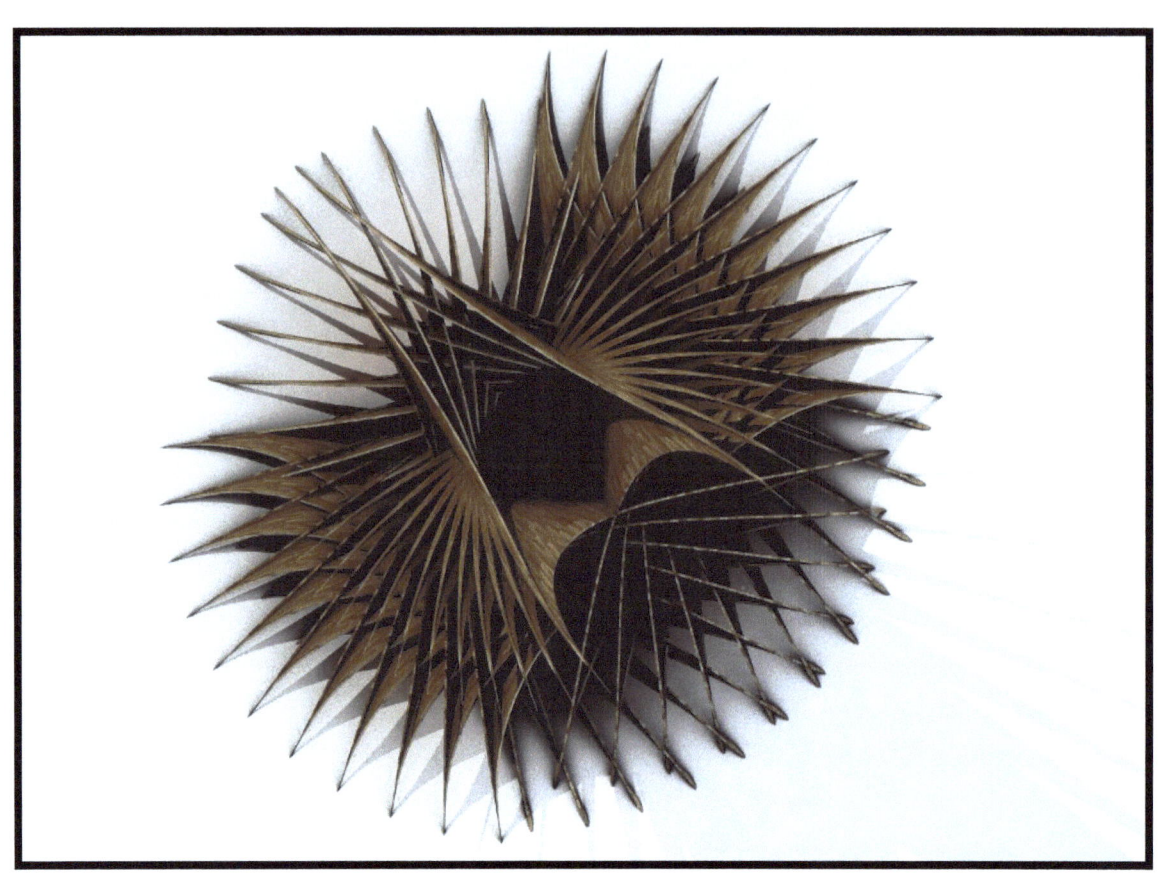

Parametric presence inside the cube

Aida Aglmand Azarian

Master of Interior Design

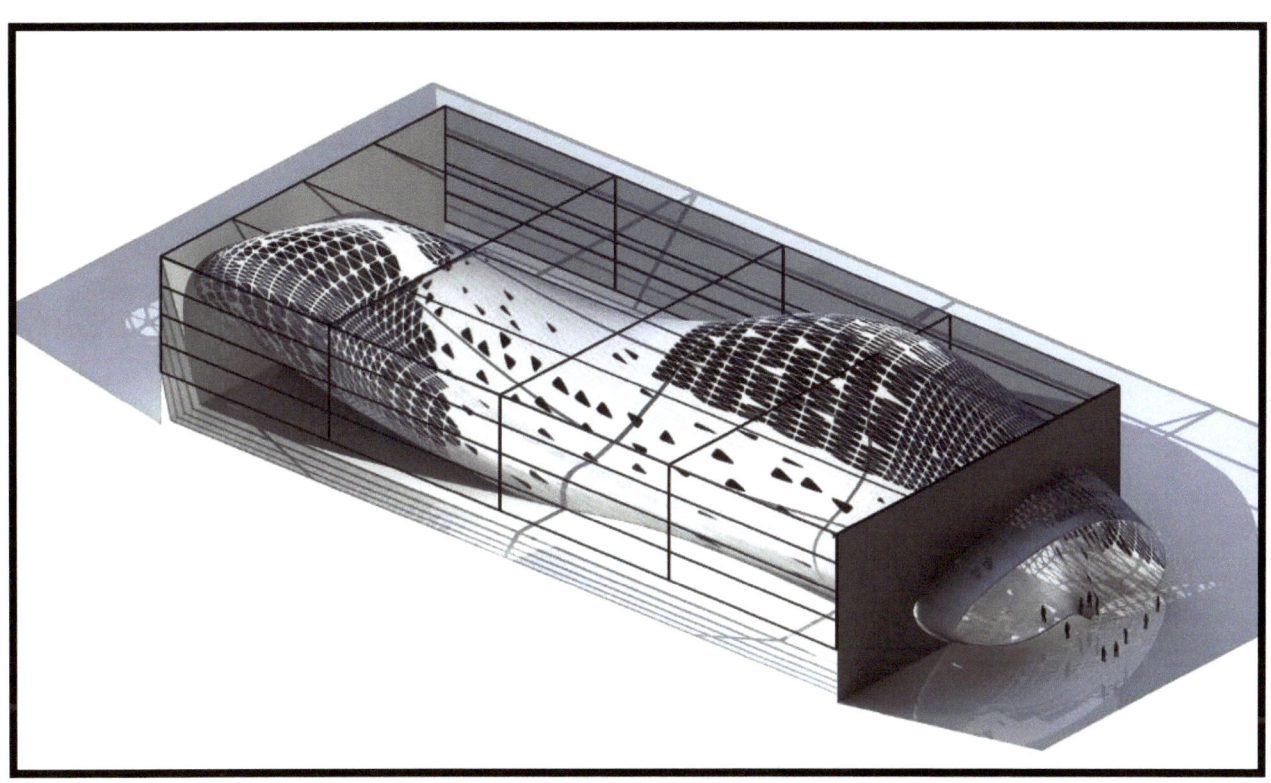
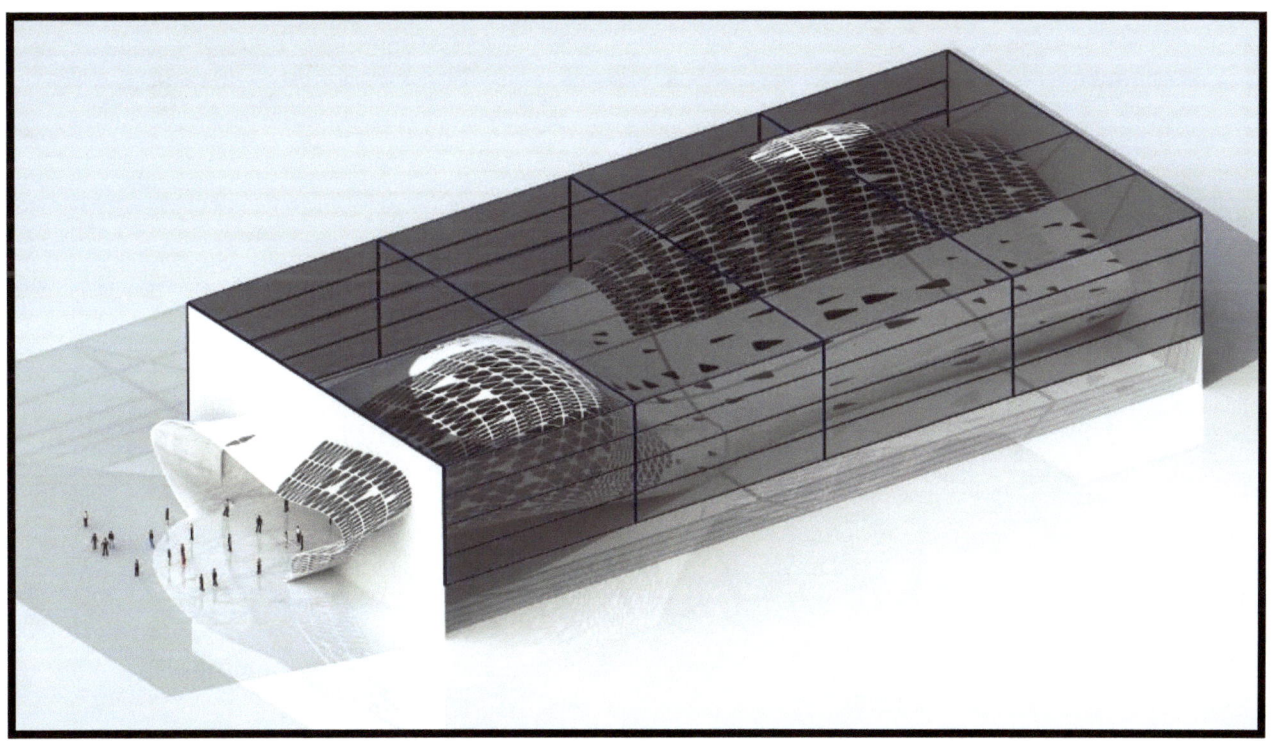

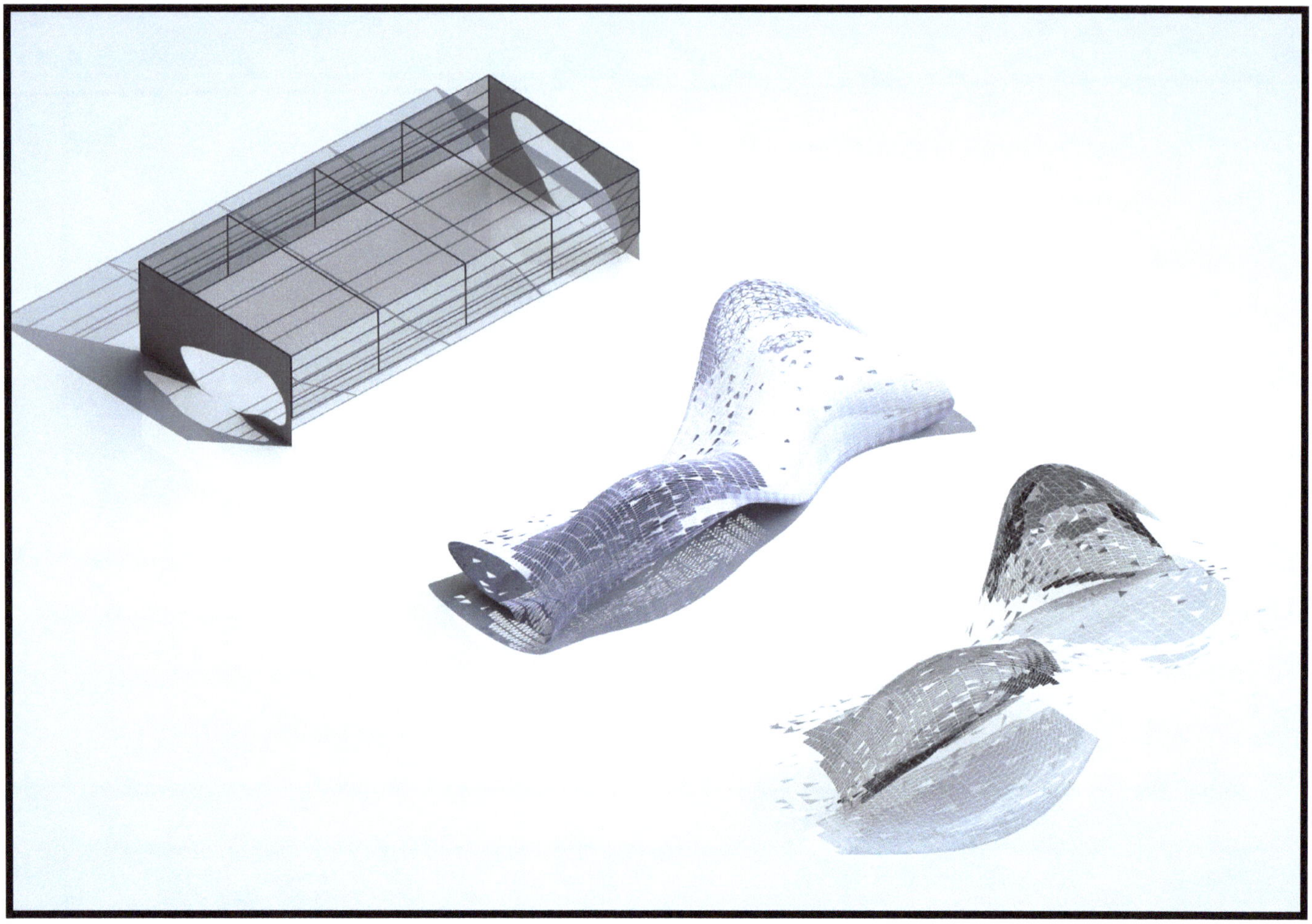

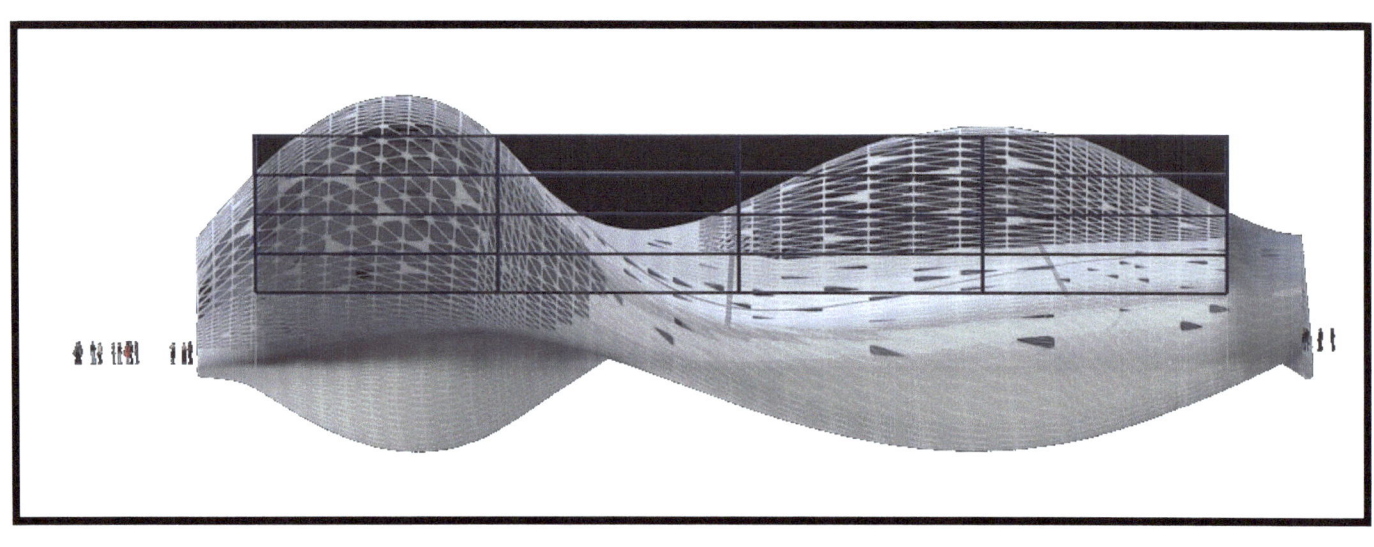

Parametric forms

Sajjad Sabour

Bachelor of Graphic

www.cgmax.ir

From patterns to parametric design

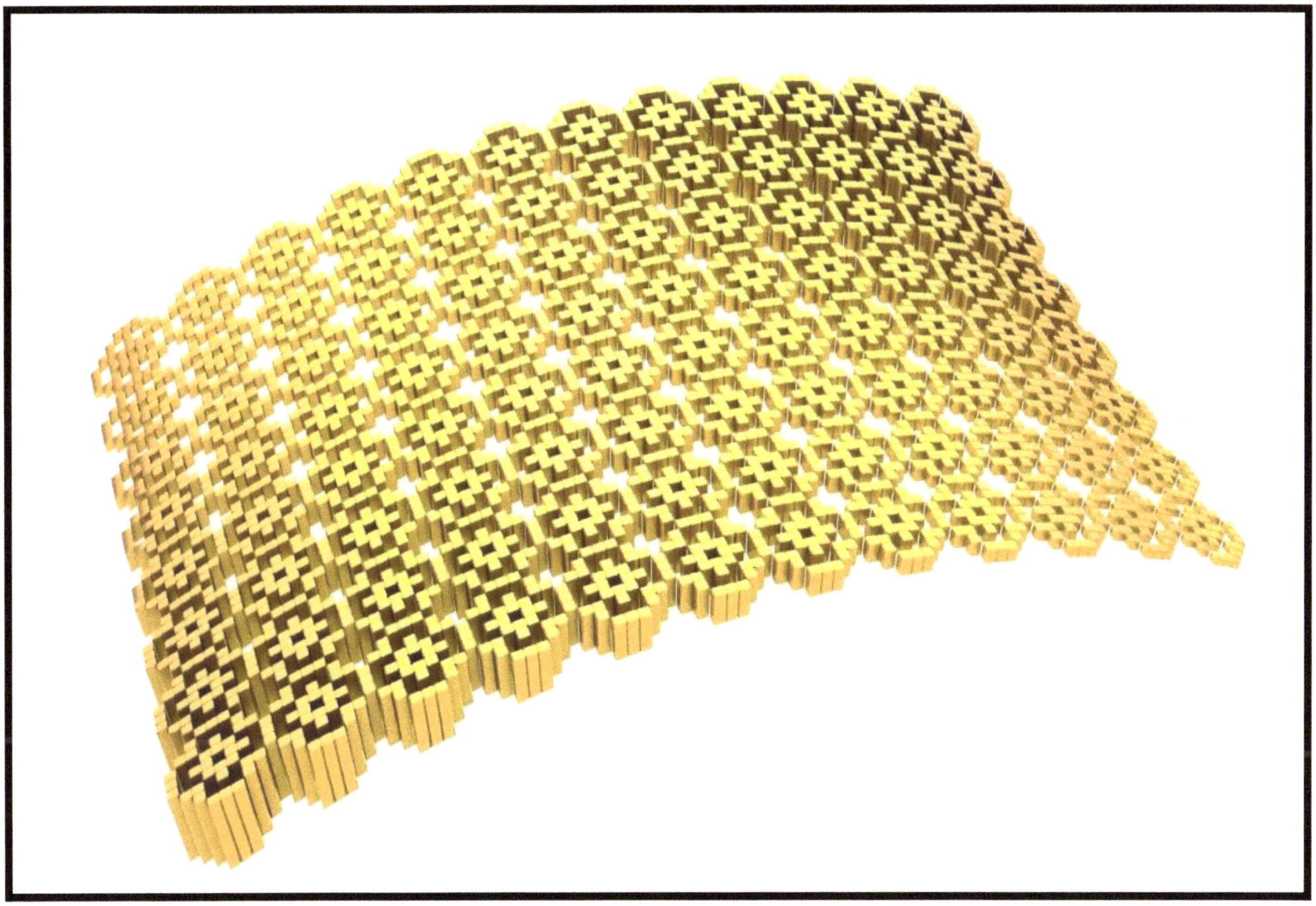

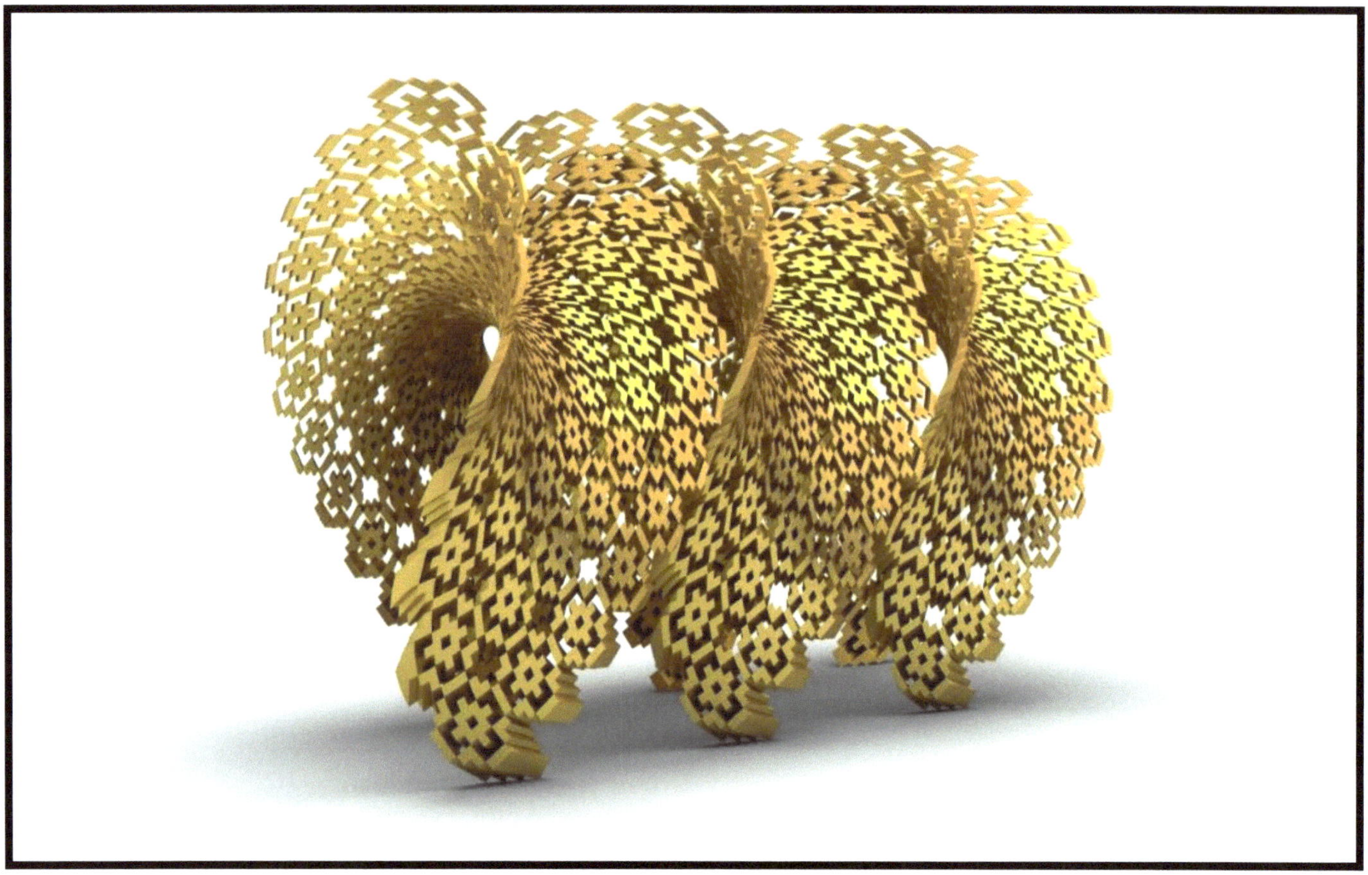

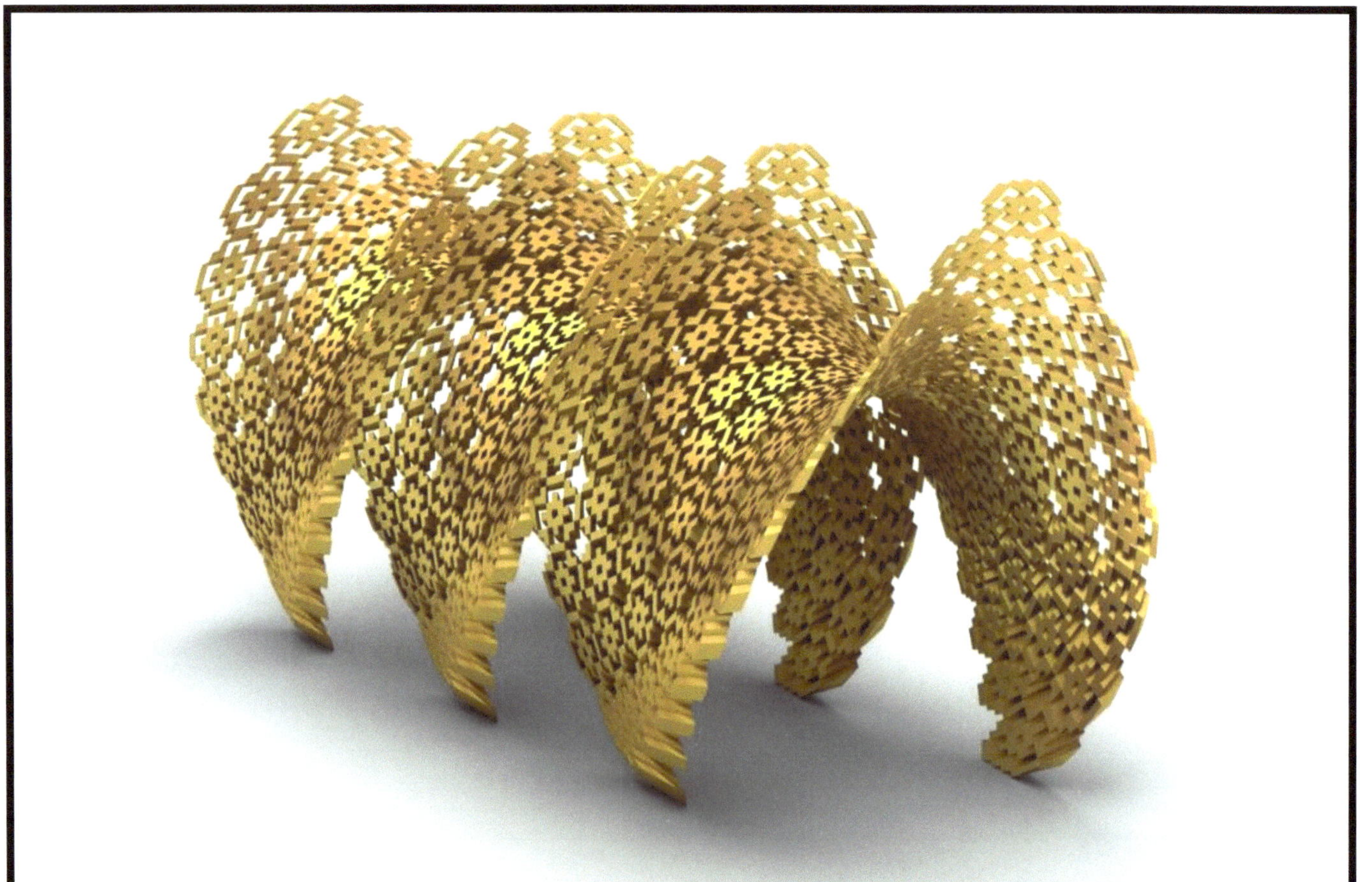

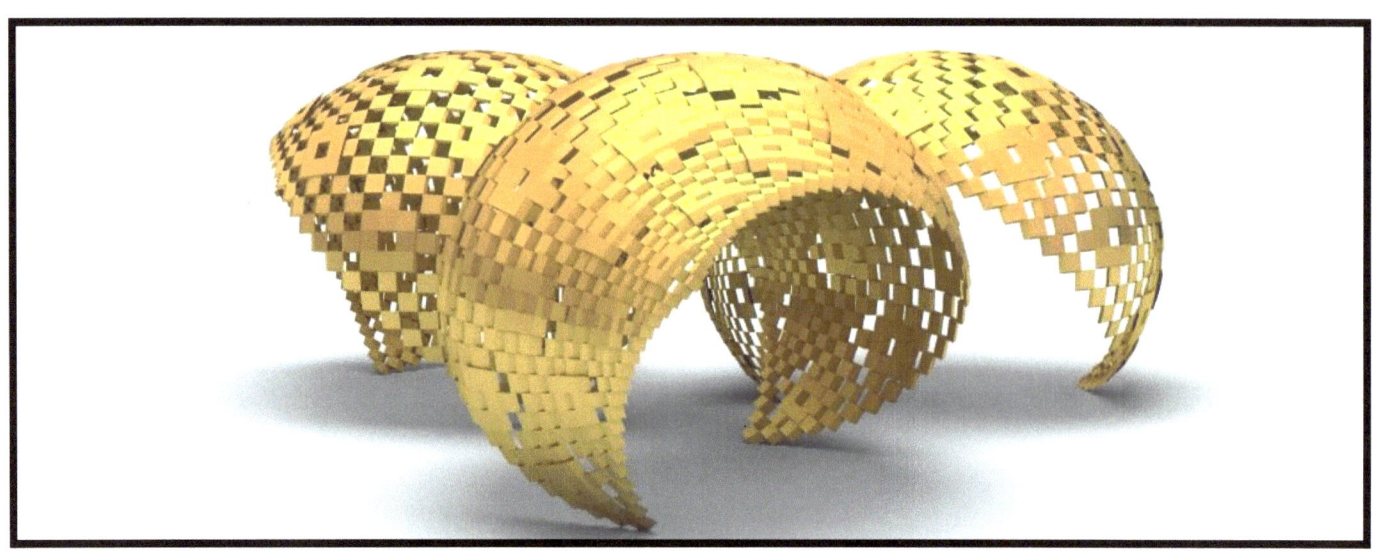

Parametric Tower

Alternatives Forms for Water museum concept

Samira Mahutchian

Master of interior design

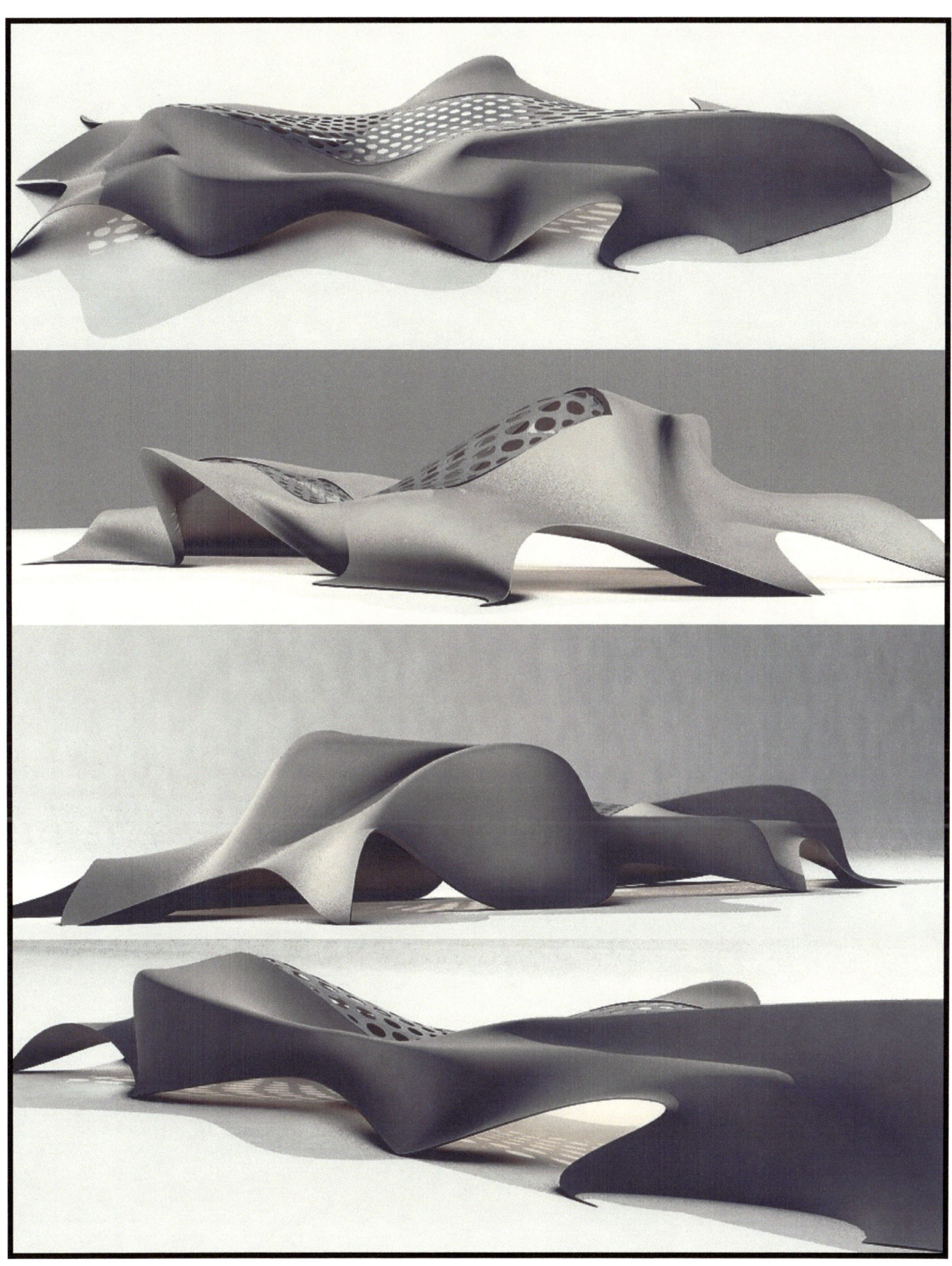

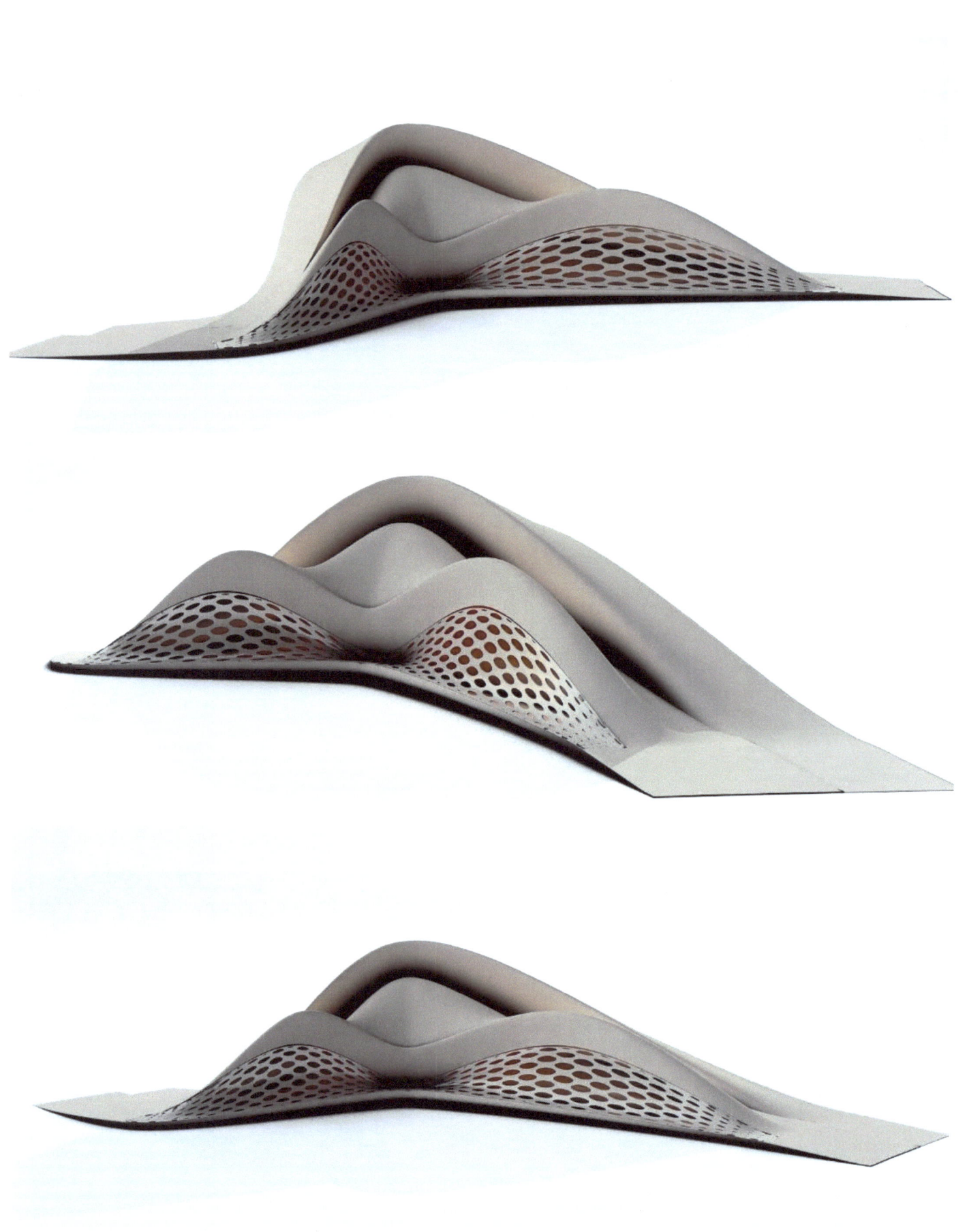

Design of semi-open exhibition space

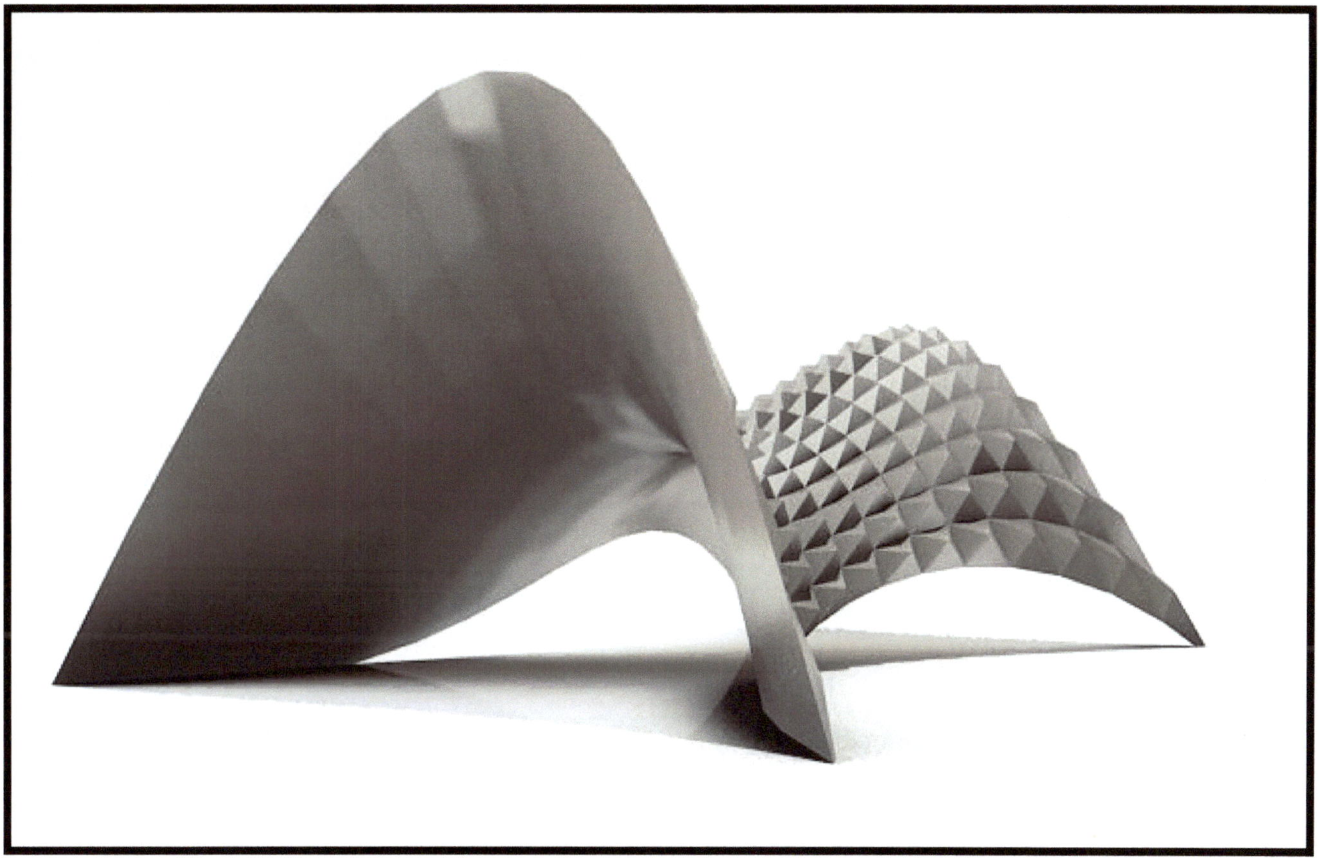

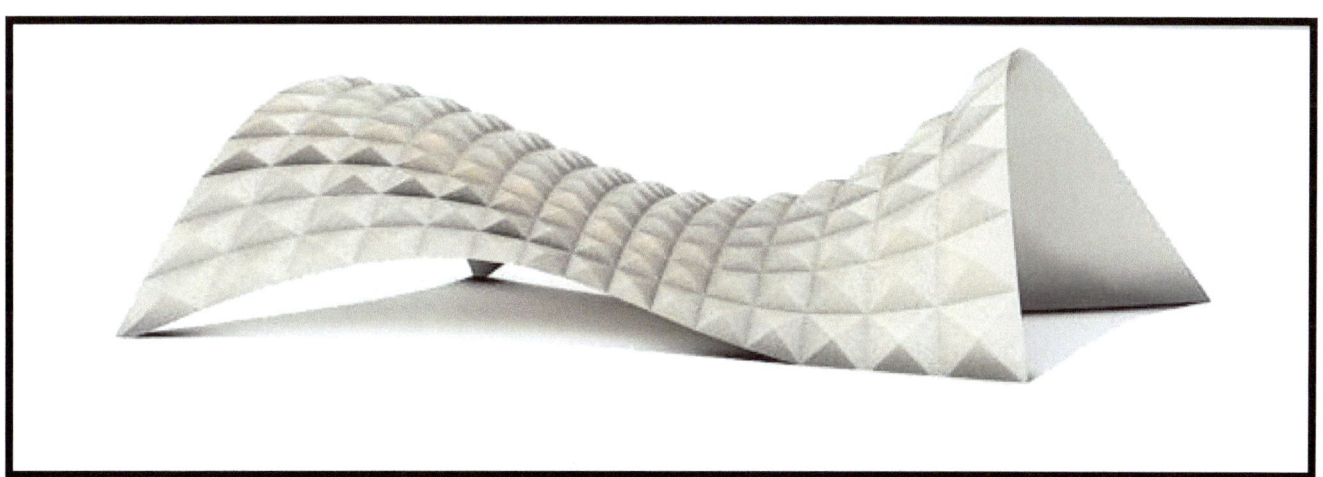

Element design inspired by bird

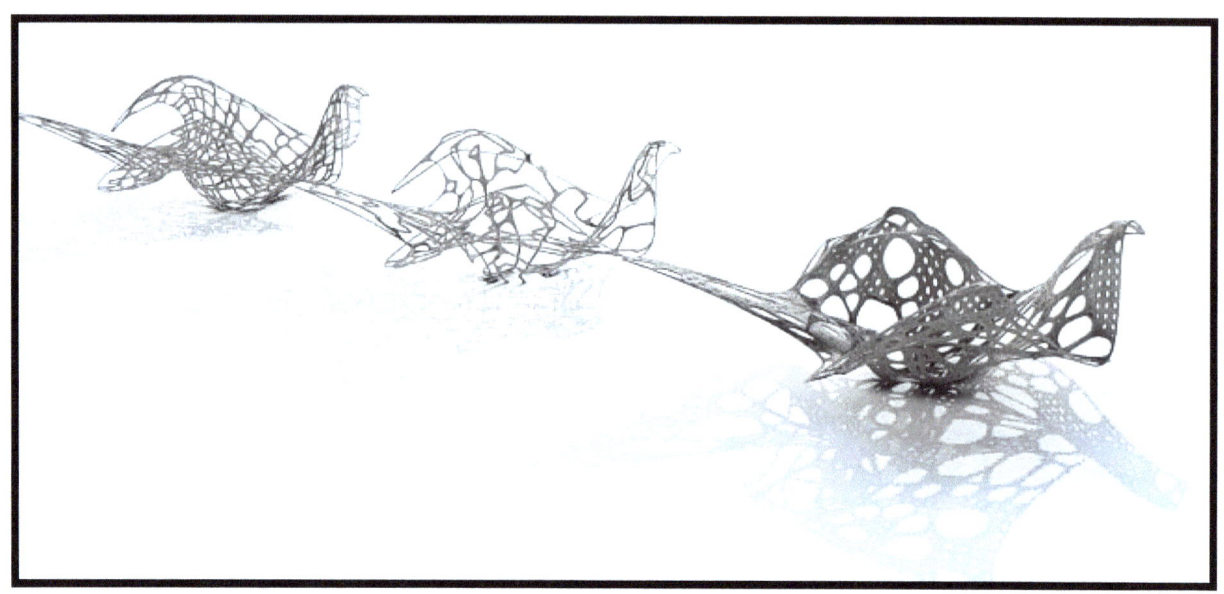

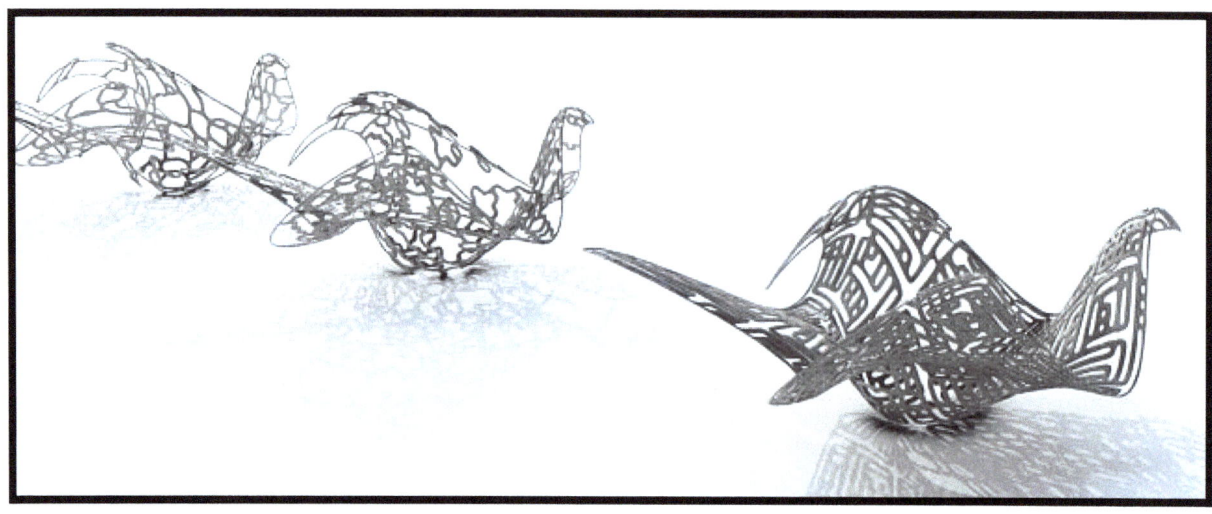

Aqua museum

Saeedeh Sadegpour

Master of Architecture

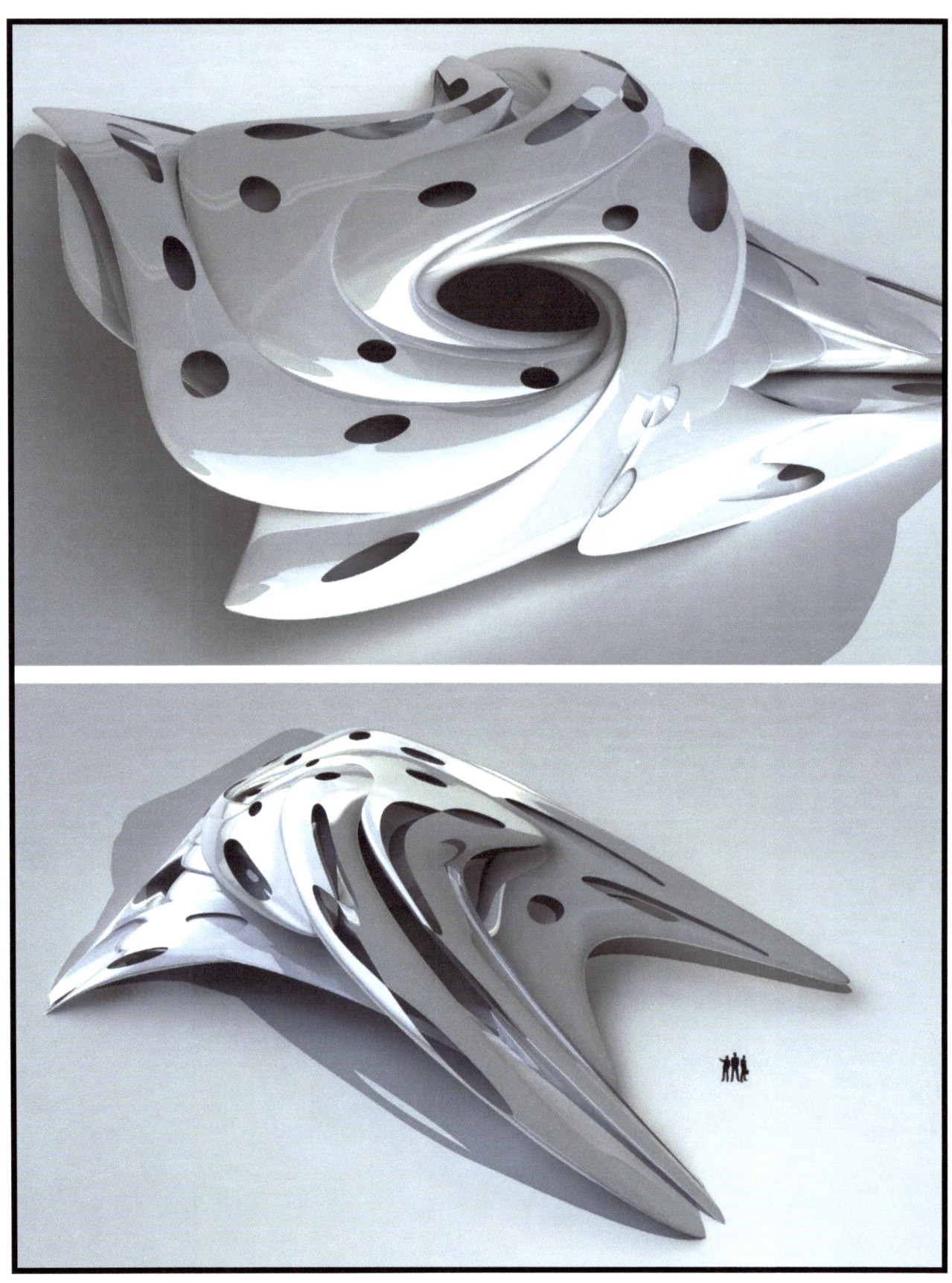

Pelagic animals' museum inspired by waves

Chapter 3

Pattern Design

Pezeshkan Tower facade design
Interdiscipline Design Universe (IDU office)

Design Process

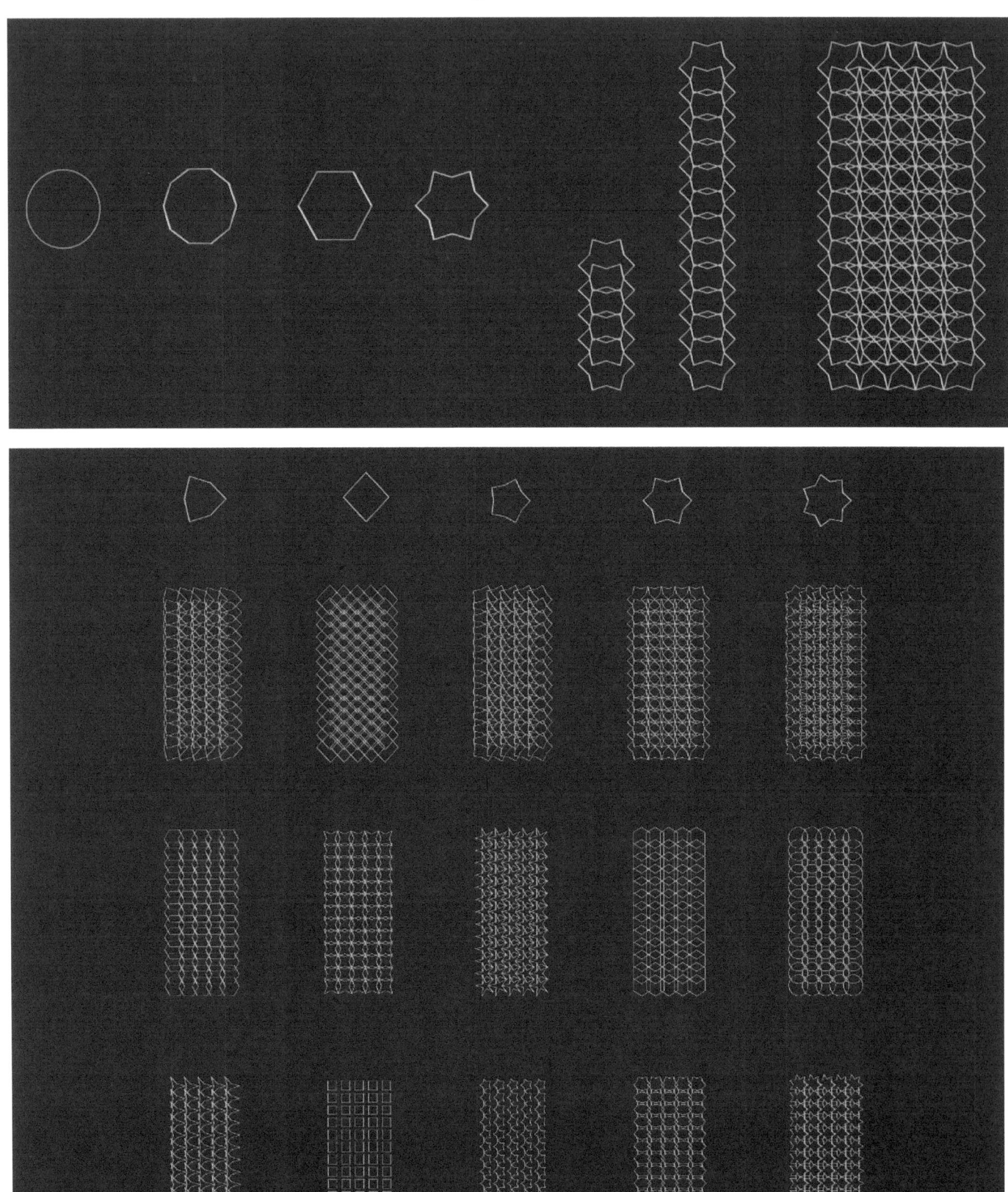

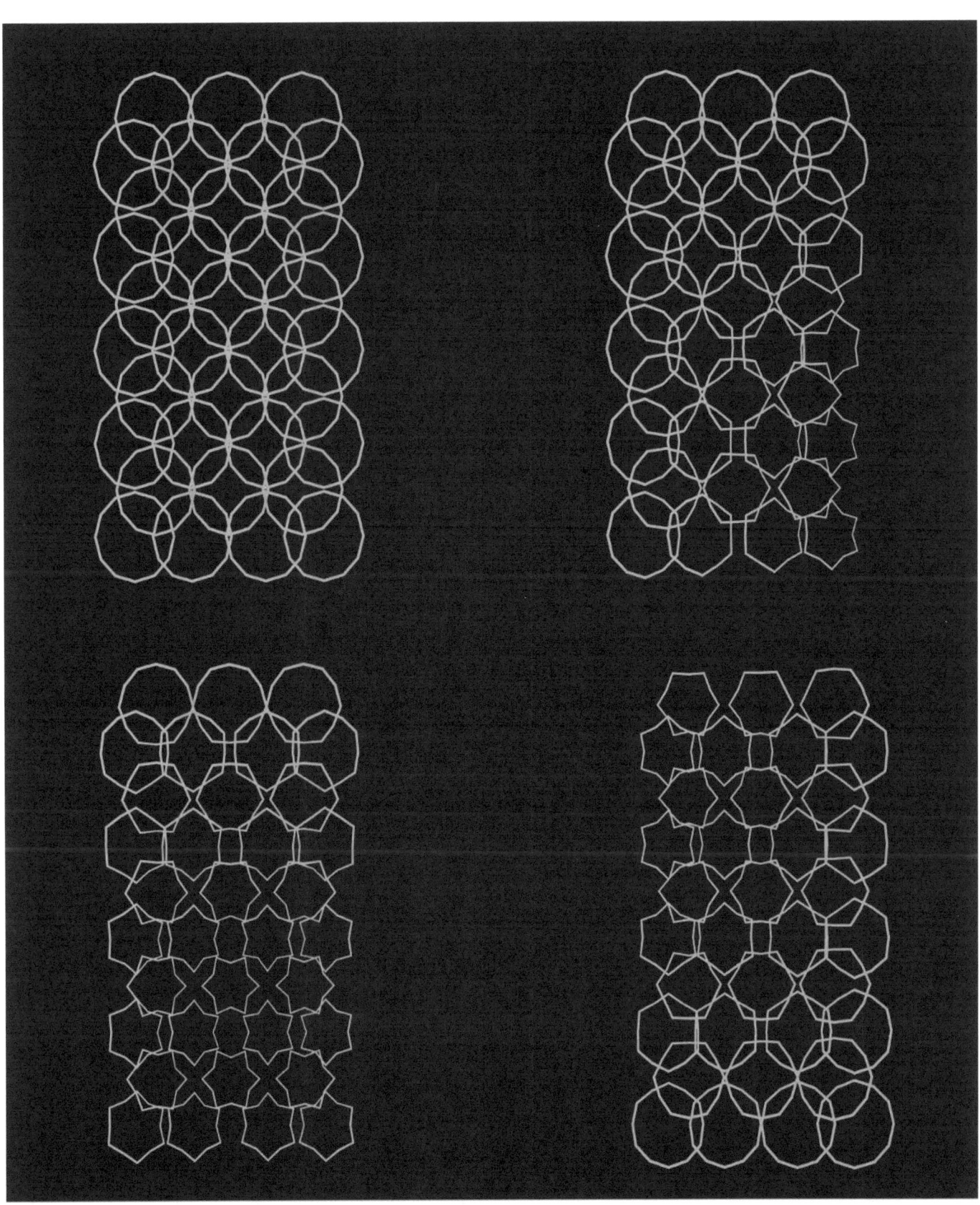

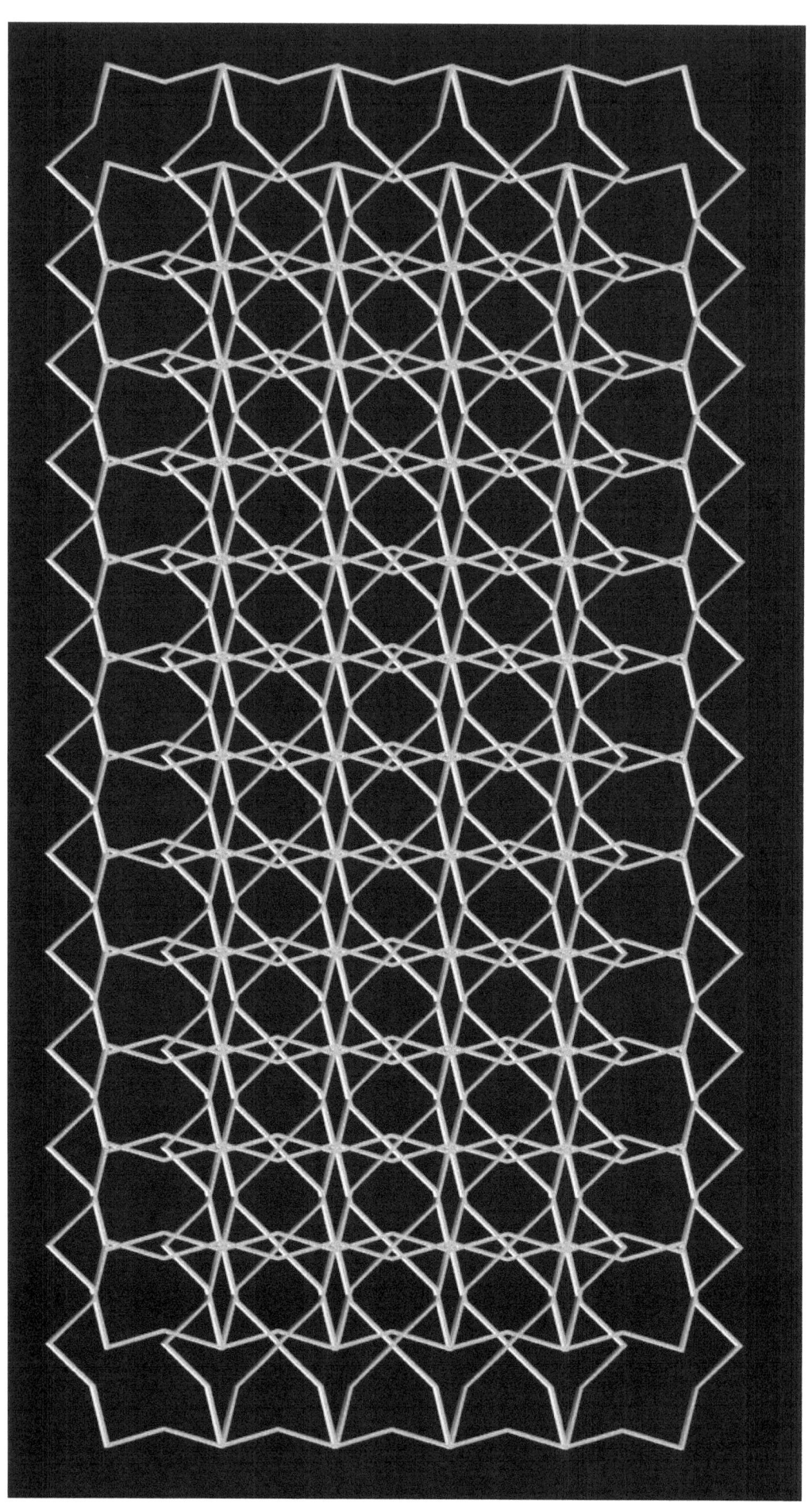

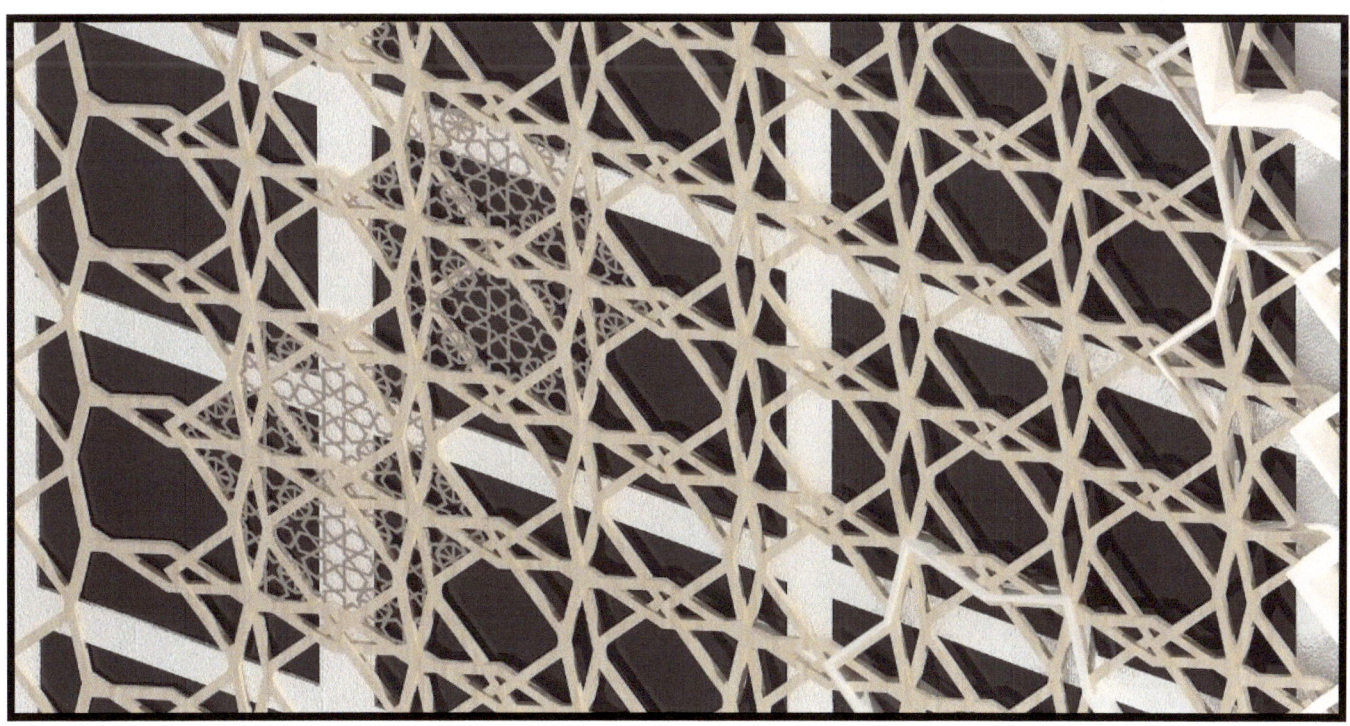

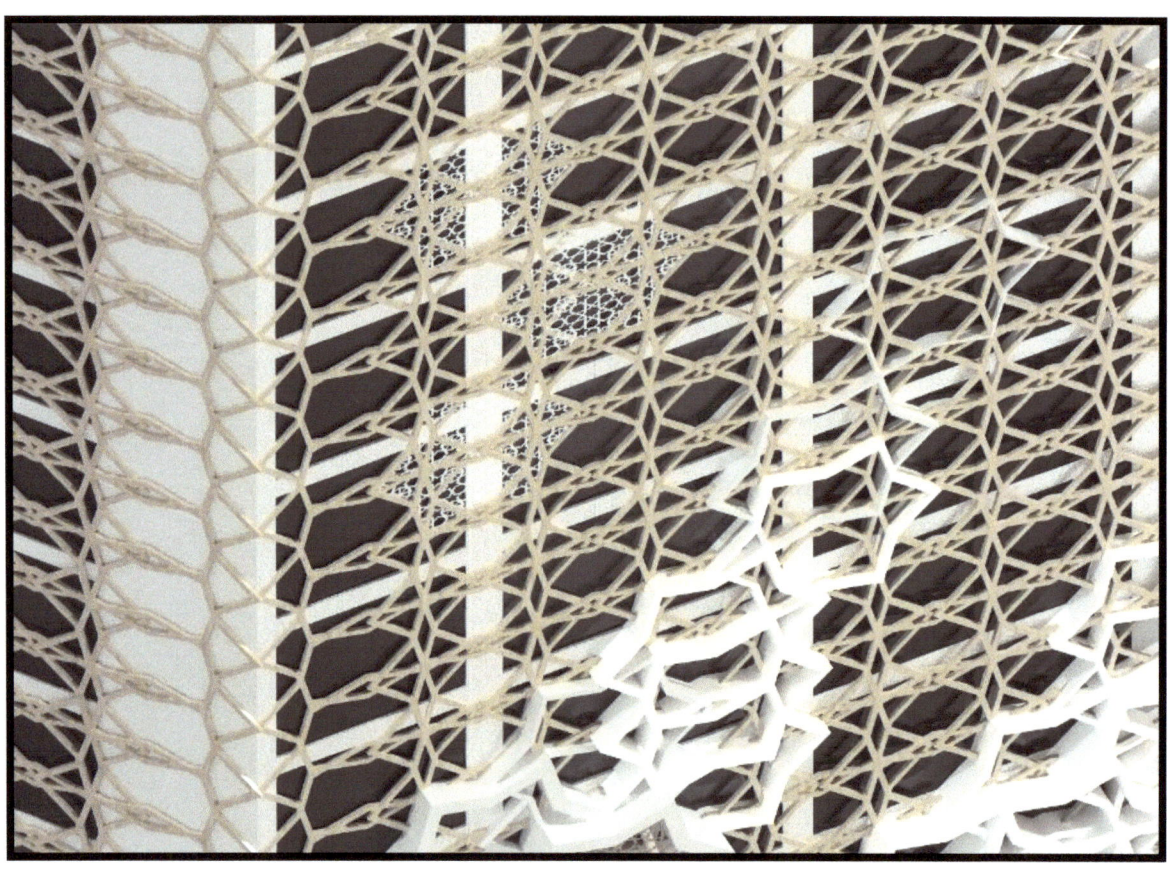

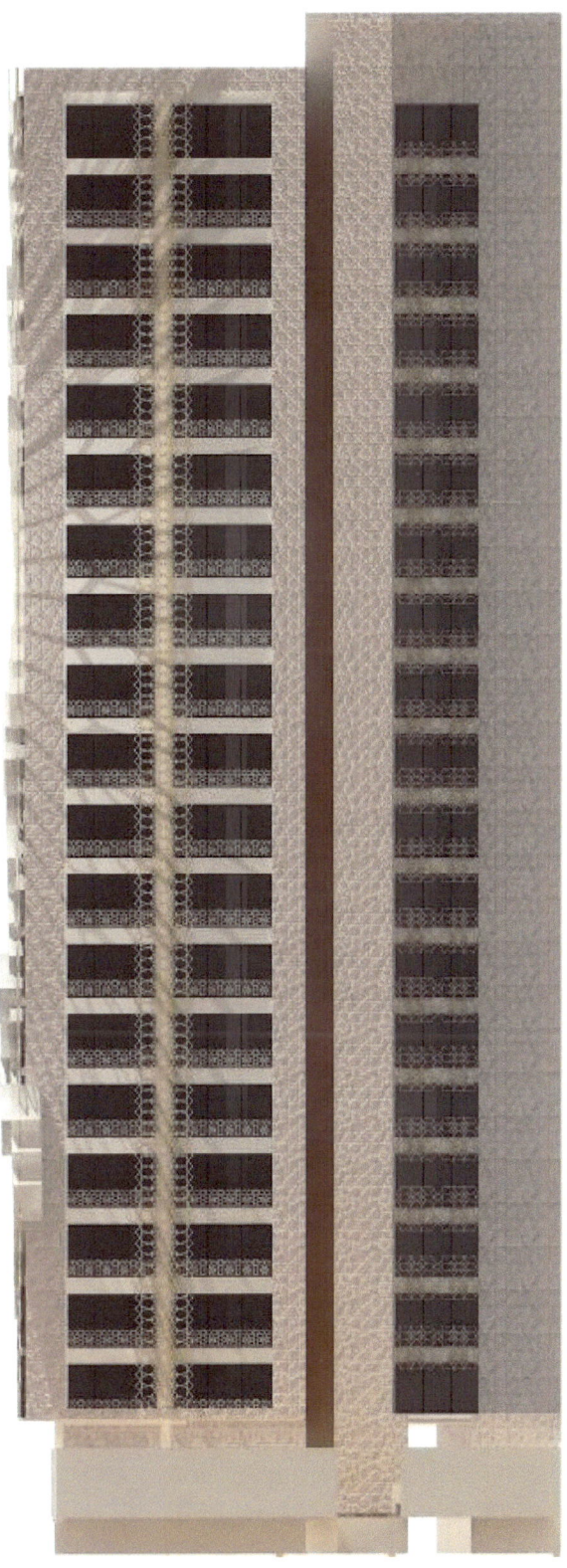
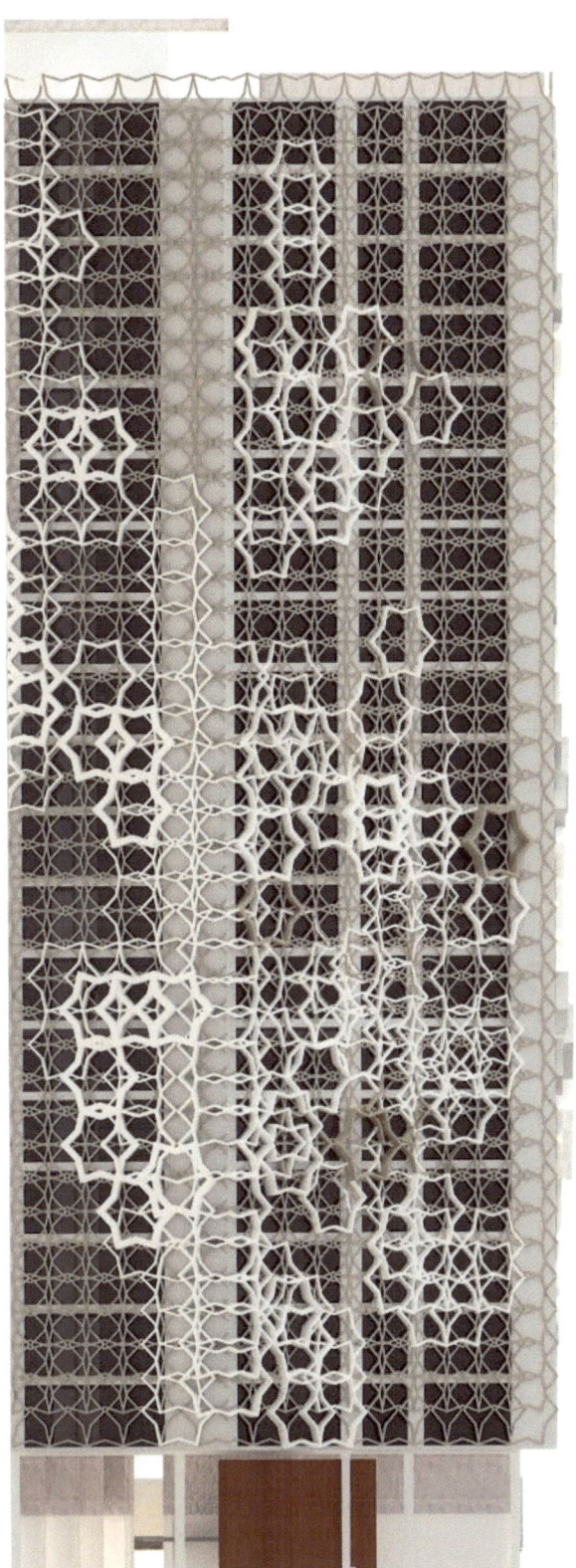

Elevation

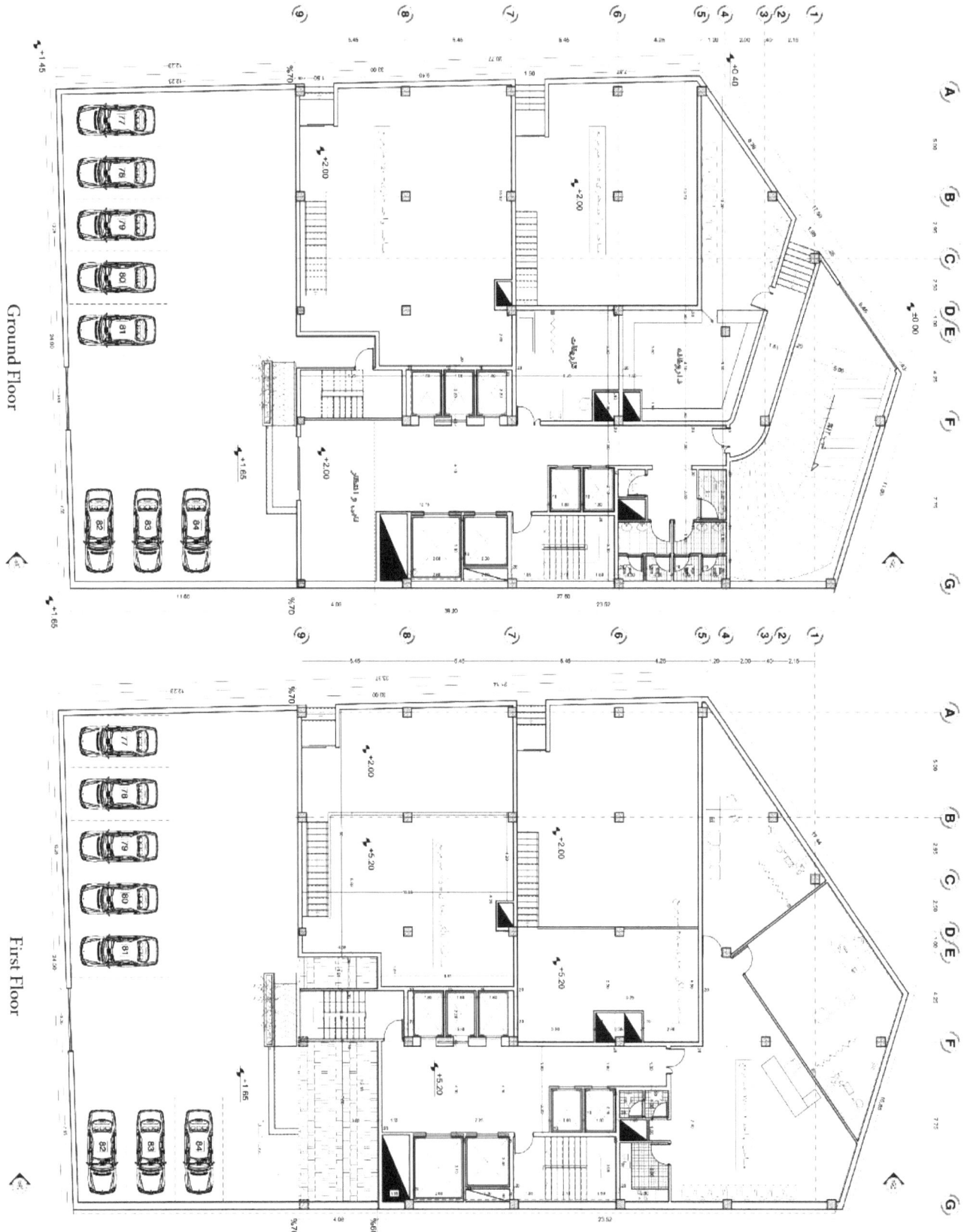

Plans

187

Façade design
based on Sheikh-Lotf-Allah Mosque of Isfahan

Foad Bonakdar

Bachelor of architecture

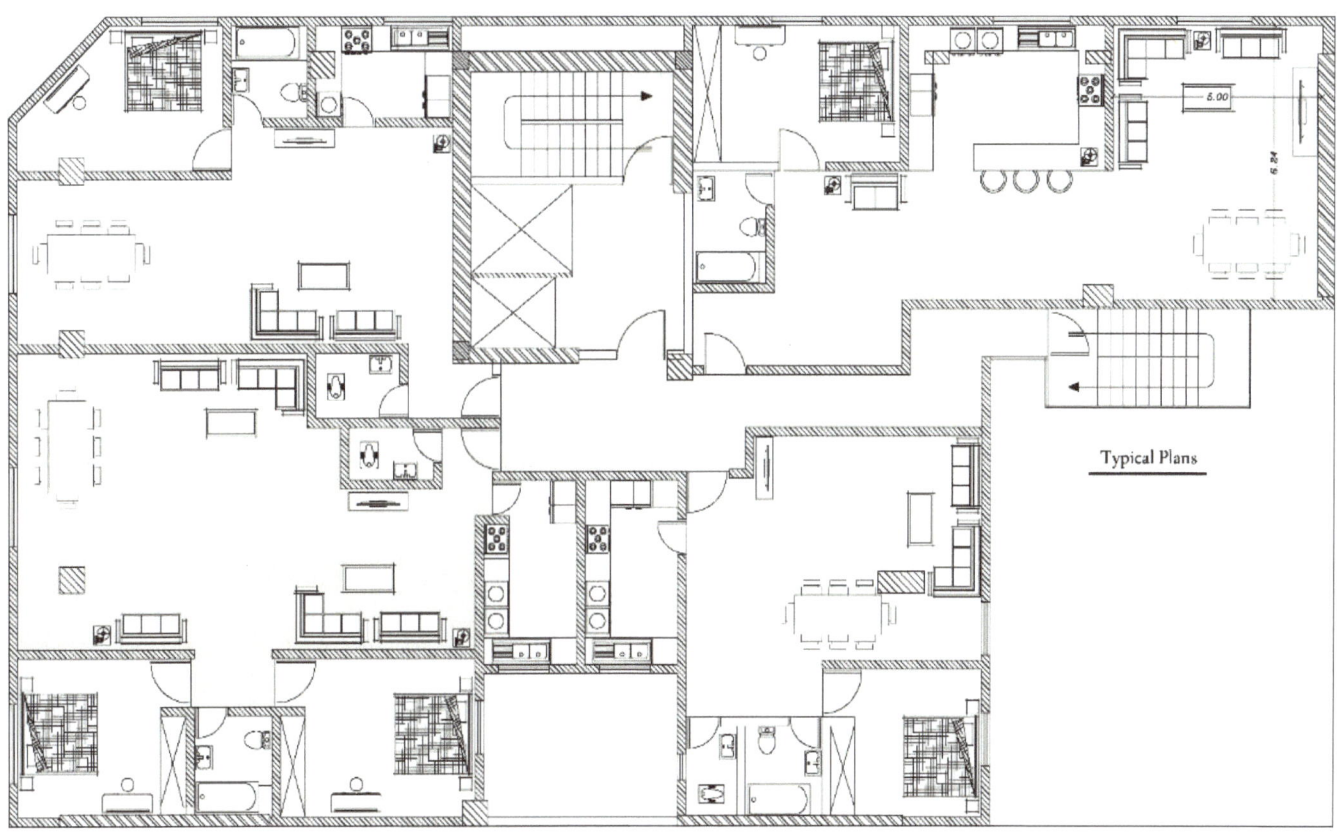

Typical Plans

Symbols designed as vault ornaments based on Persian patterns

Mohamad Reza Talebi

Batchelor of architector

Master of structural engineer

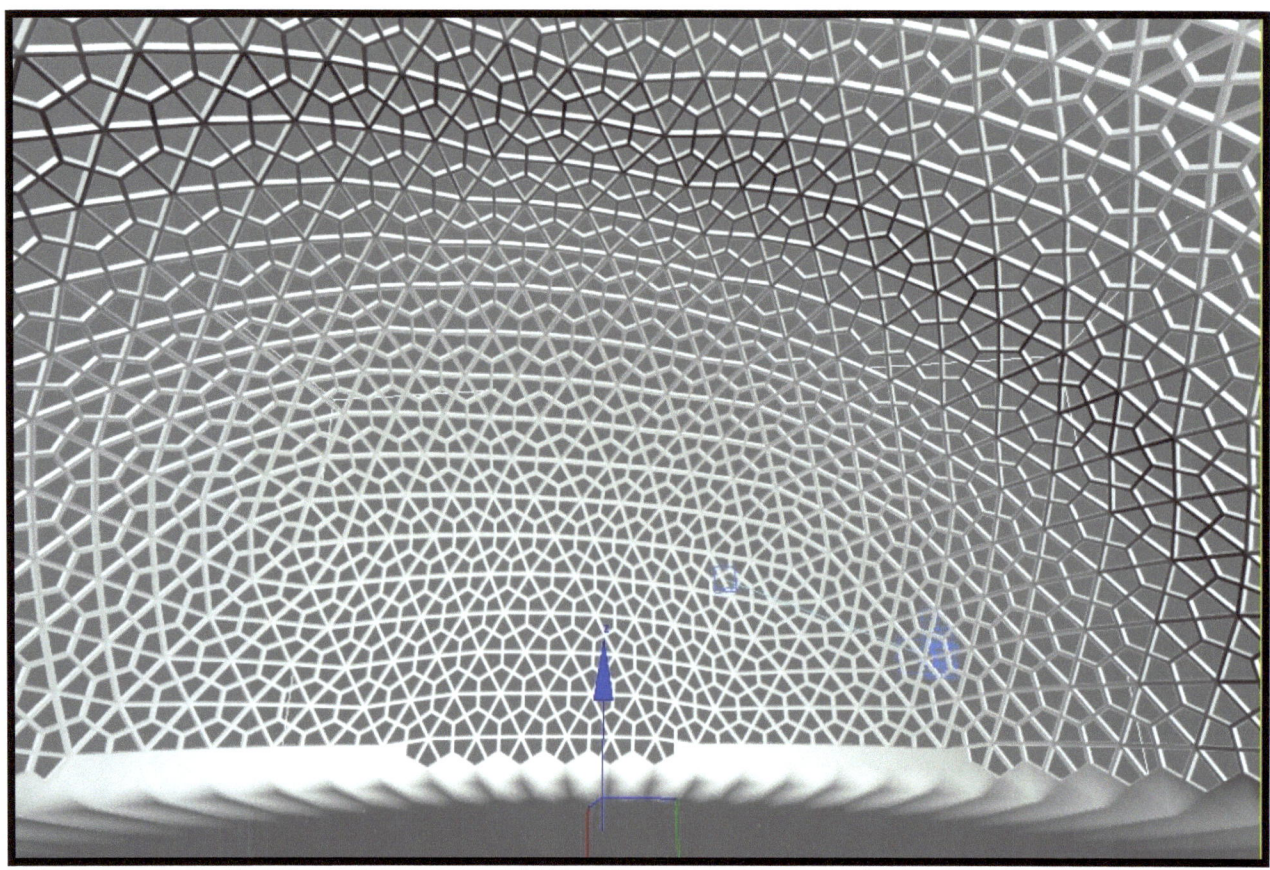

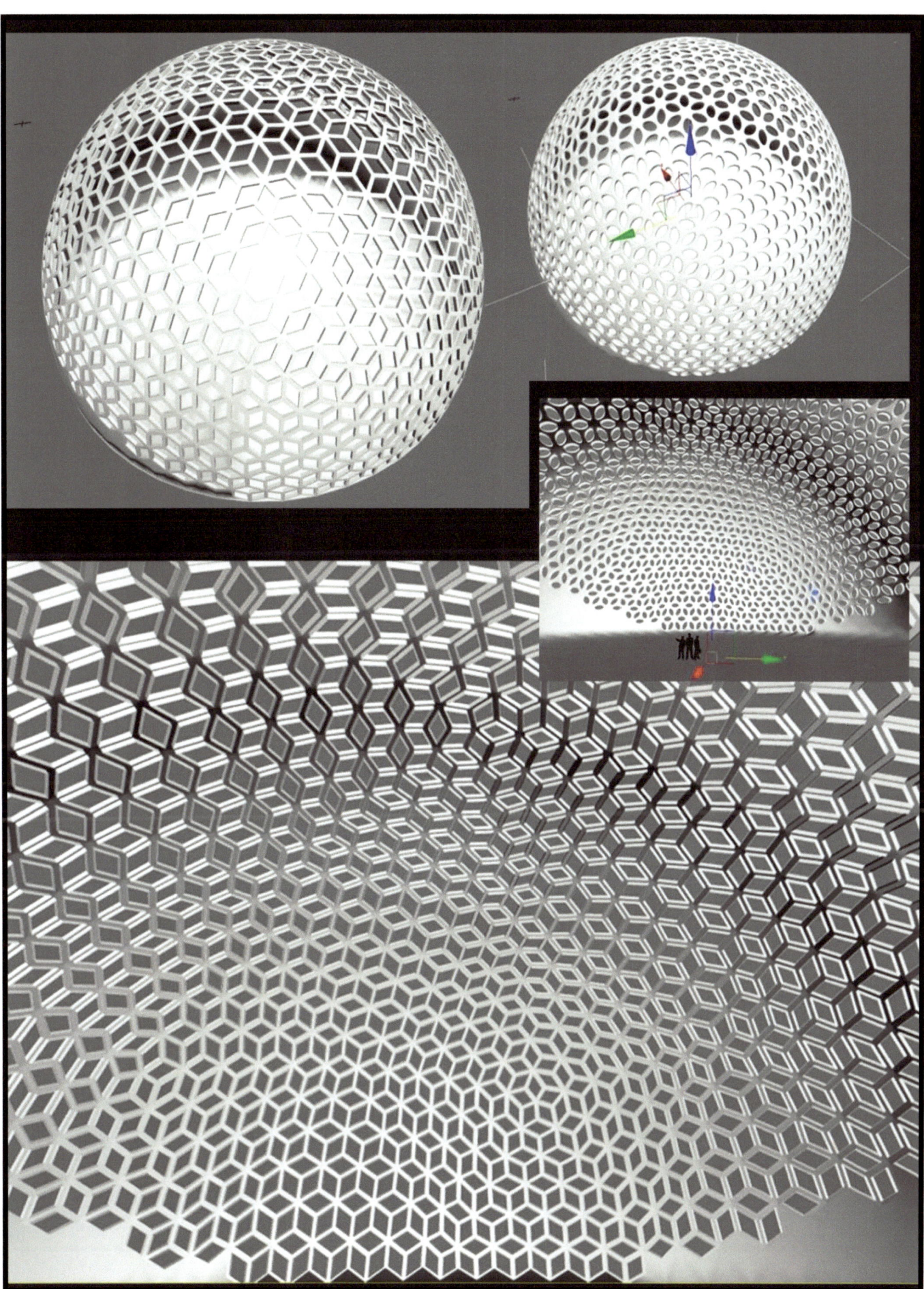

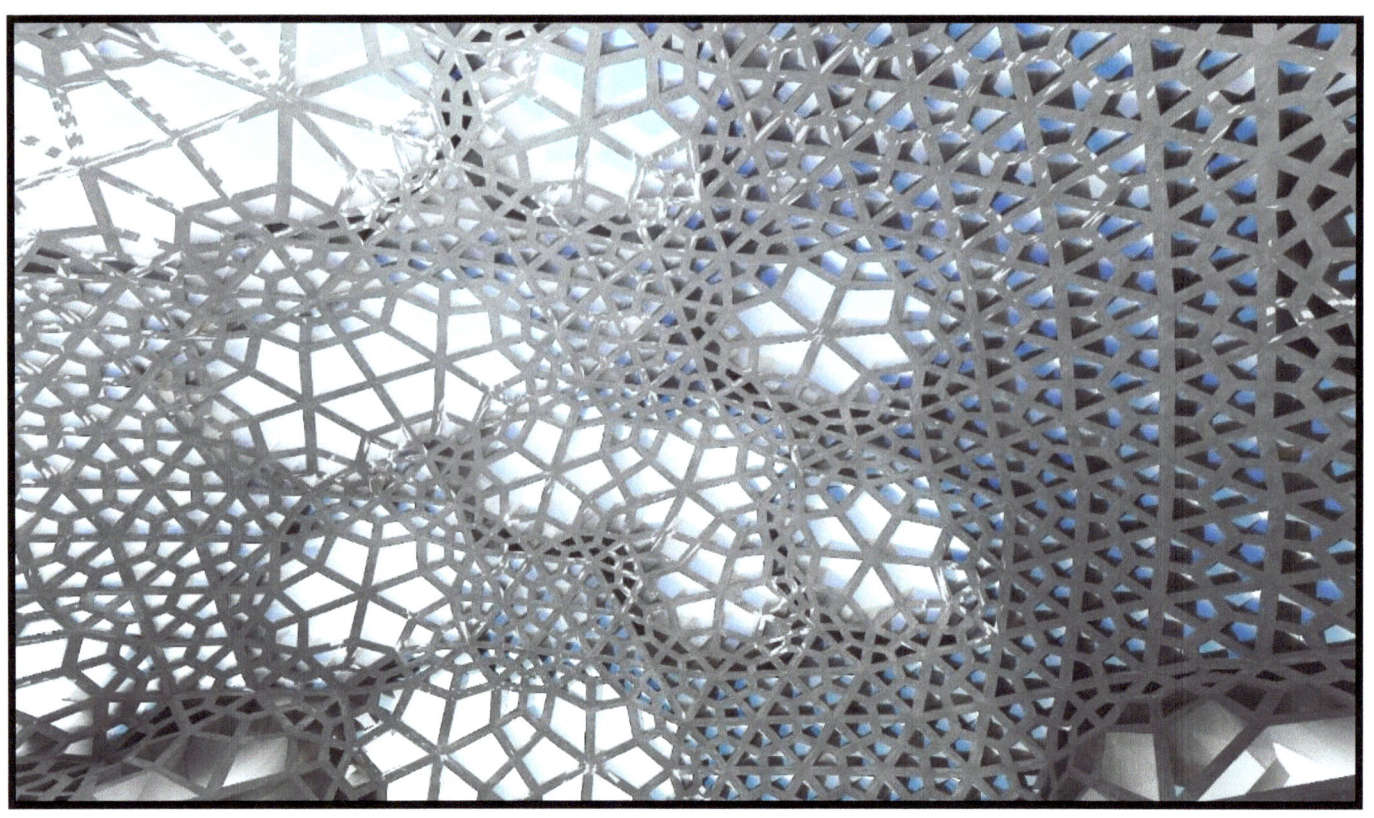

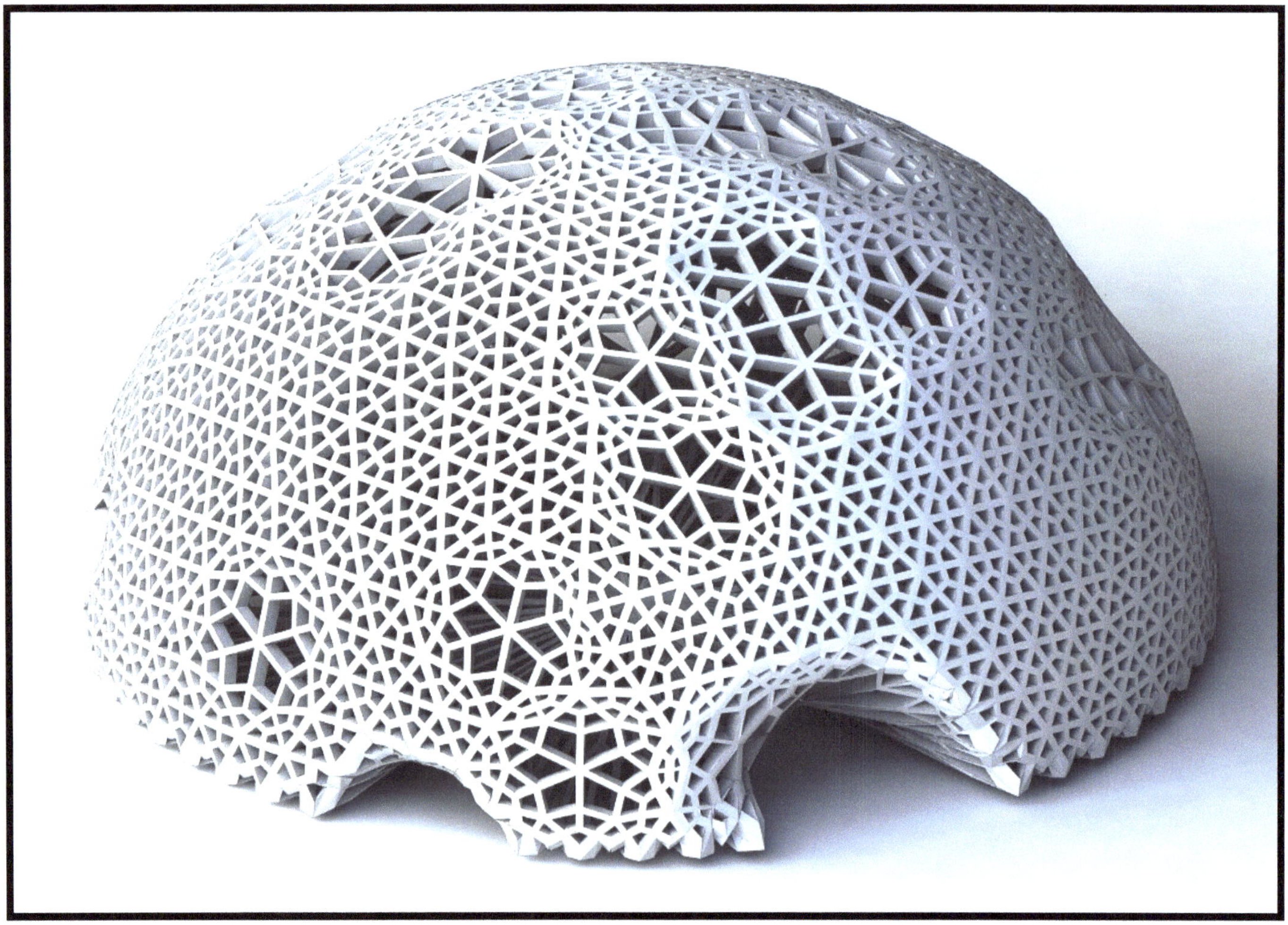

198

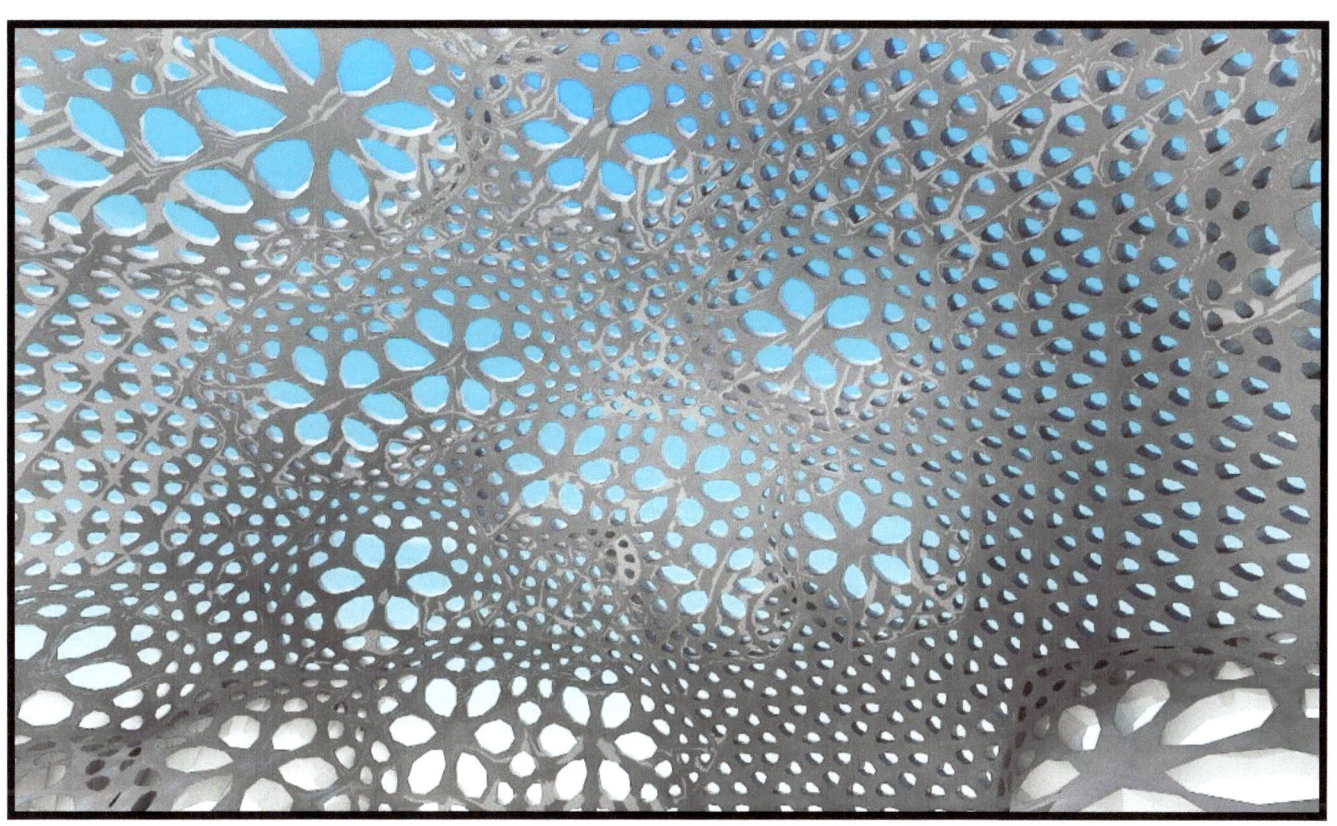

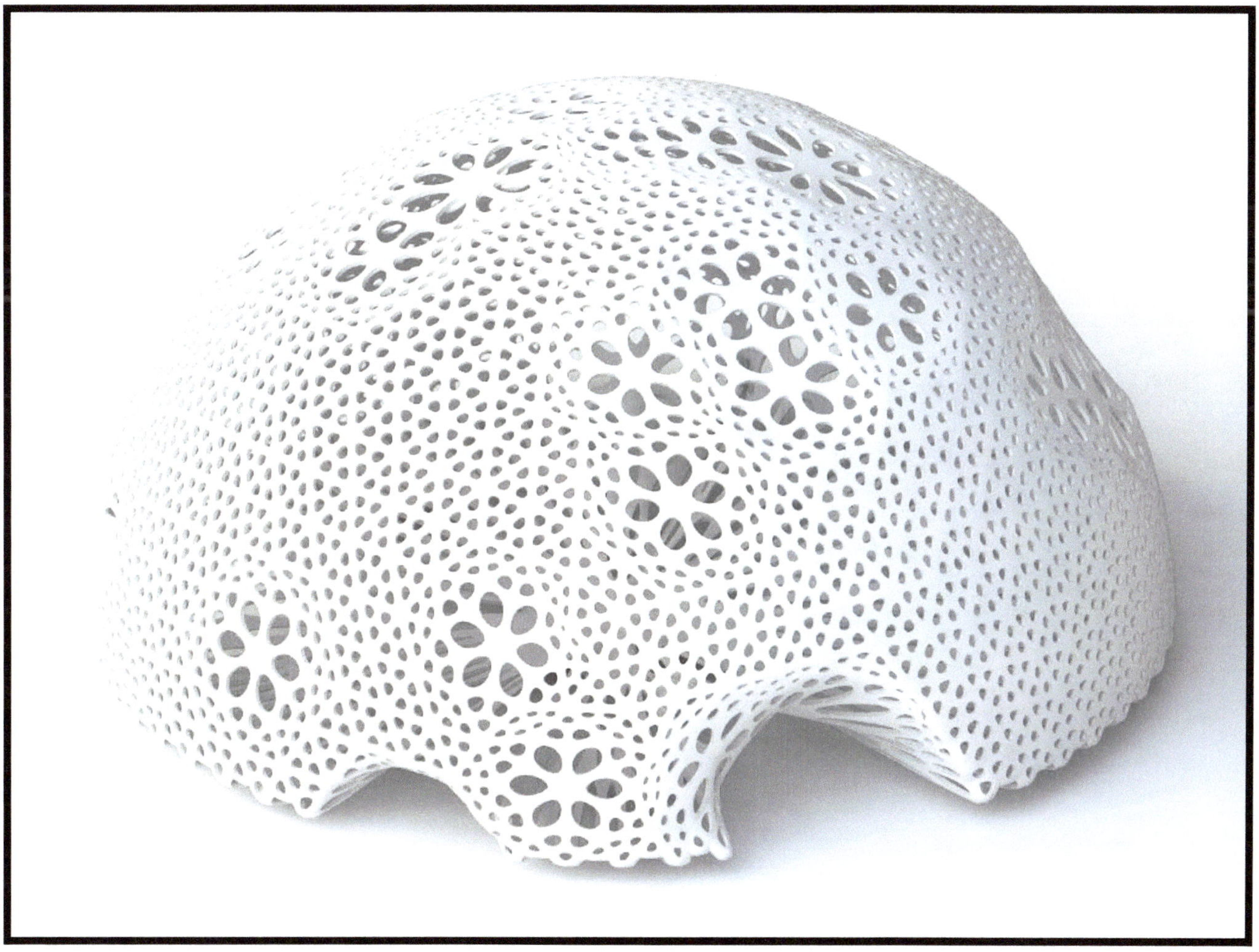

Facad Design (Store)

Sahand Latifi

Batchelor of architecture

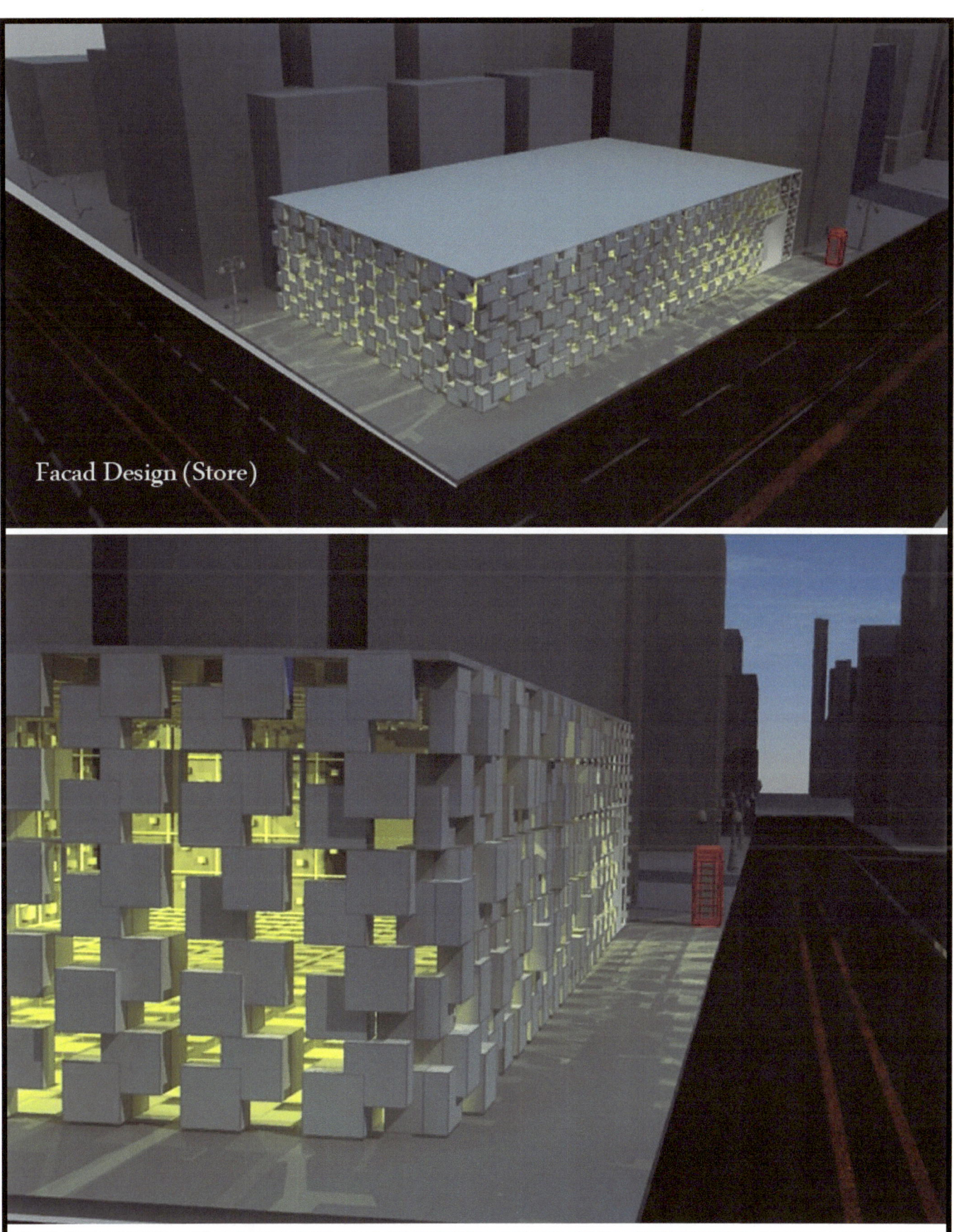
Facad Design (Store)

Table Design
Niloofar Amel

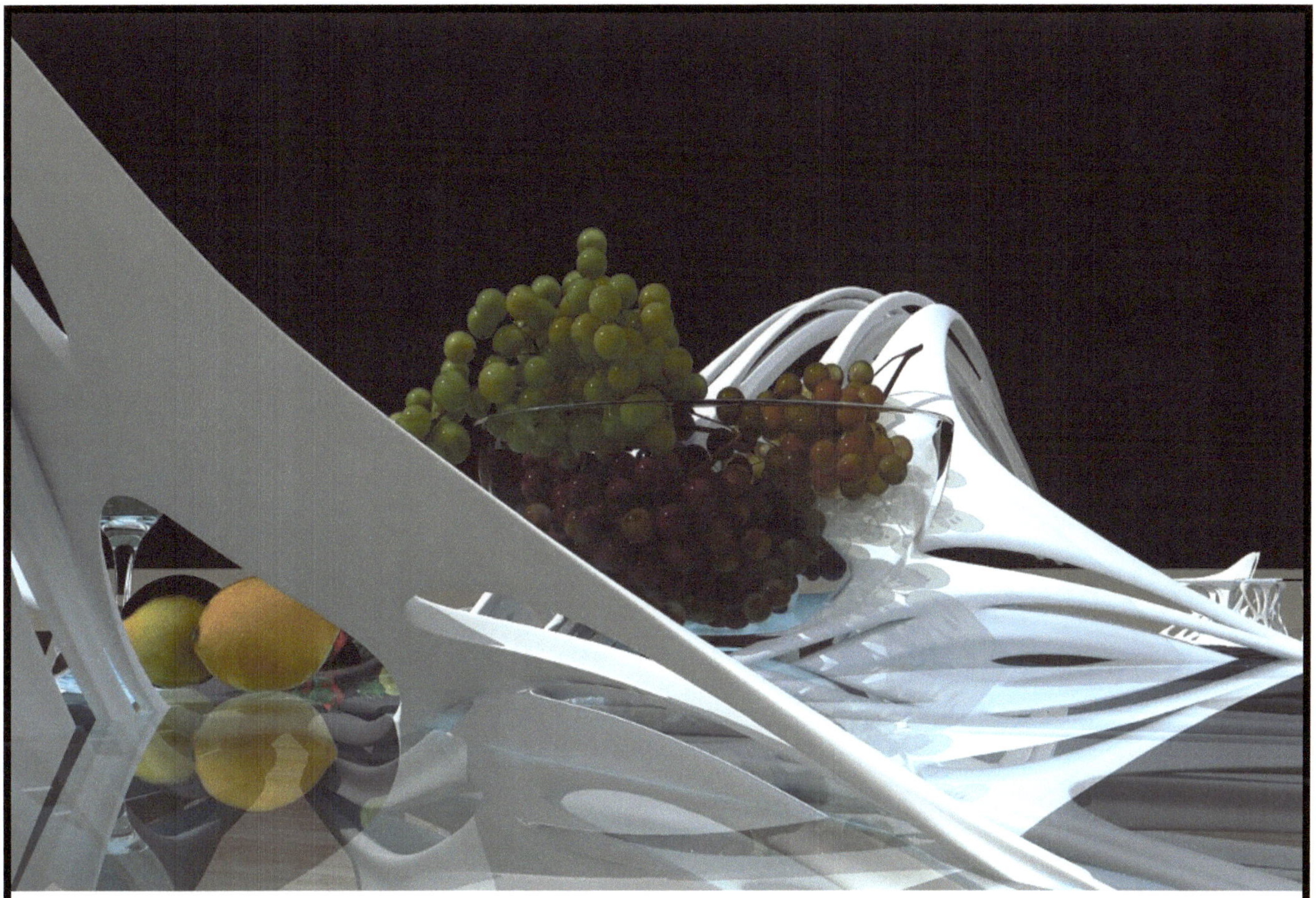

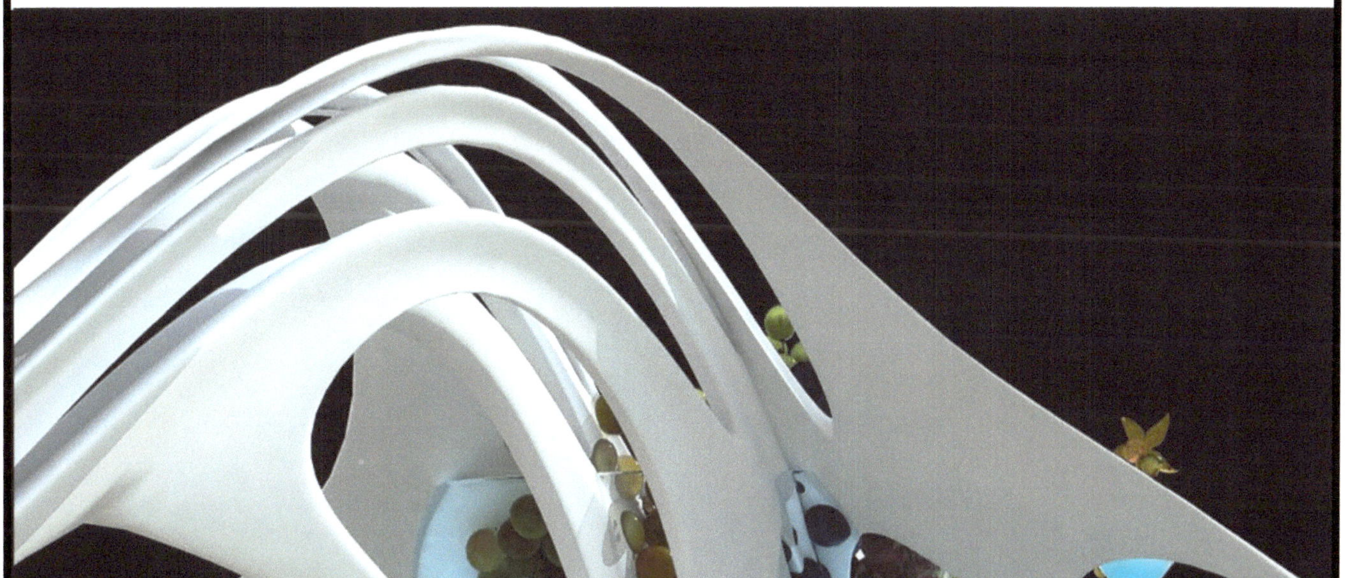

Sample of patterns designed for shapes and forms which can transform to other forms under control of parametric rules.

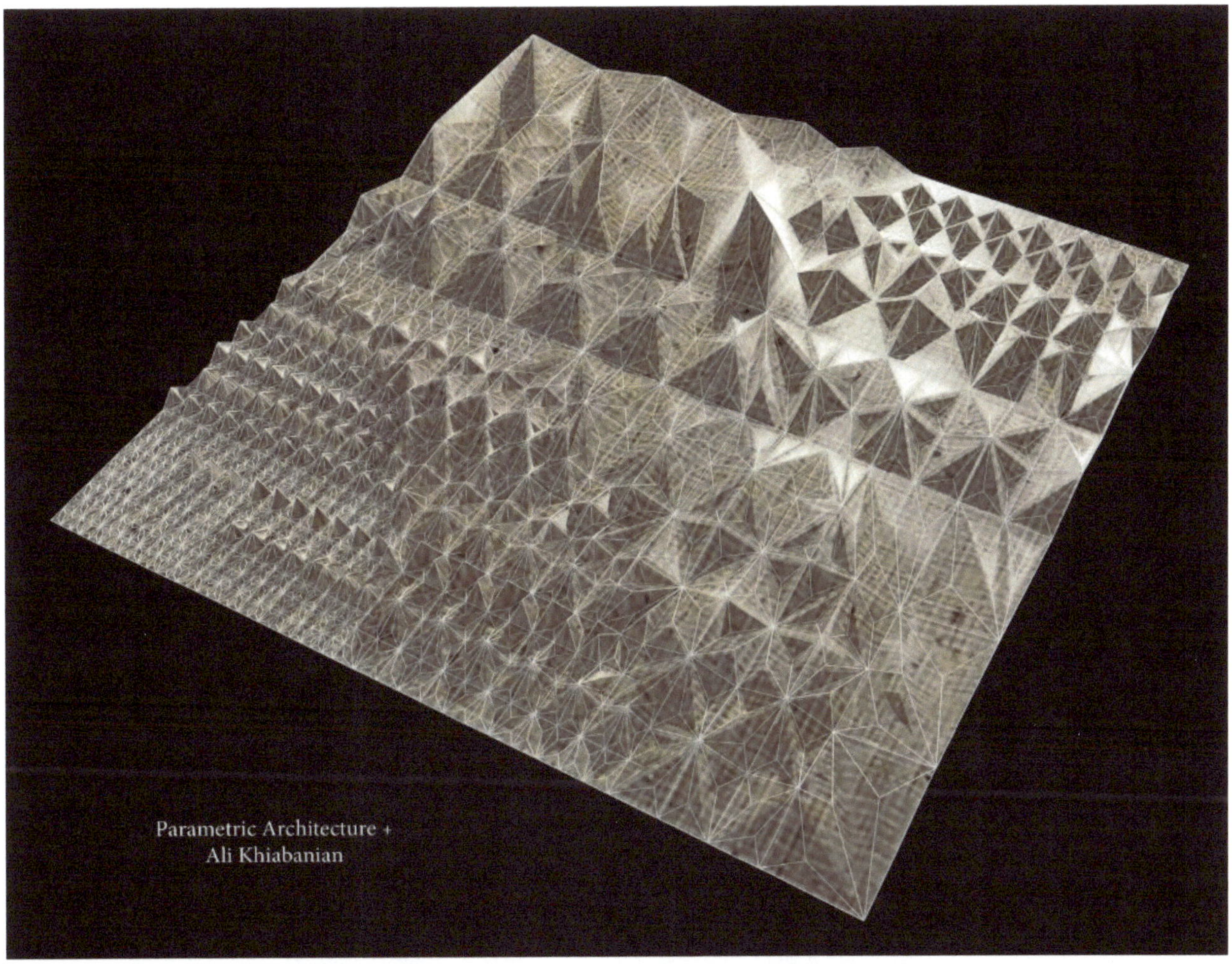
Parametric Architecture +
Ali Khiabanian

Parametric Architecture +
Ali Khiabanian

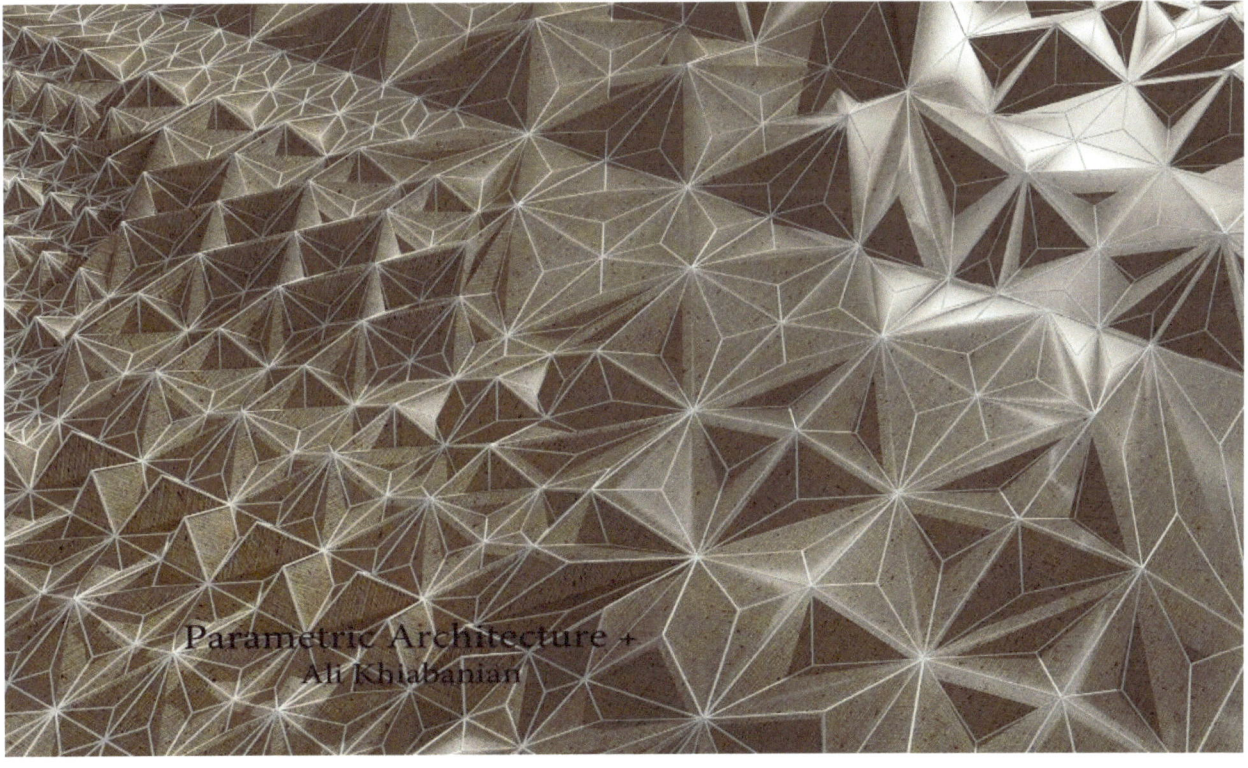

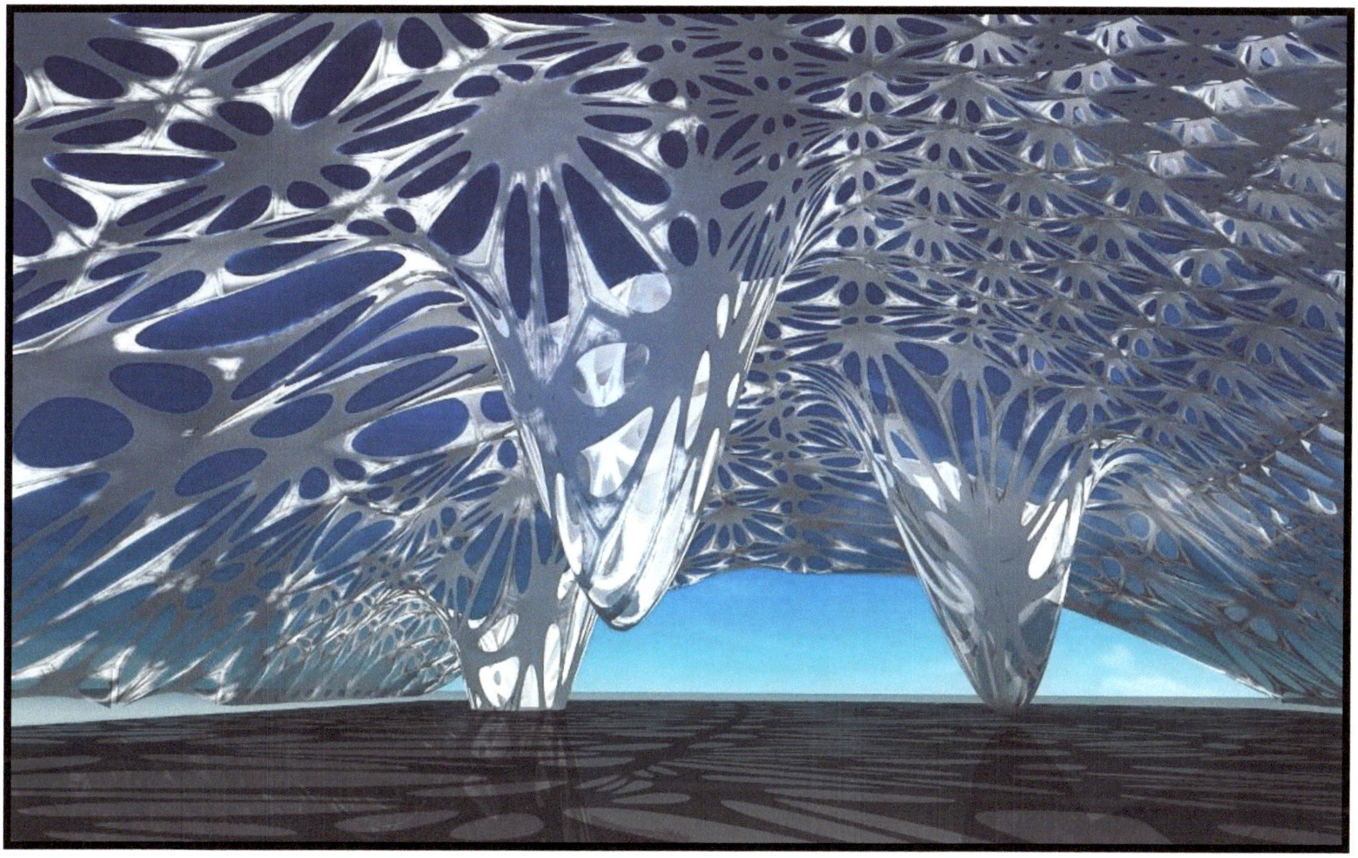

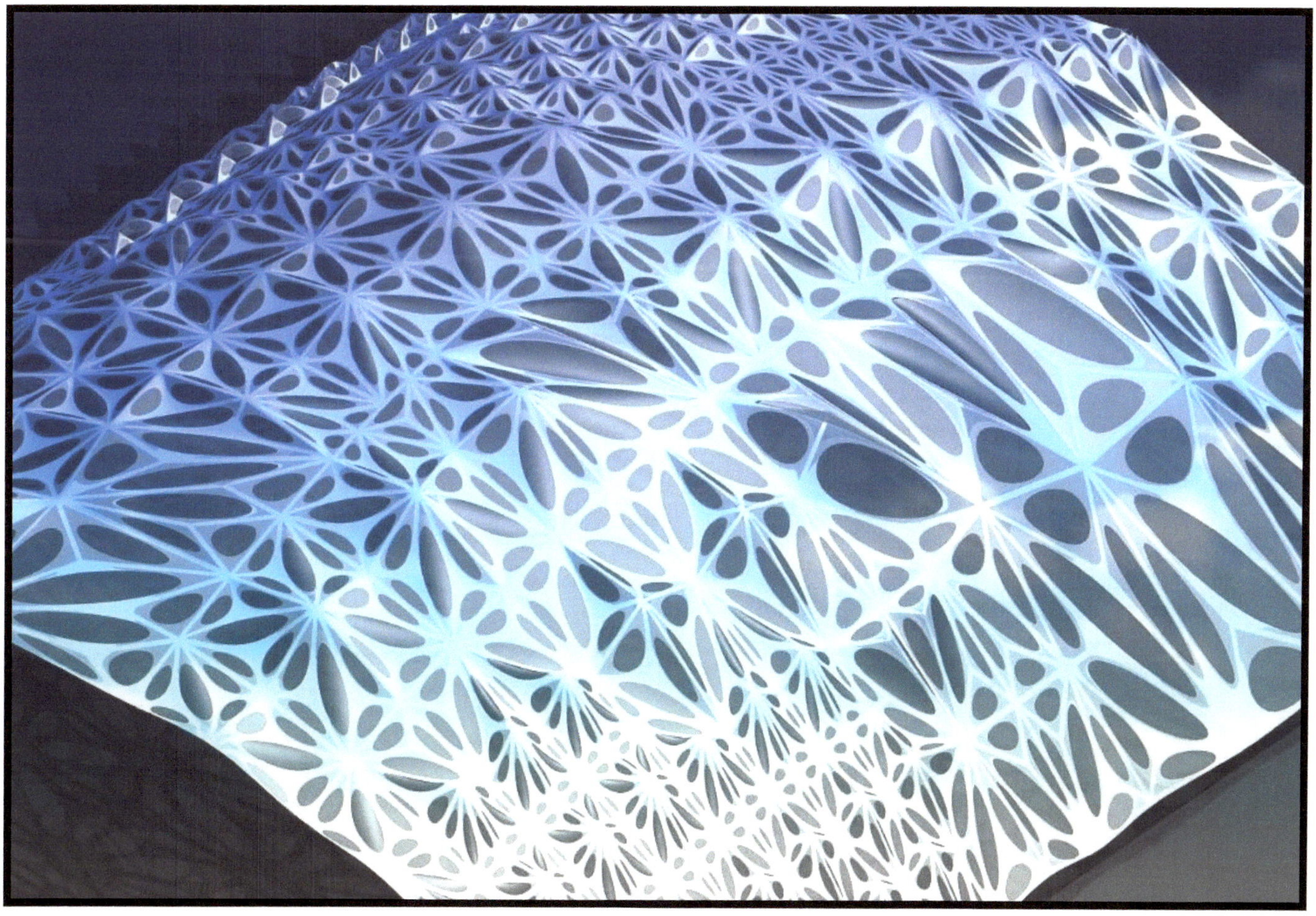

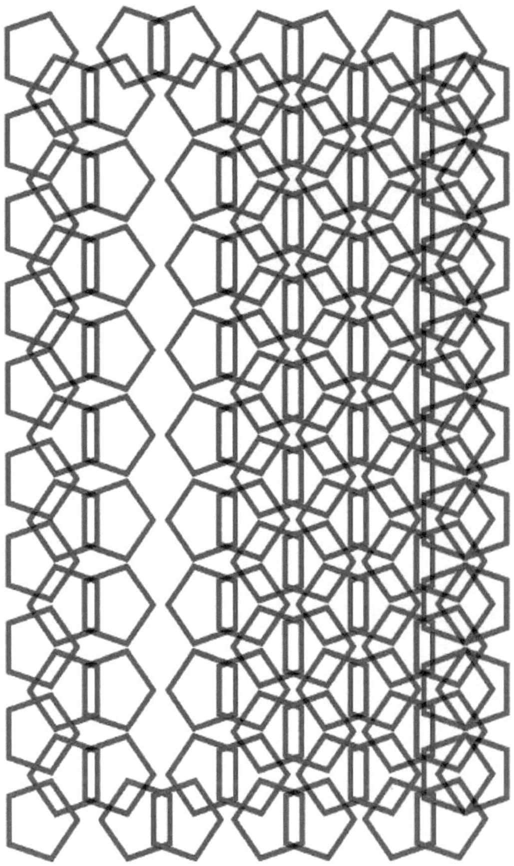

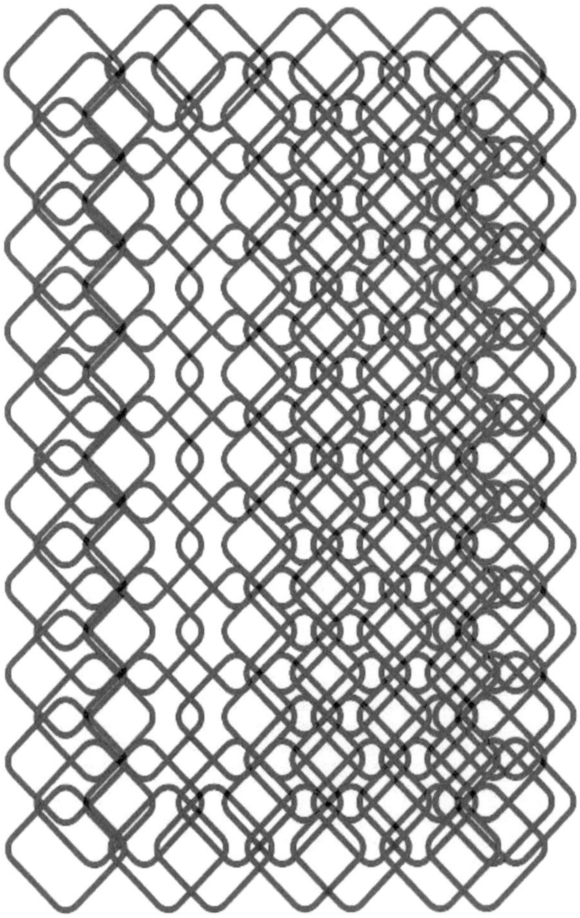

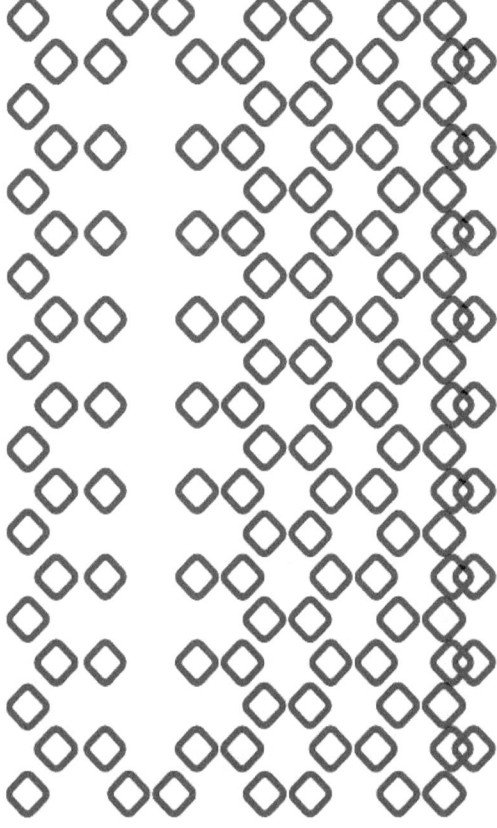

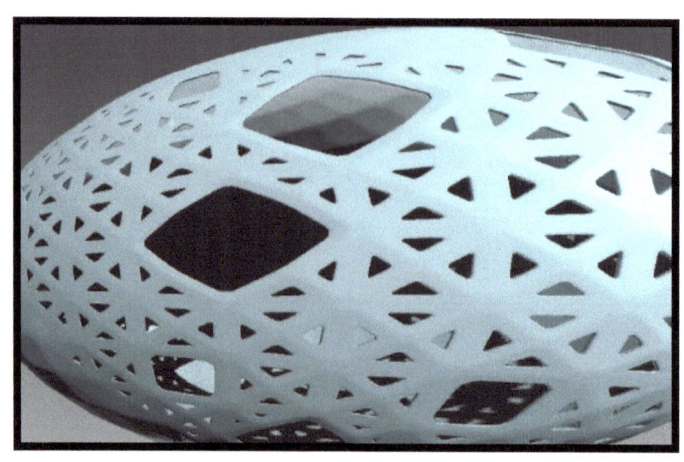
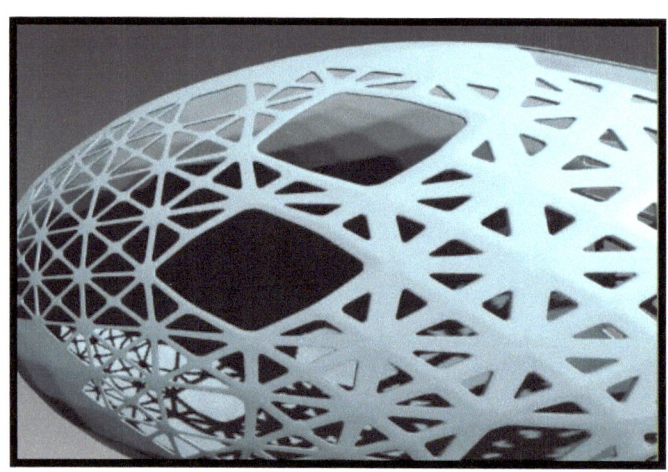

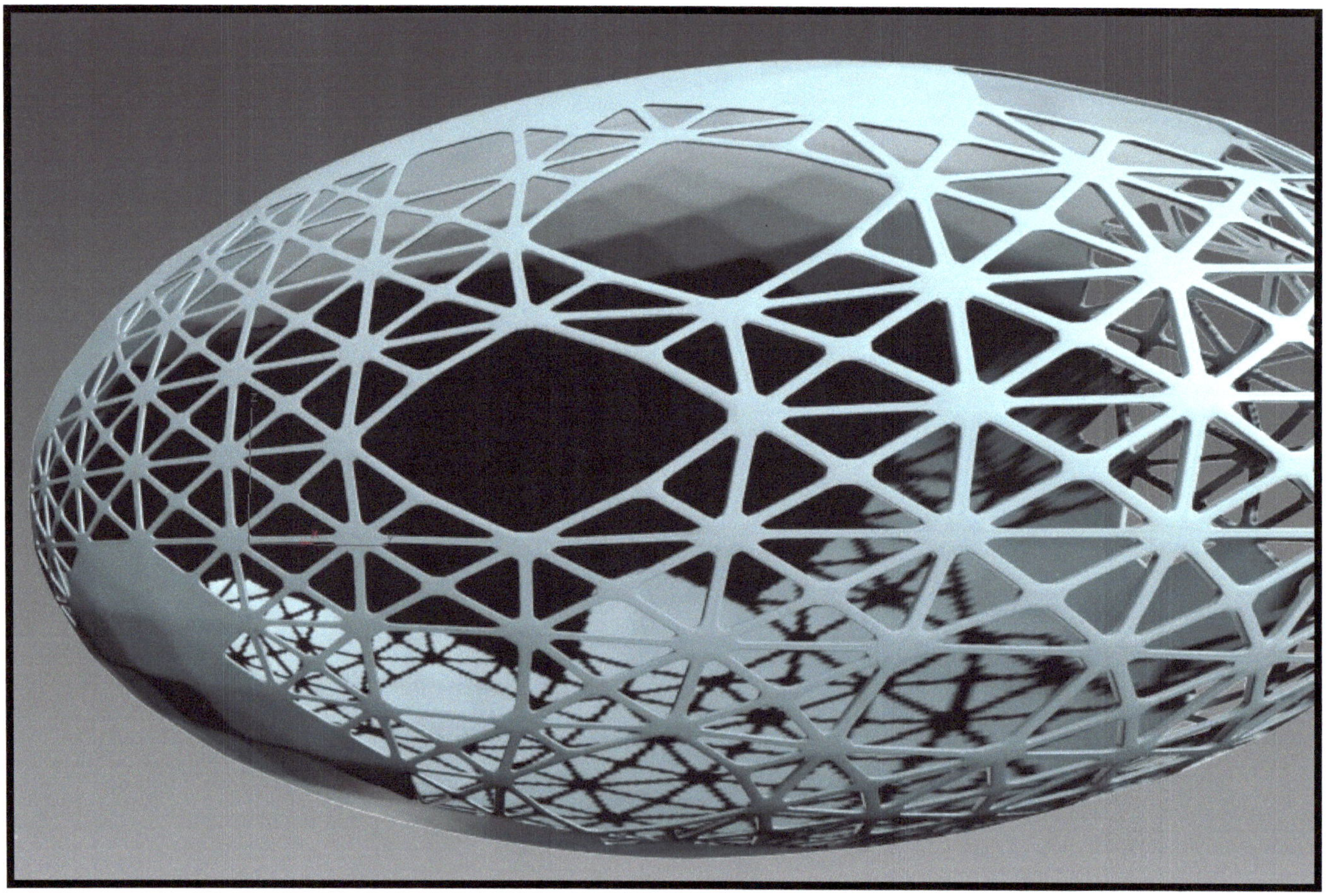

Refrences

- Arbab Keikhosrow, Sh, Zoroaster, a prophet whom should be recognized again, Tehran, 2001.
- Croner, W, Architecture for Children, Translated by Ahmad khoshnevis, Ganje Honar, Tehran, 2006.
- Falamaki, M, Architecture formation in Iran and West experiences, Faza press, summer 1992
- Falameki. M, Roots and Theoretical tendencies of architecture, Faza press, Tehran, 2002.
- Godard, A. Godard, Y, Iran Works, Translated by A. Sarv Moghadam, 1986.
- Jalali Moghadam, M, Zurvanism, Tehran, 1993.
- Khiabanian, A, Conceptal sketches in architectural design, Supreme Century, USA, 2014.
- Khiabanian, A, The role of creativity in architectural design process 2, Mehr Iman, Tabriz, 2011.
- Manzouri, L, Designing space for children, printed in "Decorasion-e- Dakheliy Daris, (Iranian Monthly on Interior Design), No 1, 2006.
- Mikani, A, Creativity and thinking in children's education, Avaye Nour, Tehran, 2013.
- Sarafraz, A Solomon Throne, Iran History & Culture Institute Press, Tabriz faculty of literature & humanitarian, 1968.
- Talebian, N. Atashi, M. Architecture functions "Museum", Herfeye Honarmand, Tehra, 2005.
- Vafamehr, M, Creative thinking in architectural design of the National Museum of Science and Technology, Shahid Rajayi University, Tehran, 2013.

www.ingramcontent.com/pod-product-compliance
Lightning Source LLC
Chambersburg PA
CBHW040903020526
44114CB00037B/38